WOMEN'S HOME MUSEUMS
OF THE NORTHEAST

Help Us Keep This Guide Up-To-Date

Every effort has been made by the author and editors to make this guide as accurate and useful as possible. However, many things can change after a guide is published—regulations change, facilities come under new management, and so forth.

We would love to hear from you concerning your experiences with this guide and how you feel it could be improved and kept up-to-date. While we may not be able to respond to all comments and suggestions, we'll take them to heart, and we'll also make certain to share them with the author. Please send your comments and suggestions to 64 S. Main St., Essex, CT 06426.

Thanks for your input!

WOMEN'S HOME MUSEUMS
OF THE NORTHEAST
A Guidebook

MARLENE WAGMAN-GELLER

Globe
Pequot

Essex, Connecticut

Globe
Pequot

An imprint of The Globe Pequot Publishing Group, Inc.
64 South Main Street
Essex, CT 06426
www.globepequot.com

Distributed by NATIONAL BOOK NETWORK

Map by The Globe Pequot Publishing Group, Inc.

British Library Cataloguing in Publication Information available

Library of Congress Cataloging-in-Publication Data available

ISBN 978-1-4930-8628-3 (paper: alk. paper)
ISBN 978-1-4930-8629-0 (ebook)

∞™ The paper used in this publication meets the minimum requirements of American National Standard for Information Sciences—Permanence of Paper for Printed Library Materials, ANSI/NISO Z39.48-1992.

The author and The Globe Pequot Publishing Group, Inc., assume no liability for accidents happening to, or injuries sustained by, readers who engage in the activities described in this book.

To the women who have homes in my heart—
my mother, Gilda Wagman, my daughter, Jordanna Geller,
and my friend Jamie Lovett.

"*A home of one's own is the want, the necessity of every human being, the one thing above all others longed for, worked for. Whether the humblest cottage or the proudest palace, a home of our own is the soul's dream of rest, the one hope that will not die until we have reached the very portals of the everlasting home.*"

—Susan B. Anthony

Contents

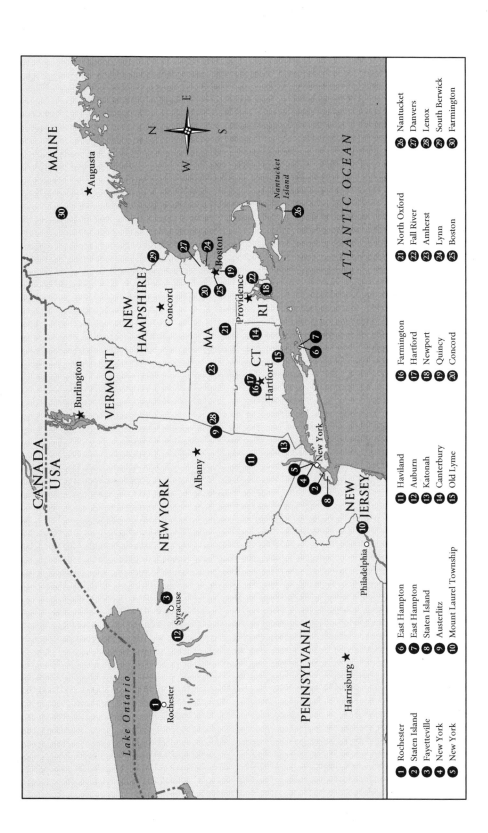

CANADA

USA

Lake Ontario

1 Rochester

3 Syracuse

12

NEW YORK

★ Albany

Harrisburg ★

PENNSYLVANIA

Philadelphia ○

NEW JERSEY

10

11

5

4

2

8

9 **28**

13

New York

VERMONT

★ Burlington

NEW HAMPSHIRE

Concord ★

MAINE

★ Augusta

30

29

27 **24**

★ Boston

20 **19**

MA **25**

23 **21**

16 **17**

CT **14**

Hartford ★

Providence ★

22

18

RI

15

6

7

Nantucket Island

26

ATLANTIC OCEAN

N
W E
S

1 Rochester
2 Staten Island
3 Fayetteville
4 New York
5 New York

6 East Hampton
7 East Hampton
8 Staten Island
9 Austerlitz
10 Mount Laurel Township

11 Haviland
12 Auburn
13 Katonah
14 Canterbury
15 Old Lyme

16 Farmington
17 Hartford
18 Newport
19 Quincy
20 Concord

21 North Oxford
22 Fall River
23 Amherst
24 Lynn
25 Boston

26 Nantucket
27 Danvers
28 Lenox
29 South Berwick
30 Farmington

Acknowledgments

The most emotional part of my book is this page, the acknowledgments. How does one find adequate words to thank those who transformed *Women's Home Museums of the Northeast: A Guidebook* from a twinkle in my eye to a reality? The first step was my literary agent, Rita Rosenkranz. She has the tenacity of a pit bull when finding a home for her clients. Thank you to my publisher, Globe Pequot, for taking me on board. Thank you to my "three musketeers" editors: David Legere, Lynn Zelem, and Felicity Tucker.

In the world according to Marilyn Monroe, "Diamonds are a girl's best friend." As she sang in *Gentlemen Prefer Blondes*, "It's then that those louses / Go back to their spouses / Diamonds are a girl's best friend." Jamie Lovett is a writer's best friend. She served as a sounding board when brainstorming ideas regarding which museums to include, she proofread the manuscript, and she provided endless encouragement. Without her, my book would have been far less, my hair far grayer.

If there is a support group for husbands of writers, Joel Geller should become a card-carrying member. He listened—albeit often reluctantly—to my endless descriptions of the women of whom I was currently writing. Because of another book's deadline that left me a slim margin to finish this one, his dinners were all encased in Styrofoam.

My final thanks to my readers. Because of your patronage, I have published twelve books, my Man of La Mancha impossible dream. My books are proof of a message I shared with my students, "Dreams don't just have to be for sleeping."

INTRODUCTION

It Took a Yankee

"Poor dull Concord. Nothing colorful has come through here since the Redcoats."
—LOUISA MAY ALCOTT

At the conclusion of *The Wonderful Wizard of Oz,* Dorothy Gale shared her wisdom with her words, "There's no place like home." She was right. There is something unique about homes, whether humble or haute, that belong to the ladies of legend. Their dwellings are as significant as traditional museums though they make for vastly different visits. Someone once remarked if something exists, it can be found in the Big Apple, and Manhattan offers world-class galleries. A trip to the American Museum of Natural History leads one to empathize with the biblical Jonah: suspended from the ceiling is a life-size ninety-four-foot-long model of a blue whale. The Morgan Library is swoon-worthy for bibliophiles: it owns the original manuscripts of John Milton's *Paradise Lost* and Charles Dickens's *A Christmas Carol.* Art lovers make a beeline to the Museum of Modern Art to view Vincent van Gogh's *Starry Night,* Monet's *Water Lilies.*

Removed from these grandiose institutions are their humbler cousins: the historic-house museums. Located in formerly private residences often staffed by volunteers, these unique institutions may have a period-clad docent, authentic décor, and a gift shop. They also display objects such as combs, cosmetics, and sewing baskets, as even the mundane takes on magical realism when associated with the famous of yesteryear.

Historians follow the breadcrumbs to Hartford, Connecticut, to witness where Harriet Beecher Stowe wrote *Uncle Tom's Cabin,* a novel that helped ignite the Civil War. Feminists are drawn to the New Jersey farmhouse of Alice Paul to pay homage to the firebrand who endured hunger strikes to obtain the holy grail of the ballot box. Fans of Lin-Manuel Miranda's hit musical gravitate to Manhattan's The Grange, the estate of Alexander and Eliza Hamilton.

Peering through keyholes of these homes hints at the nature of domestic partnerships. As Virginia Woolf wrote in her essay regarding the London residence of Thomas and Jane Carlyle, "One hour in No. 5 Cheyne Row would tell you more about the couple than all the biographies." Samuel Butler revealed what that hour of observation would deliver by his quotation, "It was very good of God to let Carlyle and Mrs. Carlyle marry one another and so make only two people miserable instead of four."

Alexander Hamilton's two-year affair, publicly acknowledged, could have prompted Eliza to remove the welcome mat from The Grange. However, not only did she remain committed to her spouse who had delivered disgrace on the House of Hamilton, following his death Eliza spent a half century resurrecting his reputation. A guest recalled that while standing in the foyer that held a bust of her slain husband, the widow leaned on her cane and moaned, "My Hamilton."

Some of the profiled ladies had living arrangements that entailed enjoying their own space, a configuration that conjures Virginia Woolf's quotation, "A woman must have money and a room of her own if she is to write fiction." Franklin Delano Roosevelt gifted his wife, Eleanor, Val-Kill, her cherished "she-shed," to escape from her controlling mother-in-law, Sarah. Although FDR often parked his 1936 Ford Phaeton in her driveway, Val-Kill was Eleanor's fiefdom.

If one dropped by at Stepping Stones, the Katonah, New York, residence of the first couple of sobriety, Bill and Lois Wilson, a visitor could glean insight into their marriage through the souvenirs from their trips and photographs of friends and family. Bill, the founder of Alcoholics Anonymous, wrote his books in a cinder-block studio he named "The Shack" and what his wife called "Wit's End." Lois, the founder of Al-Anon, enjoyed her own space, where she corresponded with those infected by their loved ones' addiction.

The Hampton home of Jackson Pollock and Lee Krasner held his-and-her studios. Jackson created his oversize canvases in his barn while Lee painted in her bedroom. Viewing each other's work was by invitation only. After Jackson's fatal accident, the barn-studio became Lee's own.

History buffs undertake a pilgrimage to locales associated with famous names which permits the past to rise once more. Clara Barton's Civil War moniker, the Angel of the Battlefield, leads to the assumption she was a Southerner, but she was born in North Oxford, Massachusetts. The two years spent caring for her bedridden brother was the catalyst for her nursing career.

Visitors to Rochester's Susan B. Anthony House can stand in the parlor where Deputy U.S. Marshal E. J. Keeney informed the supreme suffragist she was under arrest for the crime of voting. At her trial, Anthony socked it to the judge: "Resistance to tyranny is obedience to God." The dust will never settle on such a statement.

An ode to Staten Island's yesteryear is one of New York's oldest homes: The Alice Austen House. A ferry ride to the landmark rewards guests with spectacular views of Brooklyn and Lower Manhattan. Alice's beloved home is the only United States museum dedicated to a female photographer, the first designated as a LGBT historic site. The only closet Alice Austen—a woman who had the courage of her sexual convictions—ever entered was her darkroom.

While traditional museums offer the apogee of civilization, a drawback is they constitute a passive experience. The crown jewel of the Musée du Louvre is the *Mona Lisa*; however, due to shatterproof glass and dense crowds, the Lady of the Rocks keeps viewers at arm's length. The woman in the painting, known as the Enigma, remains shrouded in mystery. The only autobiographical information provided is an adjacent plaque: Leonardo da Vinci–artist; Lisa Gherardini–subject, Francisco del Giocondo–spouse; venue–Florence. To discover Mona (an abbreviation of *Ma Donna*, My Lady, a matron's title in Renaissance Italy) one need look elsewhere. In contrast, after walking the halls of women's homes and observing their art, furnishings, and bric-a-brac, the former chatelaines enter the confessional.

A peephole into the life of poet Edna St. Vincent Millay is provided by a tour of Steepletop, her hillside home in Austerlitz, New York. Dorothy Parker wrote of her fellow poet, "I was following in the exquisite footsteps of Miss Edna St. Vincent Millay, unhappily in my own horrible sneakers." In the vein of "you can know somebody by the books that line their shelves," Steepletop's second-floor library proves insightful. The room is also a nod to Edna's sense of humor: She hung a sign with the word SILENCE—she was the only one permitted entry.

My fascination with writers' homes had its genesis in my Toronto hometown where forbidding winters turned me into a lifelong reader. With my library card, I could check out as many books from The Forest Hill Public Library as I desired. Returning home with my stash, I felt like Mr. Henry Bemis from *The Twilight Zone* episode "Time Enough at Last." One morning, walking to West Prep, my elementary school, fingers numb under my mittens, I longed to be immersed in my can't-put-down novel, *Little Women*. At age twelve, having stumbled upon *The Portable Dorothy Parker*, I was smitten. In the belief Dorothy lived in the Algonquin Hotel, my pipe dream was to pay her a visit. And, if New York City wasn't on the table, then any of my cherished authors' homes would suffice. As my parents, immigrants to Canada, with limited education (my father finished high school, my mother, elementary), an excursion to literary destinations was in the wish-upon-a-star realm.

How wondrous it would be to visit author Louisa May Alcott's Orchard House in Concord, New England's equivalent to Britain's Bloomsbury. A highlight would be the semicircular desk set into the wall, looking out into the leaves of a Revolutionary-era elm tree. Louisa's inkwell had doubled as an alchemist's stone, birthing the March sisters: Jo, Beth, Amy, and Meg. Those of an imaginative nature can hear her quill scratching on parchment; a creak of a floorboard summons the Alcott ghosts. Jan Turnquist, the museum's executive director, said that when visitors ask to stay for a while to be guided by the aura of Louisa, Jan accommodates their request when possible. If a guest asked a Louvre guard if it would be OK to write at Marie Antoinette's ornate gold writing table, the response would not be as obliging.

During dreary days, I think of Emily Dickinson's words: "Hope is the thing with feathers– / That perches in the soul / And sings the tune without the words– / And never stops–at all –." To pay tribute to the Woman in White, visit Amherst's The Homestead. While studying at Mt. Holyoke Female Seminary, Emily mailed a letter to her brother, writing, "Home was always dear to me . . . but never did it seem so dear as now." Eventually, she became a recluse, and her home became her world.

The museum mansion that puts to rest the notion that one must be a starving artist to succeed is Edith Wharton's The Mound. The estate and magnificent gardens are a nod to the author's privileged upbringing. Her maiden name, Jones, gave rise to the expression "Keeping up with the Joneses." With all her wealth, The Mound was far from a house of mirth.

For a country that features the word "United" in its name, America has fault lines based on lines of latitude and longitude. Locale leaves an imprint as deep as birth order, socioeconomic status, and religion. In that vein, New England's women's home museums are far afield from their southern counterparts.

A visit to the Margaret Mitchell House in Atlanta, Georgia, illustrates regional differences. The highlights of the museum are the artifacts from Margaret's epic novel, *Gone with the Wind*—such as the door from the Tara plantation. On a wall hangs the portrait of the novel's heroine, Scarlett O'Hara, dressed in a royal-blue gown with a low-cut bodice. The painting appears so lifelike one can almost hear Scarlett exclaim, "Fiddle-dee-dee!" An example of her trademark expression, "Fiddle-dee-dee! War, war, war; this war talk's spoiling all the fun at every party this spring. I get so bored I could scream." Margaret Mitchell stated she did not discover that the South had lost the war until she was ten.

The Northern Louisa May Alcott's view of the Civil War was far different. When the fighting erupted, she was desperate to do more than make bandages and knit socks. Through her family connection to the reformer Dorothy Dix, Louisa managed to secure a position as a Northern nurse. At the time, her appointment was unique as women in the medical field were deemed unseemly. When the need became too great to continue the exclusionary policy, the ladies were paid less, had to be age thirty or over, and had to be considered plain. Training or experience was not required. The nurse from Concord described conditions at The Union Hotel: "A more perfect pestilence-box than this house I never saw." After contracting typhoid pneumonia, doctors treated her with a mercury compound. The "cure" led to poisoning that carried in its wake lifelong illness. Mitchell's Scarlett was cut from a very different cloth than Alcott's Jo. The tomboy protagonist proclaimed, "I'd rather be a free spinster and paddle my own canoe."

Fellow New Englander Emily Dickinson also wrote of the horror that left thousands of widows in its wake, "How martial is this place! / Had I a mighty gun / I think I'd shoot the human race / And then to glory run!" The regional reaction to the Civil War illustrates how geography is as much a state of mind as a physical locale.

Regardless of the reason to visit niche home museums, they are an important aspect of America's cultural landscape. The National Trust for Historic Preservation estimates there are approximately fifteen thousand of these sites (to some they are shrines) across America. The statistic is reassuring as it surpasses the number of the country's McDonald's franchises. Most of the home museums are situated on the East Coast.

In 1614 London merchants hired Captain John Smith to explore the New World. He christened the landmass New England, an area that comprises New York, Connecticut, Rhode Island, Massachusetts, Vermont, New Hampshire, and Maine. The history and landscape of the Northeast influenced the lives of its women who tended to be hard-working, dedicated to their family and church—values reflected in the homes and artifacts they left behind. Some of the influences that shaped their souls were pious Pilgrims, feisty Minutemen, whaling ships, transcendentalist philosophers.

Gertrude Ederle, nicknamed Trudy, who learned to swim on the Jersey Shore, embodied the same indomitable spirit as the women profiled in this book. As she made her watery way from France to England, fighting freezing waves and poisonous jellyfish, the crew on the accompanying boat kept asking, "Do you want to come out, Trudy?" Her repeated response of "What for?" led to her moniker, "What for?" When she arrived on the beach of the white cliffs of Dover, Trudy made history as the first woman to cross the English Channel. The Jazz Age mermaid had provided a rebuttal to John Hayward, a journalist for the *London Daily Sketch*, who had said of women conquering the channel, "No woman has ever yet been anywhere near success and wasn't likely to be." Upon her return to the States, two million New Yorkers shouted, "Trudy! Trudy!" Mayor Jimmy Walker compared her to Moses parting the Red Sea. News of her breaking the ocean's glass ceiling knocked coverage of Rudolph Valentino's funeral from the front page.

Trudy's final days were far removed from her ones of glory. At age ninety-eight, she lived in a nursing home in Wyckoff, New Jersey, confined to a wheelchair. However, when asked about her groundbreaking achievement, her eyes lit up, a reminder of the "What for?" girl. She reminisced, "It was just that everybody was saying it couldn't be done. Well, every time somebody said that, I wanted to prove it could be done. It took a Yankee."

Please refer to this chart as you plan your trips to these women's home museums. Since admission prices are subject to change, I've included a chart with a range of prices. However, I encourage you to visit the museum's website before your visit.

Admission	Symbol
0 to $9.99	$
$10 to $19.99	$$
$20 to $29.99	$$$
$30 to $39.99	$$$$
$40 to $49.99	$$$$$

NEW YORK AND NEW JERSEY

CHAPTER ONE

Failure Is Impossible

Susan B. Anthony

"Men, their rights, and nothing more; women their rights, and nothing less."
—SUSAN B. ANTHONY

National Susan B. Anthony Museum & House (opened 1945)
17 Madison Street, Rochester, New York 14608
(585) 235-6124
contact-us@susanb.org
https://susanb.org

Parking: Available in the lot next to the Visitors Center at 19 Madison Street. On-street parking is also available.

Hours of Operation: Tuesday–Sunday, 11 a.m.–5 p.m. Closed on major holidays.

Admission: Adults: $$; children/students: $

Gift Shop: Yes

Nearby Accommodations: Staybridge Suites / The Strathallan Hotel & Spa / Hampton Inn & Suites

Nearby Eateries: 1872 Café / Pane Vino / Founders Café

THE UNWAVERING FRIENDSHIP BETWEEN ELIZABETH CADY STANTON AND Susan B. Anthony helped form the foundation of the American suffrage movement. Elizabeth supplied many of the speeches that Susan delivered. Elizabeth explained, "I forged the thunderbolts and Susan fired them!" For those desperately seeking Susan, one should make a pilgrimage to the National Susan B. Anthony Museum & House.

Susan B. Anthony

A U.S. marshal arrested Anthony in the parlor for the "crime" of voting.
WIKIMEDIA COMMONS, DMADEO

The Quaker faith (so-called as members were said to quake in the presence of the Lord) shaped Susan's soul and provided the courage to slay the hydra heads of injustice. Susan Brownell was born in 1820, the second oldest of seven children of Daniel and Lucy Anthony. Along with her sisters, Guelma, Hannah, and Mary, Susan shared the same educational opportunities as her brothers. From an early age, Susan suffered from a wandering eye that made reading difficult. The family lived in Adams, Massachusetts; when Susan was six they moved to Battenville, New York, where Daniel managed a mill. As a child, Susan could not understand why Sally Anne Hyatt, her father's employee, more knowledgeable about weaving than her supervisor, Elijah, was not in charge. Daniel explained a woman could not hold a position of authority.

The depression of 1837 led to the loss of the Anthony business and home. Eight years later, with an inheritance from Lucy's father, Daniel purchased a residence in Rochester, New York. The parlor became a meeting place for abolitionists such as Frederick Douglass who was formerly enslaved and a well-known abolitionist. The two maintained a lifelong friendship; when he passed away in 1895, Susan was one of the mourners who delivered his eulogy. As an agent for the American Anti-Slavery Society (she also assisted freedom seekers travelling along Underground Railroad routes), Susan spoke at antislavery meetings. Mobs pelted her with rotten eggs, hung her in effigy, and burned her image in the streets of Syracuse. A newspaper labeled her a "Pestiferous fanatic."

Guelma married Aaron McLean, the son of a local judge, but Susan had no desire to follow her into holy matrimony as there were unholy aspects attached to the institution: women could not obtain a divorce, retain custody of their children, or own property. Rather than become a marionette to a male, Susan took a teaching position—one of the few careers open to women—at Canajoharie Academy. She was incensed that the Quaker school paid female instructors one-quarter of the salary of men. Eventually, politics took precedence over teaching, and Susan turned her attention to the temperance movement as drunken husbands were threats to their wives and children. While attending the convention of Sons of Temperance, after she attempted to speak, men demanded she "listen and learn." The misogyny led her to seek her first woman's rights convention.

Taking New England somberness to the extreme, breakfast in bed led to feelings of guilt; the first time she stepped foot on a beach was at age sixty-seven. A decade later she experienced her first football game, which led to her pronouncement, "It's ridiculous." Her thoughts on Elizabeth's pregnancies were to wonder how "for a moment's pleasure to herself or her husband, she should thus increase the load of cares under which she already groans?" The mother of six, Elizabeth was pregnant when Susan made the remark. Susan's comment to suffragist Antoinette Brown Blackwell, "Now, Nette, not another baby, is my peremptory command."

In 1848, at the Seneca Falls Convention in New York, two hundred attendees adopted the Declaration of Sentiments. They modeled the document on the Declaration of Independence, with the modification, "We hold these truths to be self-evident; that all men and women are created equal." Although Susan had not attended the historic meeting, she had found her cause célèbre.

The start of a beautiful friendship occurred on a street corner in Seneca Falls when Amelia Bloomer introduced Susan to Elizabeth Cady Stanton. The women had no idea that their friendship would last for fifty years and that together they would help birth a revolution. Susan's motto for their movement:

"Organize, agitate, educate must be our war cry." The two complemented one another. Susan possessed the organizational skills; Elizabeth was adept on a philosophical plane.

The nineteenth-century Thelma and Louise produced a newspaper, *The Revolution*, that led to *The New York Sunday Times*'s response that Elizabeth should tend to her "domestic duties," and Susan needed "a good husband and a pretty baby." In 1869 the friends formed the National Woman Suffrage Association, which demanded the vote and social, political, and economic equality. Henry Stanton remarked to his wife, Elizabeth, "You stir up Susan, and she stirs up the world."

Susan's greatest stirring of the pot occurred in relation to her holy grail: the ballot box. Her contention was that "disenfranchisement was akin to degradation." In 1872, nearly fifty years before the passage of the 19th amendment, which granted American women the right to vote, Susan, accompanied by Guelma, Mary, and Hannah, as well as several other suffragists, entered a Rochester barbershop where they demanded to be registered. When the polling officials hesitated, Susan read the constitutional passage that promised all persons were entitled to equal protection under the law. On Election Day, Susan cast her vote for Republican candidate Ulysses S. Grant due to his pro-women stance. The following morning, *The New York Times* covered the watershed moment under the heading "Minor Topics." In a microcosm of the misogyny of the era, the article referred to the women as "a little band of nine ladies."

Susan was in her parlor when a deputy U.S. marshal, E. J. Keeney, informed her that she was under arrest. She suggested he put her in handcuffs, an offer he declined. In the streetcar on the way to jail, when the conductor asked for her fare, she replied, "I'm travelling at the expense of the government." At her preliminary hearing, Judge Ward Hunt set bail at five hundred dollars. Susan had no intention of paying the fine, as prison would draw attention to her cause. To her chagrin, her lawyer put up the money because he could not stand to think of a lady languishing behind bars.

Anthony supporters argued that it was the United States that was on trial rather than Susan B. Anthony. In contrast, the Rochester Union called her a "corruptionist." The trial venue was the village of Canandaigua, New York, where one of the spectators was former president Millard Fillmore. Judge Hunt refused to let Susan argue in her defense, with the explanation that women were not competent to testify. After her lawyer, H. R. Selden, finished his argument, the judge took a paper from his pocket and read his decision, thereby proving the verdict had been a foregone conclusion. He directed the jury to find her guilty.

Of her two-day trial, Susan remarked that it was "the greatest judicial outrage history has ever recorded."

Before her sentencing, Judge Hunt asked the defendant if she had anything to say. She let a moment of what she called "sublime silence" pass before she stated, "Yes, Your Honor, I have many things to say. My every right, constitutional, civil, political, and judicial have been trampled upon. I have not only had no jury of my peers, but I have had no jury at all." As to her hundred-dollar fine, she stated, "I shall never pay a dollar of your unjust penalty." She concluded, "Resistance to tyranny is obedience to God."

SUSAN B. ANTHONY HOUSE
The suffragists fought their crusade in the nineteenth-century, red brick home, Susan's forty-year residence. When she was president of the National American Woman Suffrage Association, (the latter represents the merger with the National Woman Suffrage Association), the house was her organization's headquarters. The dining-room displays lithographs of Susan and Elizabeth, emblematic of their friendship and collaboration. Similarly, the Stanton house held Susan's portrait. At the top of the narrow stairs is the attic where she worked on the posthumously published *History of Woman Suffrage, The Life & Work of Susan B. Anthony*, and *The Revolution*. One of her favorite rooms—the study—has a photograph of the freedom fighter at her desk, surrounded by portraits of other members of The Cause. Encased in glass is the iconic alligator purse that inspired the jump-rope tune, "Call for the doctor! Call for the nurse! Call for the lady with the alligator purse!" In the guestroom are photographs of those who visited the Anthony home: Elizabeth Cady Stanton, Carrie Chapman Catt, and Ida B. Wells-Barnett. Some of the artifacts on display: a replica Singer sewing machine, typewriter, spinning wheel, and eyeglasses, and a trunk she used for her travels. A unique addition is the Anthony family pew from the First Unitarian Church of Rochester. The tour offers soul-stirring opportunities such as standing in the parlor, the site of Susan's arrest. After returning from the capital, suffering from pneumonia, Susan passed away in her room in 1906. In her bedroom, encased in glass, is her iconic black dress. On Susan's eightieth birthday, a group of Mormon women—who raised silkworms—had sent her the fabric as a gift for her role in helping their state win the vote. The Susan B. Anthony bedroom possesses the original furniture and artifacts.

The museum's gift shop offers a $250 faux alligator purse stamped with the Ms. Anthony quotation, "Every woman needs a purse of her own."

The firebrand delivered her last public words in Washington, D.C., on her eighty-sixth birthday. During the celebration, she paid tribute to those with whom she had battled injustice, "With women such as these consecrating their lives, failure is impossible."

A View from Her Window
On election days, if Susan could once more gaze through her window, she would have witnessed women laying "I VOTED" stickers on her grave in the nearby Mt. Hope Cemetery.

Nearby Attraction: Susan B. Anthony Square Park
A short walk from the Anthony house is a bronze sculpture of two old friends, fellow activists Susan B. Anthony and Frederick Douglass, sitting at a table. The name of the bronze tableau: *Let's Have Tea.*

CHAPTER TWO

It Was, It Was

Alice Austen

"I am happy that what was once so much pleasure for me turns out now to be a pleasure for other people."
—ALICE AUSTEN, SPEAKING OF HER PHOTOGRAPHY

Clear Comfort—The Alice Austen House (opened 1985)
2 Hylan Boulevard, Staten Island, NY 10305
(718) 816-4506
info@aliceausten.org
https://aliceausten.org

Parking: There is a small gravel parking lot behind the museum, accessible from Hylan Boulevard. Street parking is generally available along Edgewater Street at the corner.

Hours of Operation: Times may vary depending on season.

Admission: Suggested general admission: $; Tours: $$; Affiliate members: Free

Gift Shop: Yes

Nearby Accommodations: Hilton Garden Inn / Hampton Inn & Suites / Insignia Hotel

Nearby Eateries: Bayou / Tony's Brick Oven / Mello Bistro

SIMON AND GARFUNKEL, FOLKSINGERS FROM QUEENS, CROONED IN *BOOKENDS*, "I have a photograph. Preserve your memories. They're all that's left you." Alice Austen proved the veracity of their words. As the Klondike Gold Rush began in Alaska, Alice mined black-and-white nuggets in New York. The Alice Austen

E. Alice Austen: photographer
WIKIMEDIA COMMONS, THOMAS ALTFATHER GOOD

Clear Comfort: Alice Austen's Staten Island home
WIKIMEDIA COMMONS, NATIONAL PARK SERVICE

House is the only American museum dedicated to a female photographer; the first designated as a LGBT Historic Site.

In 1866, during a baptism at St. John's Church in Staten Island, Alice Cornell Austen christened her baby Elizabeth Alice Munn. The child preferred her middle name and rejected her last one as her father, Edward Stopford Munn, had gone AWOL shortly after his daughter's birth. Without means of support, the single mother moved in with her parents at their home, Clear Comfort, where her brother, Peter also resided.

Alice grew up in the aptly christened Clear Comfort located in the Rosebank neighborhood of Staten Island, a borough that was transforming into the Newport of New York as mansions and yacht clubs dotted its shoreline. The structure dated from the seventeenth century; her grandfather, John Hagerty Austen, who owned an auction business in Manhattan, had purchased it in 1844. After extensive renovation, the Victorian Gothic-style house with its gingerbread trim and dormer windows held elegant furnishings and interesting curios that two servants kept dusted. A third domestic was their cook. The lawn held a huge sycamore tree, and flowers carpeted the yard. Clear Comfort afforded a panoramic view of New York Harbor, and the twenty-year-old Alice witnessed the unveiling and construction of the Statue of Liberty until the landmark achieved her final height of 151 feet.

The only child in a household of adults, Alice was the axis upon which the Austens revolved. She used the expression "larky" to describe a life filled with love and security. Her favorite pastime was using her Uncle Oswald's camera, which resembled a wood box. She was so thrilled with the camera that at age ten she received her own. Peter, a chemistry professor at Rutgers University, showed her the alchemy of developing pictures. Her two uncles converted a second-floor closet into a darkroom for their niece. A maid assisted with the task of rinsing glass-plate negatives in the outdoor pump as the nineteenth-century structure had no running water. Enamored of her hobby that transformed everything into a frozen tableau, Alice made Clear Comfort, her relatives, Punch, her pug, and Chico, her Chihuahua, the objects of her photos. The siren call of the harbor was also a muse, and she photographed its ships, first powered by sail, then by steam.

A woman who dressed in the latest fashion, Alice's activities included the new sport of tennis, as well as gardening, sailing, and travelling. A horse-drawn carriage was at her disposal to transport her to skating parties and car races. Among Alice's accomplishments: the first woman on Staten Island to own an automobile, a pioneer of the women's bicycling movement, and founder of the Staten Island Garden Club. But the lion's share of her time was spent in the pursuit of photography. Just as the British Miss Austen chronicled the Regency era with her quill, the American Miss Austen captured nineteenth-century New York with her photographs. What made Alice stand out—other than being the woman who wielded a camera at a time when it was only the domain of males—she pursued action shots rather than staged studio portraits. Her camera made its appearance on sailboat outings, and she shot scenes from moving trains. A social historian, Alice snapped images of her upper-middle-class milieu and of scenic spots such as the swan boats bobbing on the Central Park pond. Intrigued by the financially disadvantaged, weighed down with fifty pounds of equipment strapped to her bicycle, Alice zoomed her lens on the denizens of the Lower East Side: fishmongers, organ grinders, child laborers, and chimney sweeps. For several years, the shutterbug visited quarantine stations where immigrants waited to be processed at Ellis Island. Other subjects that piqued her passion were horse-drawn carriages travelling along roads in proximity to early motorcars. The glass-plate negatives bore her legal initials: EAA. Her work demonstrated technical prowess; her portfolio, entitled "Street Types of New York," showcased each shot along with a title and location.

Life became ever "larkier" in 1897. While vacationing at the Twilight Park resort in the Catskills, the thirty-one-year-old Alice met the twenty-six-year-old Brooklyn-born Gertrude Amelia Tate. Due to the Tate family, who declared the women's relationship a "wrong devotion," Gertrude only moved into Clear Comfort in 1917. In contrast, the only closet Alice entered was her darkroom. Her unabashed attitude took courage; across the pond, Britain had incarcerated Oscar Wilde for acts of "gross indecency"—homosexuality.

Another treasure trove of photos would have scandalized the staid Victorian society. "The Darned Club" shows two female couples, their arms wrapped around each other's waists. In another, three women are dressed in male attire and phony moustaches; Alice's friend Julia Martin is seated with an umbrella protruding between her legs, suggestive of an erect male member. A further snapshot showcases ladies clad in underwear, hair down, smoking in a church rectory.

The "larkiness" ended when the Stock Market Crash of 1929 wiped out Alice's inheritance. Due to the Depression, Gertrude's income as a dance teacher dried up. The couple tried to bolster their flagging finances by running the Clear Comfort Tea Room where a specialty was a lobster-salad adapted from the famed eatery Delmonico's. Despite the spectacular view and high-class cuisine, *The New Yorker* wrote, "It's about what you'd expect if your oldest aunt (the one who was considered artistic rather than domestic) had started up such a business without doing a great deal about it." A desperate Alice borrowed against the house and sold the Austen heirlooms and furniture to antique dealers. A further effort to stave off debts was to rent her late Uncle Oswald and Aunt Minn's room to Dr. Richard Cannon and his wife, Mary. The court ordered Alice's eviction for failing to make her mortgage payment. The new owner allowed the couple to stay until the following year, at which time Alice and Gertrude moved to an apartment where they stayed for five years. Afterwards, Gertrude's sister allowed her to stay at her home in Queens, an invitation she did not extend to her sibling's lesbian lover. With the cramped accommodation, rather than a room of her own, Gertrude slept on the couch. Suffering from arthritis and dependent on a wheelchair, her immediate family deceased, Alice, the former girl-about-town, ended up in the municipal poorhouse at the Staten Island Farm Colony. A naked lightbulb hung over her cot. Her "golden years" were far from "larky."

Yet fortune had not entirely abandoned Alice. Before her forcible removal from Clear Comfort, Alice had safeguarded thousands of her glass-plate negatives. Oliver Jensen, an editor at *American Heritage* magazine, along with his research assistant, Constance Foulk, discovered her work in the Staten Island Historical Society while doing research for his book *The Revolt of American Women*. The forgotten cache led to a 1951 exhibition and the publication of Alice's work in *Life* magazine. During the ceremony to honor the Grand Dame of photography, Gertrude basked in her lover's glory. The exposure, that led to donations, and the sale of photographs, allowed Alice to move into a private nursing home where she died a few months later at age eighty-six. The historical society financed her burial in the Austen family plot in the Moravian Cemetery at New Dorp in her native borough. A decade later, Gertrude passed away. Despite their wishes, the Tate family did not allow the long-term lovers adjoining burial plots. Gertrude's internment was at the Cypress Hill Cemetery in Brooklyn.

Clear Comfort—The Alice Austen House

Staten Island was far more fun when Alice and Gertrude were alive, and the best way to reincarnate their vivacious spirits is to take the Staten Island ferry to their former home. The property is under the auspices of the New York City Department of Parks and Recreation, operated by the Friends of Alice Austen House, which welcomes twenty thousand annual guests. Victorian-era photographs adorn the house's patterned wallpaper, summoning the ghosts of the ladies who engaged in erotic same-sex tableaux and exchanged corsets for trousers. The wall-size photographs of the New York of yesteryear makes the present dissolve into the past.

The 1890s-era formal parlor retains its Victorian ambience, and the room holds the collection of Alice's photographs and artifacts including glass-plate negatives, and photo albums. Some of the objects are original; reproductions originated when the Alice Austen House purchased period pieces based on Alice's photographs. In contrast to the nineteenth-century parlor, Alice's bedroom is light and airy; her mother shared the room until she passed away. The Alice Austen House uses the room as a gallery to showcase Alice's work as well as contemporary photographers. There are four darkrooms in which Alice processed photographs of the quarantine stations on the immigration processing centers located on Hoffman and Swinburne Islands, situated near the Austen home. She captured the faces of immigrants standing behind a fence awaiting clearance.

While finances forced Alice to part with her treasures—an agonizing amputation—one that remains is a gold brocade-covered armchair that she sold to the Metropolitan Museum of Art in 1933. A few years ago, the Met, which changed its fabric to the current one, donated the chair to the Alice Austen House. While Gertrude and Alice's Parisienne home served as the shrine for modern art, the other Gertrude and Alice's Staten Island home is an altar of photography. From Clear Comfort's porch, overlooking her waterfront property, the waves seem to carry the cadence of *Bookends*, "What a time it was, it was . . ."

A View from Her Window
Clear Comfort's covered porch afforded Alice a panoramic view of Lower Manhattan and Brooklyn. Waves lapped the pebbled beach, while the white picket fence served as sentry from intrusion.

Nearby Attraction: The Staten Island Ferry
The famous papaya-colored ferry that traverses New York Harbor between Staten Island and Manhattan provides moving scenery of the Big Apple and a unique vantage point for marveling at the Statue of Liberty.

CHAPTER THREE

That Word Is Liberty

Matilda Joslyn Gage

"The government of the people, by the people, and for the people should be changed to a government of rich men, by rich men, for rich men."
—MATILDA JOSLYN GAGE

Matilda Joslyn Gage Foundation & Social Justice Dialogue Center
(opened 2010)
210 East Genesee Street, Fayetteville, New York 13066
(315) 637-9511
matildajgagefoundation@gmail.com
https://matildajoslyngage.org

Parking: Available along the west side of Walnut Street, directly next to the Gage Center.

Hours of Operation: May 1 through September 30: Wednesday–Saturday, 11 a.m.–4 p.m.; October 1 through April 30: Friday and Saturday, 12–4 p.m.; Sunday–Thursday, closed. Museum schedules appointments for tours on days they are closed.

Admission: Adults: $; Seniors/Children/4 and under: Free

Gift Shop: Yes

Nearby Accommodations: The Craftsman Inn & Suites / Hampton Inn & Suites / Fairfield Inn & Suites

Nearby Eateries: Apizza Regionale / The Sweet Praxis / Hong Kong Cafe

AFTER HER REALIZATION THAT THE WIZARD OF OZ WAS A HUMBUG, DOROTHY informed him that he was a very bad man. His response, "Oh, no, my dear. I'm

Matilda Joslyn Gage

MATILDA JOSLYN GAGE
NATIONALLY KNOWN ABOLITION
AND WOMEN'S RIGHTS ADVOCATE
LIVED HERE FROM 1854
UNTIL HER DEATH IN 1898

Sign outside Matilda Joslyn Gage Home
WIKIMEDIA COMMONS, DIRTDRIVER

a very good man. I'm just a very bad wizard." In contrast, Matilda Electa Joslyn Gage, the woman behind the curtain of *The Wonderful Wizard of Oz*, was both a good woman and a good wizard.

In John Steinbeck's novel *The Grapes of Wrath*, Tom Joad states, "Whenever there's a fight so hungry people can eat, I'll be there. Wherever there's a cop beatin' up a guy, I'll be there." And whenever there was an injustice, a nineteenth-century radical was there. Matilda was born in 1826 in Cicero, New York, the only child of Helen and Dr. Hezekiah Joslyn. At an early age, her parents swore her to secrecy: the visitors who arrived in a wagon, buried under hay, were what the museum terms "Freedom Takers," desperately fleeing their plantations. Dinner conversation revolved around abolition, gender equity, and outlawing alcohol. Desirous of following in her father's footsteps, Matilda applied to Geneva Medical College. Her effort proved futile as medical schools were a male domain. Upon Hezekiah's passing, Matilda had his tombstone inscribed with the words "an early abolitionist." When asked what influences shaped her, Matilda replied, "I was born with a hatred of oppression."

At age eighteen, in the Joslyn parlor, Matilda married Henry Hill Gage in a ceremony presided over by a minister from the Disciples of Christ Church. In 1854 the couple purchased a residence in Fayetteville, New York. The Gages christened the house Sunset View, where they raised their four children (a fifth died in infancy). Matilda signed a petition stating that she would face a penalty of a six-month prison term and a thousand-dollar fine rather than honor the newly enacted Fugitive Slave Law. As the Joslyns had done years earlier, and prompted by a request from Reverend Jermaine Lougen, the Gages turned their home into a station on the Underground Railroad. On the day when John Brown swung from the gallows for leading an armed resurrection against plantation owners, Matilda put out black decorations on her home. Before the 122nd Regiment left for battle, she stated she disagreed with President Abraham Lincoln's claim that the Civil War revolved around preserving the Union. For her, the battle's goal had to be emancipation for all.

In 1852 Matilda decided to "publicly join the ranks of those who spoke against wrong" by taking part in a women's rights convention in Syracuse, New York. In attendance was Susan B. Anthony, a future friend and collaborator. While other speakers outlined what women would be able to accomplish if given the chance, Matilda painted a picture of what they had already achieved. She cited Catherine Littlefield Greene who had initiated the idea of the cotton gin, an invention of which Eli Whitney took credit. She ended her speech with the rallying cry, "Onward! Let the truth prevail." A prolific writer, Matilda sent off combative letters to newspapers signed with her initial: M. In her book *Woman, Church and State*, she argued that witches were merely inconvenient females and victims of unwarranted prosecution. The Russian author Leo Tolstoy responded to her work: "It proved a woman could think logically."

Along with nine women, Matilda attempted to vote in Fayetteville for President Ulysses S. Grant, who was up for reelection. The suffragists favored his party as the Democrats opposed giving the vote to women. The official refused to allow Matilda to cast a ballot on the grounds she was married. Accordingly, she escorted a single woman to the polls; the result was the same. She described her third attempt, "Then I took down . . . war widows, whose husbands had left their bones to bleach on the field of battle, in defense of their country, and they, too, were refused, and so on through the whole nine."

Matilda and Susan strategized a future trip to the polls. During this time, Susan stayed at the Gage home so often that Matilda's children named an upstairs bedroom "the Susan B. Anthony Room." For support, Susan took her sister and a friend to register to vote in a barbershop in Rochester, New York.

When she succeeded, the act garnered national headlines. Matilda was not shocked at Susan's arrest; she had often remarked that, in America, women were "born criminals." During the trial, Matilda proved Susan's staunchest supporter and railed that the United States was on trial, not Susan B. Anthony.

In 1886, the activist staged a protest at the unveiling of the Statue of Liberty. The New York State Suffrage Association had declared, "The Statue of Liberty is a gigantic lie, a travesty, and a mockery. It is the greatest sarcasm of the nineteenth century to represent liberty as a woman while not one single woman throughout the length and breadth of the Land is as yet in possession of political Liberty."

Elizabeth Cady Stanton, Susan B. Anthony, and Matilda Joslyn Gage were the triumvirate of the women's movement until Matilda became too extreme for the Quaker Susan and the more conservative Elizabeth. They disagreed with Matilda's radicalism, especially her insistence on the separation of church and state. Matilda took umbrage with the story of Adam and Eve which blamed women for original sin, death, and labor pains. Another source of friction was Matilda insisted on including women of color in the movement, an opinion the other two suffragists did not share, likely because they felt it best to slay one hydra head at a time. Because of their divergent approaches, Susan and Elizabeth tried to excise Matilda from the women's movement.

Another behavior against which Matilda jousted was the mistreatment of Native Americans. She admired matriarchal power within the Haudenosaunee (Iroquois) Confederacy. The Wolf Clan of the Mohawk Nation offered her an honorary adoption and presented her with the name Ka-ron-ien-ha-wi, "She who carries the sky."

Matilda, mother to her children and her causes, was also the mother of Oz. Her daughter Maud had dropped out of Cornell (her class was the second to admit women) to marry L. Frank Baum. Although Matilda had been aghast at Maud preferring matrimony over education, she agreed to let the couple wed in Sunset View's parlor. The Baums had five sons, and, at his mother-in-law's urging, Baum published *The Wonderful Wizard of Oz*. Matilda's influence is apparent in the intrepid female protagonist, the witches, and Aunt Em (Em being an allusion to her initial, M).

THE MATILDA JOSLYN GAGE HOUSE

In 2000, the Matilda Joslyn Gage Foundation purchased Sunset View with the mission to transform it into a museum. For the endeavor, its members recruited Gloria Steinem who wrote, "Matilda was ahead of the women who were ahead of her time." The center provides a hands-on experience where visitors interact with exhibits, for example, by leaving notes on Matilda's writing desk, explaining how she had inspired them. The house consists of these rooms: Women's Rights, the Family Parlor Oz, the Haudenosaunee, Religious Freedom, and the Underground Railroad. The gift shop offers souvenirs that commemorate Matilda's speeches, writing, prints of her artwork, books concerning social justice, the *Wizard of Oz*, and other topics related to the principles advocated by the center. The museum counteracts Matilda's unfair erasure as a cornerstone of the women's rights movement and holds her up as a supreme suffragist.

On a visit to the Baums' home in Chicago, at age seventy-one, Matilda passed away from a stroke. She had made plans for her death and a radical minister presided over her funeral. Although unusual for the time, Matilda had requested cremation, and a famous Theosophist spoke at her funeral. Maud took her mother's ashes for burial in the Fayetteville Cemetery. The inscription on her tombstone is from Matilda's own words: "There is a word sweeter than mother, home, or heaven; that word is liberty."

A View from Her Window

Matilda and Henry had christened their home Sunset View because of the spectacular pink and lavender evening display over their Fayetteville home. However, another view from the same spot proved a pain-laden memory. Susan B. Anthony had been such a frequent visitor to the Gage home that she carved her name on the windowpane with a diamond ring—an etching that remains visible today. The inscription was a heartbreaking souvenir from the time when the three musketeers were one.

Nearby Attraction: The Women's Rights National Historic Park

There are no falls in Seneca Falls; however, it does have a three-acre park that witnessed the beginning of an American Revolution, and the birth of the women's movement. The remnant of the old church is a sacred spot, a monument to its role in history. Elizabeth Cady Stanton's home is part of this historical site.

The two-story visitor center has an interactive exhibit that poses questions on sex discrimination, sexual harassment, and gender equality. There are life-size bronze statues of five of the women organizers. One is of Sojourner Truth alongside an excerpt from her speech "Ain't I a Woman?" Near the chapel is the text of the Declaration of Sentiments engraved on a bronze wall, over which water flows.

CHAPTER FOUR

The Other Hamilton

Eliza Hamilton

"No lapse of time, no nearness to the grave, makes any difference."
—ELIZA HAMILTON ON HER REFUSAL
TO FORGIVE PRESIDENT JAMES MONROE

Hamilton Grange (opened 1924)
St. Nicholas Park, 414 West 141st Street, New York, New York 10031
(646) 548-2310
hagr_info@nps.gov
https://www.nps.gov/hagr/index.htm

Parking: There is no street parking on West 141 Street between Convent Avenue and St. Nicholas Avenue. Limited street parking is available. Alternate side parking is normally in effect.

Hours of Operation: Wednesday–Sunday, 10 a.m.–4 p.m.; Monday and Tuesday, closed.

Admission: Free

Nearby Accommodations: Opera House Hotel / The Surrey / The Wallace

Nearby Eateries: Momoya Soho / Fumo Harlem / Grill on the Hill

AT THE CONCLUSION OF THE MEGAHIT MUSICAL *HAMILTON*, ELIZA HAMILTON lets out a gasp, followed by the chorus breaking into the haunting lyrics, "Who lives, who dies, who tells your story?" A way to discover Eliza's story is to visit the Hamilton Grange house-museum.

Traditional weddings echo the words of the biblical Mark, "What therefore God hath joined together, let no man put asunder." When Eliza recited her vows,

Ralph Earl painted Eliza Hamilton's portrait while he
was serving time in the New York City Jail, 1787.
WIKIMEDIA COMMONS, RALPH EARL

she never fathomed a vice president would separate her from her beloved. The
woman behind her great man was born in 1757, the daughter of senator and
Revolutionary War leader Major General Philip Schuyler. Through the death of a
childless uncle, Philip became the third richest man in the Upper Hudson region.
Coffers further overflowed, as her mother, Catherine (Kitty) van Rensselaer, was
a descendent of the elite Dutch settlers. Eight of her fifteen children died young.

When Eliza was eight, Philip purchased thirty-two acres on which he built
The Pastures, perched on a bluff overlooking the Hudson River. Eliza and siblings
Angelica and Margarita (Peggy) strung wampum, a Native American tradition
to record agreements. The Pastures did not prove the same idyll for its enslaved.

The Schuyler sisters shared commonalities with the Bennet sisters of Jane
Austen's *Pride and Prejudice*: they fussed over their finery, attended balls, and
longed for a Mr. Darcy. Eminent visitors were Benjamin Franklin—who taught
Eliza how to play backgammon—his wife, Martha, and James Madison.

Hamilton Grange National Memorial
WIKIMEDIA COMMONS, AJAY SURESH

Gertrude Cochran invited her twenty-two-year-old niece, Eliza, to her home in Morristown, New Jersey, to find a suitor amongst the ten thousand soldiers of the Continental Army. Hamilton was also in Morristown serving as an aide-de-camp for General Washington, who referred to his assistant as "my boy." At an officer's ball, Eliza experienced a *coup de foudre*—love at first sight. Cynics held Hamilton was courting Eliza due to her wealth and connections; however, a love letter paints a different picture, "You not only employ my mind all day, but you intrude upon my sleep—I meet you in every dream." In a letter far different from one a Bennet sister would have penned, Angelica wrote Eliza regarding her swain, "I love him very much and if you were as generous as the Old Romans you would lend him to me for a while." Angelica did not pursue Hamilton due to his poverty and roots as an illegitimate West Indian orphan. The Schuyler-Hamilton nuptials took place in 1780 in the living room at The Pastures. The bride sported a gold double-band wedding ring (currently in the Columbia University library). Her parents were pleased with the ceremony as Angelica and Peggy had eloped.

The Hamiltons purchased their forever home, which Alexander named The Grange after his aunt's plantation in St. Croix or his ancestral home in Scotland, where they raised their six sons and two daughters, as well as Fanny Antill, an orphaned toddler of a Revolutionary War colonel. Eliza assisted as Hamilton worked on "Washington's Farewell Address." Upon Philip's passing, his children freed the Schuylers' enslaved servants.

While his family was vacationing in Albany, Hamilton was in Philadelphia canoodling with the twenty-three-year-old blonde Maria Reynolds. His paramour had likely seduced Hamilton for financial gain rather than for passion. Exploiting his wife's adultery, James Reynolds demanded a thousand dollars in exchange for his silence: Hamilton ponied up the money. After his arrest for forgery, James turned to Hamilton for help, and when none was forthcoming, he dished the dirt. Aware his enemies would claim he had financed his affair with taxpayers' funds, a fact that would have repercussions on his career as secretary of the treasury as well as the fledging nation's economy, Hamilton confessed. When the truth came out, Hamilton's ninety-five-page booklet "The Reynolds Pamphlet" stated that his only crime had been an "irregular and indelicate amour." He admitted that trysts had occurred in the Hamilton home, that he had encouraged his wife to remain in Albany. The sordid situation cost Hamilton any chance at the presidency. Another part of the pamphlet was a mea culpa to Eliza, "I can never cease to condemn myself for the pang which this confession may inflict in a bosom eminently entitled to all my gratitude." Eliza was pregnant with her sixth child when the infidelity became public. The wronged wife never publicly commented on the affair, though privately she mourned that her husband had broken the covenant of the wampum. Hamilton blamed Monroe for leaking the scandal and challenged him to a duel. Maria sued James for divorce: her attorney was Aaron Burr.

The Hamiltons found contentment at The Grange—whose architect also worked on New York's City Hall—until their chorus delivered another tragic lyric. Their nineteen-year-old son, Philip, died in a duel in Weehawken, New Jersey. His pregnant mother honored his memory by giving her baby his slain sibling's name. Her daughter, Angelica, suffered a breakdown, and would only communicate with her brother's ghost. Later in life, Angelica resided permanently at a New York psychiatric ward. Three years later, Eliza lost her husband in the same place, in the same fashion, in a duel with Vice President Aaron Burr. (The pistols are on display at the New York Historical Society.) Hamilton's farewell letter explained he had not told Eliza of his intention in advance, as that would "unman" him. Eliza kept a lock of her husband's hair, and never remarried.

Her necklace was a bag that held two pages: a sonnet Hamilton had composed during their courtship and a hymn he left her on the fateful morning.

While Hamilton participated in the duel to save his honor, his death left his family without means of support. Had it not been for the help of her family and friends, his widow would have lost The Grange. Her final years were spent in New York and Washington where she socialized with presidents Tyler, Polk, Pierce, and Fillmore. A chief executive with whom she never spoke was Monroe. The founding mother spent her long life resurrecting Hamilton's reputation, which included buying back reprints of "The Reynolds Pamphlet." She instituted New York's Orphan Asylum Society, currently known as Graham Windham. Eliza Schuyler Hamilton passed away at age ninety-seven.

HAMILTON GRANGE

Alexander Hamilton's home on the range, in his case, The Grange, was the embodiment of Hamilton's American Dream. When his home was a twinkle in his eye, he teased his wife about a secret "sweet project," and in a letter wrote, "You may guess and guess and guess again / Your guessing will be still in vain." Ironically, the Founding Father only lived there for two years before his death. The house, like its owner, had a dramatic past. Originally, the structure sat on a thirty-two-acre property that afforded views of both the Hudson and Harlem Rivers. The Grange had two subsequent locations; the first move was when Eliza sold it in 1833, and a developer donated the residence to St. Luke's Church. The church transported the Grange 250 feet, at which time it became a house of worship. In 2008, the historic residence moved to St. Nicholas Park, its current location.

The foyer of The Grange holds a white marble bust of Hamilton when he was treasury secretary, sculpted by the Italian Giuseppe Ceracchi, who fashioned his image in the likeness of a Roman senator. A Grange guest recalled that the widow "always paused before it in her tour of the rooms, and leaning on her cane, gazed and gazed and remembered her husband as 'My Hamilton.'" Looking out from the dining room walls are the portraits of Eliza and Alexander.

The Hamiltons often hosted dinners, as evidenced by an 1802 letter Alexander sent his wife, "My dear Eliza, on Sunday Bonaparte & wife with the Judges will dine with you. We shall be 16 in number if Morris will come." Bonaparte referred to Jerome Bonaparte, Napoleon's brother; Morris was the governor. The room has yellow walls and mirrored doors; the table is elegantly set, awaiting eminent visitors. A replica of the four-bottle Sheffield—named after the city in England—silver wine cooler was a gift from Washington. Accompanying the present was a note, "Not for any intrinsic value the thing possesses, but as a token of my sincere regard and friendship for you, and as a remembrance of me; I pray you to accept a Wine cooler for four bottles. I pray you to present my best wishes, in which Mrs. Washington joins me, to Mrs. Hamilton & the family; and that you would be persuaded, that with every sentiment of the highest regard, I remain your sincere friend." The gift coincided with the Reynolds Pamphlet, and perhaps softened the blow brought on by the scandal. The Hamilton family had kept the Washington gift until 2012 when they put it up for auction; the identity of the buyer is not known.

The parlor holds Angelica's Clementi pianoforte (a name that means "soft-loud in Italian), which was a present from her namesake aunt. During the years Angelica stayed in her New York City facility, her pianoforte remained with her. A gold mantel clock bears the relief of an ancient god. The clock chimes on the hour and the half hour. Reproductions include Hamilton's desk; the original resides at the Museum of the City of New York. Hamilton's study sports green walls; its secretary is a faithful production of the original that resides in the Museum of the City of New York. An avid reader of history, the room retains many of Alexander's books such as *The Antiquities of Rome*, and *The History of Modern Europe*. The basement has an exhibition that explores Hamilton's biography and includes an interactive video display in which questions are answered by an avatar using Hamilton's own words. The garden has been reproduced according to Hamilton's written instructions. In 1802 he wrote, "A garden, you know, is a very usual refuge of a disappointed politician." The gardens bloom with hyacinths, tulips, and daffodils, along with many other flowers. The Grange explains the story of the man who stares out from the ten-dollar bill, and allows visitors to walk in the footsteps of an American Founding Father, along with his soulmate, Eliza.

Lin-Manuel Miranda, by ending his musical with Eliza, makes the audience realize the play is also about the other Hamilton.

A View from Her Window
When Eliza gazed from her window, she saw the thirteen gum trees her husband had planted in a symbolic nod to the thirteen colonies.

Nearby Attraction: Trinity Church
The graveyard holds the remains of Eliza and Alexander Hamilton. Her grave is a plain white marble slab at the foot of the far grander monument of her husband.

CHAPTER FIVE

Queen of Sugar Hill

Eliza Jumel

"Vice Queen of the United States" (How Eliza Jumel introduced herself in Paris)

Morris-Jumel Mansion (opened 1904)
65 Jumel Terrace, New York, New York 10032
(212) 923-8008
info@morrisjumel.org
https://morrisjumel.org

Parking: Street parking is available on 160th and 162nd Streets, on Jumel Terrace (cobblestone street) in front of and behind the museum on Edgecombe Avenue. A parking garage is on 161st Street between Broadway and Amsterdam Avenue.

Hours of Operation: Thursday, 1–4 p.m.; Friday–Sunday, 11 a.m.–4 p.m.

Admission: Mansion and Grounds Tour: $$; Museum members, Military: Free; Self-guided interior tour: $$; Paranormal Historical Investigation: $$$$

Nearby Accommodations: Teaneck Marriott / The Mark Hotel / The Wallace

Nearby Eateries: Blue Mountain Heights Café & Bar / Fort Washington Public House / Ramen Kuraku

IF WALLS COULD INDEED TALK, MANHATTAN'S OLDEST REMAINING HOME would provide a tantalizing tale. And one would be of Eliza Jumel who defeated Aaron Burr in a duel. To experience the historic house that doubled as a nineteenth-century soap opera, head over to the Morris-Jumel Mansion.

New York City's oldest home. The famous who walked its halls: General George Washington and Aaron Burr.

While the Cockney Eliza Doolittle longed for "a room somewhere/far away from a cold night air," the Yankee Eliza Jumel's appetite increased with the eating. Her mother, Phebe, married sailor John Bowen, and gave birth to John Thomas, followed by Mary. Her youngest, Betsy, arrived three weeks before the start of the American Revolution. As her husband, away at sea, provided only a pittance, Phebe worked in a "disorderly house," situated on the site of a former jail. When Betsy was seven, she awoke in terror as rioters burned down the brothel to rid Providence, Rhode Island, of its citadel of sin.

The homeless mother and daughters relocated to a shelter before they found lodgings with Patience Ingraham. Phebe and Patience ended up behind bars for "plying their flesh." For the next three years, Betsy endured the workhouse until she became an indentured servant for Samuel Allen and his wife, Charlotte. Misfortune dogged the Bowens: John drowned at sea, and Phebe and John Thomas passed away, likely from yellow fever.

As an adult, Betsy moved to New York, where she worked as a stage actress. In a bid at reinvention, she transformed to Eliza Brown, a moniker possibly chosen for its association with the wealthy Brown brothers who founded Brown University.

The man who impacted Eliza's destiny, Étienne Jumel, fled France at the outbreak of the revolution. In America, he anglicized Étienne to Stephen and fell for the actress. A week after Eliza's twenty-ninth birthday, she married the thirty-eight-year-old Stephen. In the same spirit as Henry of Navarre's philosophy, "Paris is worth a mass," Eliza, a member of the Congregational Church, wed Stephen in a ceremony officiated by Father William W. O'Brien, the pastor of Manhattan's only Roman Catholic church. Prominent New Yorker John Pintard wrote to his daughter that Eliza had tricked Stephen into marrying her by pretending to be terminally ill, and her dying wish was to be made an honest woman. The animosity stemmed as the era's zeitgeist held that men of the mercantile class did not marry actresses with murky pasts. Later in life, for upper-class acceptance, she became an Episcopalian. Without children of their own, they raised Mary, Eliza's illegitimate niece.

The Jumels purchased a bluff-side estate that had long stood empty—except for its gallery of ghosts. British Colonel Roger Morris and his Anglo-Dutch heiress wife, Mary, whose family had made their fortune in the slave trade, had built Mount Morris as their summer residence. When they left the city at the onset of the Revolutionary War, General George Washington commandeered the estate as his headquarters. He remained there for five weeks, and the second-story octagonal-shaped room served as his office till British troops necessitated his departure. For a brief period in 1790, when a tenant farmer, John Bogardus, rented the premise, the house transformed to an inn and tavern. At that time, Washington threw a lavish banquet on its grounds. His guests included Thomas Jefferson, John and Abigail Adams, Alexander and Eliza Hamilton, Martha Washington, and Major General Henry Knox, the latter the namesake of Fort Knox.

Twenty years after the who's who of American history dinner, Stephen and Eliza Jumel changed the name of Mount Morris to Mount Stephen. The Jumels purchased the property and its 104 acres for $9,927.50. Eliza managed to knock two thousand dollars off the price as local lore held a Hessian soldier's ghost hung around the mansion's stairway. Mary refused to stay alone in the house. Their real estate portfolio included property on Broadway, located three blocks from Wall Street, purchased for $14,700. Further acquisitions made the once penniless Eliza one of New York's richest women. Their cook, Anne Northrup, was the wife of Solomon Northrup, author of *Twelve Years a Slave*. She worked as Eliza's cook for one to two years in the 1840s.

To spend time with Stephen's family, the Jumels boarded the *Maria Theresa* for France. In Paris, over the next eighteen months, Eliza purchased more than 240 paintings that dated from the sixteenth through the early nineteenth century. Souvenirs of her travel abroad were the works of art, armoires, sofas, and chairs. When she returned to the States, what she left behind was Stephen Jumel. Despite the distance, Stephen's matrimonial fire remained strong. He wrote to his wife, "Since your departure, my bedchamber has become insipid to me. I stayed on the jetty until I could no longer see the ship." Stephen granted Eliza power of attorney to handle business transactions during his absence. Her real estate investments and aggressive lawsuits increased their fortune.

A relationship that remained constant throughout Eliza's life was the one she shared with Mary. Eliza gave her blessing when her attorney, Nelson Chase, married her niece. Nelson might have been partially attracted to the fact that Mary was an heiress. Stephen, who had returned from the continent, acted as witness. Shortly afterwards, travelling in a one-horse wagon, he suffered a fatal fall. The story that made the rounds was Stephen's death had resulted from impaling himself on a pitchfork and the missus had intentionally not bandaged his wounds. In either scenario, Stephen expired at his namesake home, leaving the fifty-seven-year-old Eliza a widow. His passing resulted in a famous addition to Mount Stephen's guest book.

Nelson began working for attorney Aaron Burr, whose curriculum vitae included a stint as Thomas Jefferson's vice president and the killer of Secretary of State Alexander Hamilton. Eliza invited Burr to Mount Stephen for a banquet, and he charmed his hostess when he led her to seat with the words, "I give you my hand, Madame; my heart has long been yours." Burr proposed with a Machiavellian agenda: as he was always in debt, he felt Eliza was the key to an economic kingdom. The widow's calculation was that marriage to a former vice president would bring her entry into the societal circle for which she had long sought entry. They were wed in her home's front parlor.

The matrimonial bubble burst when Eliza grew alarmed at the rate at which her husband was going through her fortune. Eliza's divorce lawyer was Alexander Hamilton Jr., who may have hoped he would win the case in a bid at karmic retribution. A judge dissolved their marriage in 1836, a few hours before Burr's death. His passing freed Eliza from her inconvenient second husband and allowed her to present herself as the widow of the vice president. On this occasion, gossip needed no embellishment. The saga of Betsy Bowen, Eliza Brown

Jumel Burr, ended when she died, alone, at age ninety, at Mount Stephen. The woman who had started life in a brothel passed away as one of America's wealthiest women and the country's first major collector of European art.

MORRIS-JUMEL MANSION

Constructed in 1765, the Morris-Jumel Mansion is Manhattan's oldest remaining home whose age alone renders it a revered address. The estate's senior status, along with the fact that presidents, first ladies, and a vice president walked its halls, makes it a notable landmark. Gazing at the balcony, one can visualize George Washington pacing its length, contemplating a strategy to drive the British back to their shores. Contemporary accounts hold that Eliza, a Manhattan Miss Havisham, suffering from dementia, rode around her property on horseback, attended by a contingent of homeless men, armed with sticks for rifles, in a mock parade. The entrance hall holds a painting of the chatelaine, along with her two grandchildren, commissioned in 1854 while in Rome. If one wants to sit and gaze upon her portrait, there is a sofa upholstered in gold with claw feet. Another canvas is of the evicted Aaron Burr. In the parlor, adorned with light-blue brocade, lies the furniture Eliza maintained had once belonged to Napoleon. A French Empire armchair, carved with a floral motif, has engravings of dolphins, with an upholstered seat and back. Equally ornate, the pianoforte displays a brass lion head. The dining room holds a French porcelain basin with a blue floral decoration. A French-style candelabra with three candles rising from a laurel wreath held aloft by a figure of winged victory resting on an orb is an embellishment of the octagon room. From the wall of the octagon room is an oil painting of the mistress of the manor whose brass plaque reads: "Eliza Jumel 2nd wife of Aaron Burr Vice President of the United States." On the second floor is Eliza's bedroom which holds a canopied bed with a covering of navy fabric. Aaron Burr's room retains a cast-iron bootjack in the shape of a beetle, and his gaming table.

When Roger and Mary Morris constructed their summer home, an architectural flourish was a grand Tuscan portico. The Georgian-style mansion, situated on the second highest point of Manhattan, is reminiscent of a Southern plantation, a Tara transplanted to the East Coast. In 2014 writer and composer Lin-Manuel Miranda sat in Aaron Burr's bedchamber where he wrote songs such as "The Room Where It Happened" for his hit musical *Hamilton*.

Visitors come to gaze upon rooms that exhibit furniture from various time periods, including Second Empire pieces that Eliza brought from France. Aaron

Burr's writing desk holds several cubbyholes. Eliza is buried five blocks from her old haunt, in the Jumel mausoleum in Trinity Cemetery.

In the 1930s, Duke Ellington moved into the area referred to as Sugar Hill and pronounced the Morris-Jumel Mansion its crown jewel. Eliza Jumel reigns as the queen of Sugar Hill.

A View from Her Window
Looking out at her domain, Eliza would have had views of the Harlem and Hudson Rivers, Westchester County, and Staten Island.

Nearby Attraction: The Apollo Theater
Harlem's Apollo Theater has impacted American musical history more than any other venue. The neo-classical music hall was originally slated for burlesque, when Harlem was predominately white and black Americans were not admitted, except as performers.

CHAPTER SIX

Nevermore

Lee Krasner

"I don't feel I sacrificed myself."

—LEE KRASNER

The Pollock-Krasner House (opened 1988)
830 Springs-Fireplace Road, East Hampton, New York 11937-1512
(631) 324-4929
https://www.stonybrook.edu/commcms/pkhouse/index.php

Parking: Limited

Hours of Operation: May through October; Group tours: Thursday–
Saturday, 12 p.m., 2, p.m., and 4 p.m.; Sunday, 2 p.m.

Admission: Children: $$; Infants: Free

Nearby Accommodations: Hartman's Briney Breezes Beach Resort /
Journey East Hampton / Baron's Cove

Nearby Eateries: Lobster Roll Restaurant / Vine Street Café /
The Blend at Three Mile Harbor

A WELL-KNOWN TROPE POSTULATES, "BEHIND EVERY GREAT MAN IS A GREAT
woman." History tends to forget these ladies, as great men can be reluctant to
provide spousal credit. Ultimately, the artist formerly known as Mrs. Pollock
became Lee Krasner. To experience Lee's paint-bedecked studio, follow the
turpentine fumes to The Pollock-Krasner House.

If anyone did not seem destined to make her mark in the avant-garde
art world, it was the Brooklyn-born Lena Krasner, one of seven children. Her
parents were Orthodox Jews from a Russian shtetl who had fled after the 1903
Kishinev pogrom. She changed her name from Lena to Lenore because of Edgar

Lee Krasner

The house-studio where Jackson Pollock created his masterpieces
WIKIMEDIA COMMONS, AMERICASROOF

Allan Poe's poem "The Raven," which portrays a man tormented by the loss of his beloved. Poe described the man's angst: "Vainly I had sought to borrow / From my books surcease of sorrow-sorrow for the lost Lenore". The rebel settled on the American, androgynous Lee, and removed an 's' from her surname. Family drama transpired when Rose, her older sister, died, leaving her husband, William Stein, and two young daughters. In keeping with Jewish tradition, as the next oldest daughter, her parents expected Lee to marry William, a movie-projector operator. Upon her refusal, the responsibly fell to her sixteen-year-old sister, Ruth. As a result, the siblings' relationship suffered.

The Girls High School expelled Lee for refusing to sing religious Christmas carols, something she objected to as a Jew. At age thirteen, Lee attended Washington Irving High, the only school in New York to permit females in art classes. Postgraduation, she enrolled in the National Academy of Design which she described as a place of "congealed mediocrity." During the Great Depression, Lee painted murals for the WPA artists' project where she met Willem de Kooning. A scholarship allowed her to study with Hans Hofmann, a German émigré abstract expressionist painter who had known Matisse, Mondrian, Kandinsky, and Picasso. He commented on her canvas, "This is so good, you would never know it was done by a woman." Until he ended the relationship, Lee lived with a Russian art student, Igor Pantuhoff.

In 1940 Manhattan's McMillen Gallery was putting on an exhibit featuring Pablo Picasso, Henri Matisse, and Georges Braque, and invited an equal number of unknown American artists: Willem de Kooning, Paul Jackson Pollock, and Lee Krasner. As Jackson lived a block away, Lee dropped by, although Willem had described Jackson as looking like "some guy who works at a service station pumping gas." She recognized him as the man she had met four years earlier at an Artists' Union loft party and had refused to go out with him because he was a "lousy dancer." Then she saw his paintings and recalled, "I almost died." Falling for the artist as well as his art, lousy dancing no longer mattered. Lee moved in.

Weeks after V-J Day, after they were married in Marbel Collegiate Church in Manhattan, they visited Springs, East Hampton, Long Island, and swooned under its spell. For five thousand dollars they purchased a nineteenth-century farmhouse on the Accabonac Creek, replete with a barn and five acres. Heiress Peggy Guggenheim provided the two thousand-dollar down payment; she adored Jackson, though she never cared for Lee. Peggy was equipped with a sex drive as huge as a Pollock canvass. She tried to seduce Jackson, but he later remarked, "You would have to put a towel over Peggy Guggenheim's head to have sex with her." Other men were not as discerning. When asked by an interviewer how many husbands she had, Peggy replied, "Mine or other people's?" The home lacked heat, hot water, and an indoor bathroom, but it provided—if not Poe's raven—a crow they named Caw-Caw. In their isolated sanctuary, the couple dug for clams, rode their bikes to the beach (they did not own a car), and painted. A Hampton Mother Hubbard, Jackson traded art for food with the proprietor of the nearby Springs General Store; it displays a reproduction of the Pollock painting that the store obtained in the deal of deals. Local lore holds that the Jackson Pollock canvas sat behind the couch of the store's owner for years as he did not know what to make of the paint-splashed painting. Lee harbored the hope their rural retreat would distance her husband from the siren call of the Greenwich Village bars. As the first of the post–World War II artists to settle in the Hamptons, the Pollocks were the founders of its legendary art colony.

Initially Jackson painted in their bedroom; however, requiring more space, he turned their barn into his studio whose open space allowed him to lay a giant canvas on the floor, resulting in his breakthrough "drip method." *Life* magazine declared Pollock was the greatest living artist in the U.S. During their hungry days, they would have been astounded that a Lee Krasner painting would be sold for $11.6 million, a Jackson Pollock for $200 million.

The paradigm in their marriage was while he was the one with the fame, she was the watchdog of his reputation. She recalled, "There were the artists and then there were the 'dames.' I was considered a 'dame' even if I was a painter too."

As Jackson's success skyrocketed, he proved he was not only adept with his paintbrush. When Lee learned of her husband's infidelity, she again—but in a different way—felt "I wanted to die." While intoxicated, he could also make her the target of his verbal grenades: "Imagine being married to that face." Deeply hurt at his cruelty, womanizing, and drinking, Lee commuted to Manhattan to consult with her psychiatrist. Still, she sacrificed at his alter and only denied him a child. As she explained, she "married him to become an artist, not a mother." In addition, her plate was overflowing from dealing with her mercurial husband: she was his promoter, cheerleader, and secretary. Her mission became to save Jackson from Jackson. With his oversize ego and gargantuan neediness, Jackson sucked all the air from their farmhouse. How different life would have been had Lee married William Stein.

By 1954 Jackson had begun to drink more and more, paint less and less. Compounding the troubled Krasner-Pollock marriage, physical adultery morphed into an emotional one when he developed feelings for the twenty-six-year-old Ruth Kligman, who saw herself as the Jersey-Jewish Elizabeth Taylor. After catching them together, Lee sailed for Europe. On August 11, 1956, Jackson possessed enough self-awareness to defend his wife to his mistress with the admission, "I'd be dead without her." Highly intoxicated, that evening Jackson crashed his Oldsmobile into an oak tree on Firestone Place Road. The forty-four-year-old Jackson and Ruth's friend Edith Metzger died at the scene; an injured Ruth survived. Capitalizing on their relationship, she published *Love Affair: A Memoir of Jackson Pollock*. Lee remarked that the book should have been called, "My Five F**** with Jackson Pollock—because that's all there were!" A big-game hunter of artists, Ruth went on to have an affair with Willem de Kooning. Willem said of Ruth, "She really puts the lead in my pencil." Upon hearing of her husband's death, Lee returned from France and found Ruth's clothes in her closet, her painting *Prophecy* turned against a wall. Although she never got over the loss of her great, flawed husband, she returned to painting. Her room of her own was the barn studio where she came into her own as an artist, a time when she was not merely Mrs. Jackson Pollock. Lee said, "I painted before Pollock, during Pollock, after Pollock." She never remarried and remained the dragon at the gate of the Pollock legacy. As she had once been dismissed as the great artist's wife, she fought against being viewed as the great artist's widow.

THE POLLOCK-KRASNER HOUSE

To visit the clapboard house in Springs is to be transported into a home that encompasses a love story, the history of a Goliath of modern art, a mid-century artist's retreat. Lee Krasner Pollock's will led to the creation of the Pollock-Krasner House and Study Center. The property is under the jurisdiction of the Stony Brook Foundation, a private, nonprofit affiliate of Stony Brook University. Although initially a weather-beaten farmhouse, Jackson and Lee gave their house a facelift so that it resembled a white-walled, Manhattan loft. The home, where it is 1948 forever, is so homey one can almost smell the scent of Jackson's apple pies; he was a mean baker. The kitchen displays a pair of greasy oven gloves hanging on a hook. Above the refrigerator are china pots decorated with whimsical windmills, which held sugar, rice, pepper, and cloves. The windowsill displayed the couple's garden tomatoes, waiting to ripen. Hanging over a kitchen cupboard is Pollock's painting Untitled (Composition with Red Arc and Horses). The image appears to be a ritual scene, possibly a sacrifice. The back of the canvas bears Jackson's signature and his address, 46 East 8th Street. The phonograph conjures the image of a needle rotating on vinyl, the echo of jazz drowning out the wind. White shelves hold their extensive books. A fascinating piece is a rusty anchor the couple found on the beach and utilized as wall decor. Lee's bedroom window retains her shell collection, the bed holds her plum-colored silk robe, and a rack displays her necklaces. By the mirror is a white sleeveless dress with a silver pattern. On the bedside table is a white rotary phone, vintage radio, jumble of pills, sewing kit, and a pack of cigarettes. Lee's portrait, sketched by her college boyfriend, gazes upon her former domain. Two vintage suitcases, one printed with the letters J.P. and the other with L.K., souvenirs of husband-wife travels before liquor and other women encroached on their Eden.

While the holy grail of the Vatican is the Sistine Chapel, the sacred relic of The Pollock-Krasner House is the floor on which visitors can only walk with fabric booties, which still allow for the feel of congealed paint. After Jackson became an art-world icon, the artist winterized the studio and covered the floor with pressed wood squares. After Lee's passing, when the foundation undertook renovations, workers unearthed the original flooring that preserved the artist's footprints on its paint-spattered surface. The discovery was a visual diary of Jackson at the peak of his creativity, and one can see remnants of his most famous poured paintings: "Autumn Rhythm: Number 30" (the property of the Metropolitan Museum of Art), and "Lavender Mist: Number 1" (National Gallery, Washington, D.C.). Walking on the sacred graffiti, one can summon Jackson crouched over his canvas, wearing a black T-shirt, cigarette dangling from his mouth. Standing on the perimeter, Lee watched her husband with a mixture of love and loathing. Off to the side are her weathered boots.

The final resting place of the couple is in Green River Cemetery in Springs. Their headstones are made of locally quarried granite; Lee's is substantially smaller.

Perhaps Jackson's final bender occurred because he felt he had lost his Lenore, a sentiment echoed in the closing line of "The Raven": "And my soul from out that shadow that lies floating on the floor / Shall be lifted-nevermore."

A View from Her Window
The view was of the Accabonac Creek where blue heron waded.

Nearby Attraction: Grey Gardens
The 1897 property became infamous as the residence of Little Edie and her mother, Edith Ewing Bouvier Beale, the first cousin and aunt of Jacqueline Kennedy Onassis.

CHAPTER SEVEN

Never Pass into Nothingness
Judith Leiber

"Hitler put me in the handbag business."

—JUDITH LEIBER

The Leiber Collection (opened 2008)
446 Old Stone Highway, East Hampton, New York
(631) 329-3288
info@leibercollection.org
http://www.leibermuseum.org

Parking: On premises

Hours of Operation: Open Saturday, Sunday, and Wednesday, 1–4 p.m.
Private and group tours available. Individual appointments available by
texting 917-885-0626 or by email

Admission: Donations

Nearby Accommodations: The Roundtree / Journey East Hampton / Sag
Harbor Inn

Nearby Eateries: Harvest on Fort Pond / East Hampton Grill / Felice's
Italian Restaurant

THE NINETEENTH-CENTURY BRITISH POET JOHN KEATS WROTE "A THING OF
beauty is a joy forever." The sentiment holds true for the glittery, gorgeous minau-
dières (bejeweled clutch bags) created by Judith Leiber. To enter a museum that
is a kaleidoscope of a love story, a slice of history, and art set amidst magnificent
gardens, take the meandering road to The Leiber Collection.

Heavy handbags were never associated with the handiwork of Judith
Leiber, who stated her creations were to hold only lipstick, a handkerchief, and a

Lovers brought together by World War II

hundred-dollar bill—a reasonable sum for one who could afford her artistry. When asked about space for eyeglasses, keys, and other sundries, Judith's response: "What's an escort for?"

A high priestess of handbags started out worlds away from Springs' serene landscape. Judith Marianne was born in Budapest, Hungary, in 1921, to Emil and Helen Peto. Judith and her sister, Eva, played with expensive Lenci dolls, their parents' souvenirs from Italian vacations. When Emil visited Austria, he brought home handbags for Helen. Her parents wanted Judith to become a chemist and emulate her Romanian aunt who had developed a complexion cream. After Miklós Horthy placed restrictions on Jews in universities, Judith left for King's College in London. While on vacation, World War II erupted. She refused to leave her parents and sister for refuge in Britain.

Judith apprenticed at Pessl, the eminent handbag company, where she swept the floors and prepared the glue. In 1944 she became the first woman to be admitted as a master by the Hungarian Handbag Guild, which awarded her a green toolbox. The factory closed when the government deported the Jewish owners. The same year, Nazi troops collaborated with the Hungarian Arrow Cross. When the Nazis discovered Judith's two uncles outside their home without wearing the Star of David, they killed them and dumped the corpses in the Danube. Through a friend at the Swiss Consulate, Emil obtained a *Schutz* pass which allowed refuge for himself, and eventually, through a machination, his family, in a building under Swiss jurisdiction. (The pass is now in the U.S. Holocaust Museum.) A far different donation to the Holocaust Museum was a ticket to the 1916 coronation of Emperor Karl IV. As the Red Army closed in on Budapest, the Nazis herded the Jews from their protected houses and forced them into the Jewish ghetto. On one occasion, Helen hacked off hunks of a horse's carcass to feed her family. To keep the horror at bay, Judith designed handbags in her head. After the war, having endured the occupation of Germany and the Soviet Union, the Petos were desperate to emigrate. En route to the U.S. Embassy, shrapnel pierced Judith's left arm, and she feared her career was over before it had begun. A surgeon operating in a cellar saved her arm, though she was left with lifelong scars.

While peddling purses made from salvaged scraps on the bomb-riddled streets of Budapest, Judith met Sergeant Gerson (Gus) Leiber who took her to the opera. Although her mother opposed the match to a poor soldier, Gerson and Judith married in 1946 in the Petos' home. Every day of their honeymoon, Helen phoned her daughter, imploring her to change her mind. The

Leibers sailed to New York on a bride ship—a transport for soldiers and their foreign-born brides. In her hand, she clutched her green toolbox.

The Leibers rented a mouse-infested apartment in the Bronx; Judith's culinary skills were such that smoke rose from the pan when she fried an egg. While Gerson took art classes, Judith worked for various companies. Success beckoned when First Lady Mamie Eisenhower appeared at Ike's inaugural ball holding a Judith Leiber minaudière embellished with pearls and rhinestones. Gerson told his wife that she should "not work for those *schnooks* anymore," and in 1963, they established Judith Leiber, Inc., which specialized in small bags for thick wallets. The new owner claimed her mission was to create the Rolls Royce of handbags. Though her first season was not a success because of her green-leather line (customers did not care for the color), serendipity stepped in with the arrival of dented brass minaudière from Italy. To camouflage the defect, Judith covered the bags with rhinestones, thus birthing her classic Chatelaine edition that made her the ultimate Bag Lady.

Walt Disney stated, "Always remember that this whole thing was started with a dream and a mouse." While Judith's imagination did not conjure a rodent, she did create a penguin, frog, horse, and food—without the calories: a tomato, eggplant, and kiwi.

In addition to Mamie Eisenhower, other First Ladies embraced the objects d'art. Barbara Bush carried a Leiber at her husband's inaugural ceremony. She ordered another to resemble Millie, her springer spaniel. To improve Russian relations, Barbara gifted a purse to Raisa Gorbachev, the wife of the Soviet leader. Raisa claimed it was the most breathtaking bag she had ever owned and that she would leave it to the Hermitage Museum. Nancy Reagan ordered white satin bags for both inaugural balls of her spouse. After Kitty Kelley's biography eviscerated Nancy, Judith sent her a handbag to soften the sting. Hillary Clinton requested a model based on Socks, the family cat. Lady Bird Johnson clutched the iconic clutch. Rosalyn Carter declined to do so, as she desired to project a down-to-earth-image. During the Kansas City Chiefs' Super Bowl win, Taylor Swift carried a custom Judith Leiber handbag that resembled a football, designed in the team's iconic red and gold colors. A further adornment was the crystal number 87, a nod to her boyfriend, Travis Kelce's, number.

Hollywood likewise had a love affair with the handbags. In the 1996 Academy Awards ceremony, Christine Cavanaugh, the voice of the title character in the Oscar-nominated *Babe*, carried Judith's jeweled pig minaudière (price tag: three thousand dollars). Two years later, in a scene from the film *Sex and the City*, when a frantic Mr. Big calls Carrie, Charlotte's daughter answers. After hanging up, she drops the pink phone into her Judith Leiber cupcake-shaped minaudière. The character's innocuous action set off a chain reaction that led to the cancellation of the Big-Bradshaw wedding. Audiences were appalled by both Big's behavior and the fact that the five-year-old Lily Goldblatt owned a $4,000 purse.

Celebrities have also indulged in the guilty pleasure: Greta Garbo, Barbara Walters, Beverly Stills, Elizabeth Taylor, Joan Collins, Jacqueline Kennedy, Ivana Trump, and Joan Rivers. Queen Elizabeth II received one as a gift; Judith stated, "But I look and look, high and low, and I never see her carry it." Despite her success, when Andy Warhol described her creations as works of art, Judith demurred, "Truthfully, I don't consider them art. I'm an artisan."

When not in their respective studios (Judith's held her green toolbox), home for the Leibers was their seven-room retreat in East Hampton where Judith raised orchids in her greenhouse. In Manhattan, they owned an eight-room triplex on Park Avenue. Judith loved attending the Metropolitan Opera, where she paid attention to the number of Judith Leiber bags in the audience. At an event held in her honor in Bangkok, she counted 220 bags in a crowd of 250 women. She added, "And you should have seen the jewelry on them. It was the size of lollipops." When an interviewer asked if she ever carried bags from another designer, Judith responded, "I either carry my own or a paper bag, and I won't carry a paper bag, so you figure it out." Trouble intruded into the handbag kingdom with the government's ban on the use of alligator skin. Judith, who had eaten horseflesh to survive, railed against the injunction. In 2005 she fashioned her last handbag, a Buddha's rhinestone-encrusted hand. More than eighty Leiber masterpieces are in the collection of the Met's Costume Institute.

When asked why they never had children, Judith explained that early in their marriage they could not afford any. Pointing to her collection, she said, "These are my children." Her latest was a coiled snake—the serpent's head serving as the bag's clasp. To show she had no regrets about not having procreated, she remarked of her purses, "And they never spoke a harsh word to me." As always, Gerson was on the same page as his wife and explained that their joint progeny "hang on the walls and from arms and shoulders. As a couple we feel complete and still do." However, they were the parents of Sterling, a Norwich terrier.

Although Judith had vowed, "I'll work until I drop," the Leibers sold their business in 1993 for a purported $16 to $18 million to the British firm Time Products. At age ninety-six, Gerson whispered to his wife of seventy-two years, "Sweetheart, it is time to go." Hours later, Judith joined Gerson. The couple embodied King Solomon's biblical words, "I am my beloved's and my beloved is mine." Husband and wife passed away in their Springs estate.

THE LEIBER COLLECTION

Desirous of leaving a legacy of their work, lives, and love story, Judith and Gerson established, at a cost of five million dollars, The Leiber Collection, a Renaissance-style Palladian-style museum on 464 Old Stone Highway. The building lies adjacent to their Springs estate.

Visitors to the collection can feast their eyes on the Fabergé of handbags on display in glass-fronted cabinets. On the walls are Gerson's oil and watercolor canvases. A 2000 Will Barnet portrait showcases Gerson holding a paintbrush and Judith holding her handbag. A touching tribute to the Leiber partnership is Gerson's oil painting *The Much Admired*, which portrays a woman and man in a nightclub; Judith reproduced the scene on her minaudière. The museum also holds their Chinese porcelains dating back five thousand years. The museum is the venue for exhibits of hundreds of works by twentieth-century artists.

To add as many Leiber bags as possible to their brick museum, Judith scoured vintage markets, high-end consignment shops, and online auctions. Donations supplemented the inventory, including The Hollywood purse, a black clutch with silver stars that emulated the iconic mountainside sign. Opera star Beverly Sills bequeathed her two hundred purses to the collection.

The words that followed the Keats line "A thing of beauty is a joy forever" encapsulates the Leiber collection: "Its loveliness increases, it will never pass into nothingness."

A View from Her Window

When Judith gazed from the window of her museum, she saw their six Gerson-designed gardens and works of art. A notable sculpture, *The Human Condition*, depicts six heads with gnarled fingers gripping the neck.

Nearby Attraction: Long Island Museum of American Art, History & Carriages

The museum houses the Carriage Museum that displays a collection of American horse-drawn carriages, a one-room schoolhouse, and a blacksmith shop.

Chapter Eight

Staten Island Shangri-La

Jacques Marchais

"It stands as a great monument to our love!"
—Jacques Marchais (letter to Harry Klauber)

The Jacques Marchais Museum of Tibetan Art (opened 1947)
338 Lighthouse Avenue, Staten Island, New York 10306
(718) 987-3500
https://www.tibetanmuseum.org/

Parking: Street parking

Hours of Operation: Thursday–Sunday, 1–5 p.m.

Admission: $; Culture pass: Free

Gift Shop: Yes

Nearby Accommodations: Victorian Bed & Breakfast / The Harbor House / The Staten Island Inn

Nearby Eateries: Guyon Superette / Piece of Cake / Amadeus Restaurant & Bar

In 1933 James Hilton published *Lost Horizons* whose backdrop, the Himalayas, are known as "the rooftop of the world." For those unable to travel to the fabled kingdom, take the ferry to Staten Island's The Jacques Marchais Museum of Tibetan Art.

Johnny Cash's 1969 song "A Boy Named Sue" revolves around a man who has spent his life with upraised fists, infuriated that his father had saddled him with a female name. In a similar vein, John Coblentz christened his daughter Jacques Marchais. In the Cash song, the adult Sue reconciles with his father

Jacques Marchais Garden
WIKIMEDIA COMMONS, CISC

when the old man explained his rationale: his effeminate moniker would teach him to be tough. Jacques never had the opportunity to inquire why her father had bequeathed her a French boy's name as John passed away when she was a toddler.

Jacques Marchais Coblentz was born in 1887 in Cincinnati, Ohio. Her mother, Margaret, a widow without means of support, entrusted Jacques to an orphanage run by nuns, although she was not Catholic. When Jacques was three, Margaret reclaimed her daughter and put her on the vaudeville circuit. As a male name would cause confusion, she billed Jacques as Edna Coblentz or Edna Norman (her maiden name). Wealthy Chicago families requested private performances—one of whom was Mike Cassius McDonald, who introduced organized crime to Chicago.

When she was five years old, Jacques opened a chest that had gathered decades of dust in the family's attic. The Pandora's Box held thirteen bronze deities her great-grandfather, John Joseph Norman, a Philadelphia sea merchant, had received from an Indian lama in Darjeeling. The discovery of the mysterious objects fascinated Jacques far more than any doll, and they would be instrumental in shaping her destiny.

At age sixteen, Jacques travelled to Boston to star in the comedy *Peggy from Paris*, where she met Brookings Montgomery, a student at MIT. When Brookings married the destitute teen, his prominent St. Louis family disowned him. The couple had children Edna May, Jane, and Brookings Jr.; they divorced in 1910. Six years later, Jacques married hotel manager Percy S. Deponai, a union that came with a one-year expiration date.

While Horace Greeley had admonished, "Go West, young man," Jacques left for the East hoping to make it big on Broadway and leaving behind her two former husbands and children. What she did take with her were the thirteen bronze figurines. Although she never found success as an actress, she was to excel on a different stage.

In Manhattan, Jacques met Harry Klauber (nicknamed "the Governor"), who proved opposites do attract. The Brooklyn-born Jewish entrepreneur and the midwestern Christian spiritualist married in 1918. The third marital try proved the charm though Jacques was very different than the women in Harry's circle, for whom mink stoles were de rigeur.

In the early 1900s, Staten Island developer William Platt had remarked the neighborhood carried "unimagined possibilities; a land of paradise. Have you the desire to be your own Landlord, to own your home on a grand picturesque plateau with the most magnificent view of the Ocean and Bay?" The answer to his question: a resounding yes for the Klaubers. In 1921, with the income from Harry's chemical business, the couple purchased a residence on three acres on a hill on 340 Lighthouse Avenue (then Seaview Avenue).

As Harry worked with his chemicals, Jacques pursued her studies of all things regarding Himalaya, the land she felt was her spiritual homeland. Because of health issues, the dangers associated with travelling to the world that mingled with the clouds, and the Tibetans' unwillingness to admit foreigners, Jacques transformed into a dedicated armchair traveler. She earned a black belt in shopping in her relentless pursuit of Tibetan art, statuary, and relics. Her Staten Island home became—to borrow a title from a Charles Dickens novel—a little curiosity shop filled with exotic finds.

When she ran out of space for her treasures, to house the overflow and to educate the West about the East, she opened the Jacques Marchais Gallery at 40 East Fifty-First Street in New York City. After a decade, she closed her store's doors to create a Tibetan temple. The inspiration stemmed from an exhibition dedicated to the Lama Temple Potala at the 1933 Century of Progress International Exhibition in Chicago.

In contrast to the Potala Palace in Lhasa (the home of the Dalai Lamas) that held more than a thousand rooms and ten thousand shrines, Jacques determined to do what she could to make her museum emulate a slice of Himalaya. The building's interior would be conducive to meditation; a huge Buddha would serve as benevolent deity.

In 1945 the world gained a macabre geography: Dachau, Treblinka, Auschwitz. In the same year, in Staten Island, Jacques planned what she referred to as the "Portola of the West" which she envisioned would be an enclave of peace, spirituality, and compassion. Along with local mason Joseph Premiano, who constructed the edifice, she drove around Staten Island in her pickup truck, hauling stones to embed in the temple's walls.

In 1947, a grand dedication ceremony marked the opening of the Jacques Marchais Center of Tibetan Art, an event covered by *Life* magazine in its article "New York Lamasery." An accompanying photograph showcases Jacques in a long blue gown, seated in an antique red-lacquer Chinese chair that rests in front of an altar flanked by two bronze Nepalese lions.

Tragically, Madame Marchais had little time to revel in her dream. Four months later, she passed away in her home at age sixty from complications of diabetes, cerebral embolism, and coronary disease. Her burial was in a Christian cemetery on Staten Island. An adherent of reincarnation, perhaps Jacques was in her museum in 1991 when His Holiness the Fourteenth Dalai Lama, Tenzin Gyatso, blessed the premises. His scarf graces the neck of one of the buddhas. In her will, Jacques left everything to Harry. Her husband survived her by seven months and bequeathed the property and its collections to the museum as a memorial to his wife.

THE JACQUES MARCHAIS MUSEUM OF TIBETAN ART

Pilgrims who visit the "Jewel on the Hillside" are initially taken aback by the two stone buildings that resemble a Tibetan lamasery incongruously sitting on Staten Island. The structures were the first to employ Himalayan-style architecture in the country and the first devoted to Tibetan art. The museum claims to possess America's only Bhutanese sand mandala, the multicolored sand design that represents the dwelling of a deity. The tranquility is such that one can hear the chirping of the birds. The terraced Samadhi Garden derives its name from the Sanskrit for the cycle of birth, the principle of karma. The museum's vantage point affords a vista of Lower New York Bay. In a pond, oversized goldfish make their rounds around lotus flowers. Stone elephants and rocks are inscribed with mantras. Nearby is an enormous Chinese gong. The smell of incense leaves a heady scent.

Although Madame Marchais did not journey to the East, she amassed some of its treasures. The temple-museum holds over five thousand objects; visitors can gaze upon sculptures, ritual objects, musical instruments, scroll paintings, and furniture. The relics originated in Tibet, Nepal, Bhutan, Northern China, Mongolia, and Southeast Asia. The museum maintains a permanent exhibit of 125 objects; the remainder is showcased on a rotating basis. The exoticism of the exhibits is enhanced with their ties to antiquity: they span from the twelfth through the twentieth century. The grounds hold brightly colored prayer flags, chanting rooms, and meditation cells.

Photographs of historic interest are also part of the appeal. In 1942, after months of slogging through mountains and snow, the grandson of novelist Leo Tolstoy, Lieutenant Colonel Ilia Tolstoy, arrived at the palace of the Dalai Lama. Tolstoy's black-and-white photograph of the eight-year-old god-king's picture now resides worlds away in Staten Island.

The oldest section houses a library with two thousand books on the topic of the Far East as well as a gift shop. A few steps away, a second building has a five-level stone altar, in keeping with Buddhist tradition, that takes up an entire wall. On the altar rests many-armed sculptures of gods, Chinese cloisonné braziers, and three Tibetan tankas—paintings depicting items of religious significance. Nearby reside reliquaries and a Japanese folding shrine that consists of wood and gilt doors. The central sculpture depicts a bronze figure of Tsong-kha-pa, a religious reformer and the founder of the Yellow Hat sect of Buddhism. A few of the artifacts are made from human bones, such as a skull bowl—hopefully not for sale in the gift shop.

For those with a hankering for Eastern mysticism in a New York borough, head to the museum created by an American woman with a Frenchman's name. The Jacques Marchais Museum of Tibetan Art is Staten Island's Shangri-La.

A View from Her Window

When Jacques gazed from her window at the embodiment of her dream, she must have marveled at the magic carpet that had transported her from an orphanage to the owner of a museum.

Nearby Attraction: Snug Harbor Cultural Center

The eighty-three-acre center holds a Chinese Scholar's Garden with magnificent rocks, which conjures the poetry of Confucius—the image of Buddhist monks, hands clasped in prayer.

CHAPTER NINE

A Lovely Light

Edna St. Vincent Millay

"I do not think there is a woman in whom the roots of passion shoot deeper than me."

—EDNA ST. VINCENT MILLAY

Steepletop (opened 2010)
440 East Hill Road, Austerlitz, New York
518-392-3362
https://millay.org/

Parking: There is limited parking in the visitor's lot in front of the Garage/Studio next door to the Visitor's Center. Additional parking is available down the road.

Hours of Operation: When open for tours, the hours are 9 a.m.– 5 p.m.

Admission: Guided house tour: $$$; Grounds and picnic pass: $$

Gift Shop: Yes

Nearby Accommodations: Hampton Terrace Inn / Garden Gables Inn / Lakehouse Inn

Nearby Eateries: Peace, Love and Chocolate / Once Upon a Table / Inn at Silver Maple Farm

DOROTHY PARKER, AT HER SELF-DEPRECATING BEST, WROTE, "I WAS FOLLOW-ing in the exquisite footsteps of Miss Edna St. Vincent Millay, unhappily in my own horrible sneakers." When Ms. Parker, the mistress of acerbic wit, paid a fellow poet a compliment, it was high praise indeed. To walk in Ms. Millay's "exquisite footsteps," take a trip to Steepletop.

Edna St. Vincent Millay
WIKIMEDIA COMMONS, CARL VAN VECHTEN

The expansive grounds of Steepletop was worlds away from Edna's modest roots in Rockland, a rocky-coast town in Maine, where she was born in 1892. Her middle name came from New York's St. Vincent Hospital where her uncle had received life-saving care.

Her father, Henry, gambled away his meager income, and when Edna was eight, her mother, Cora, obtained a divorce. Henry and Edna did not meet again for eleven years. To support her daughters, Edna, Norma, and Kathleen, Cora worked as an itinerant nurse. The Millays likened themselves to the struggling March family in Louisa May Alcott's *Little Women*.

Edna St. Vincent Millay's home for the last twenty-five years of her life
WIKIMEDIA COMMONS, DANIEL CASE

The Millays moved around New England until they settled in Camden, Maine, where they rented a small house in, as Edna described it, "the bad section of town." While Cora was away, Edna's life centered on chores and siblings. She entered poetry contests under the name E. Vincent Millay, in the belief publishers would take a man's work more seriously. With the prize money from *St. Nicholas,* she purchased a collection of the poetry of Robert Browning. In her diary, she wrote that for her eighteenth birthday, her mother bought her a book on the poetry of Omar Khayyam's *Rubaiyat.*

In 1912 her poem "Renascence" appeared in *The Lyric Year,* an eminent anthology. Further laurels arrived when the editors discovered the poet was a twenty-year-old whose education ended after high school. After Edna recited "Renascence" at the Whitehall Inn in Camden, a guest, Caroline Dow, was so impressed she arranged the financing of Edna's college education.

At Vassar Edna Vincent was the party-girl poet around which the campus's literary lights revolved. The college also assuaged her isolation as she embarked on relationships with two female classmates. Regarding the school's women-only policy, Edna groused, "A man is forbidden as if he were an apple." Her behavior almost led to her banishment from commencement.

Upon graduation, Edna migrated to Greenwich Village; the embodiment of the starving artist, she lived hand-to-mouth, bed-to-bed. Critic Edmund Wilson thought he was Edna's one and only; he was one of four—or more. In addition to writing, she acted with the Provincetown Players in their converted stable on MacDougal Street. Her hungry years led to her poem in which she wrote of a couple in love, "We looked into a fire, we leaned across a table." The poignancy, the pain was only apparent in its title, "Recuerdo"—Spanish for "I Remember."

Part of the roar of the Roaring Twenties emanated from the poet-flapper who drank, partied, and had affairs. In contrast to the romanticism of nineteenth-century poetry such as Elizabeth Barrett Browning's sonnet, "And, if God choose / I shall but love thee better after death," Edna's pen dripped with the transience of romance, "And if I loved you Wednesday / Well, what is that to you? / I do not love you Thursday— / So much is true."

Desirous of "new grass to feed on," Edna was thrilled to set sail for Europe as *Vanity Fair*'s first female foreign correspondent. Her love of travel was evident in her words, "But there isn't a train I wouldn't take / No matter where it's going." She was part of the American colony in Paris where she posed for Man Ray, dined with Brancusi, and caroused with F. Scott Fitzgerald. She shared she was not impressed with the author of *The Great Gatsby*. In 1923, after two years abroad, Edna returned to New York.

Six years earlier, Hungarian-born publisher Joseph Pulitzer had established the Pulitzer Prize; Edna St. Vincent Millay was the first woman to win his award for poetry. Harriet Monroe of *Poetry magazine* referred to her as "the greatest woman poet since Sappho." The public lionized the literary light, and crowds gathered to hear the words of the woman with the flame-colored hair. British author Thomas Hardy remarked that Millay's poetry, along with the skyscraper, was America's greatest contribution to the 1920s. Inspired by her affair with much younger George Dillon, her book *Fatal Interview* sold more than fifty thousand copies, despite the Great Depression. Dorothy Parker wrote, "We all wandered in after Miss Millay. We were all being dashing and gallant, declaring that we weren't virgins, whether we were or not. Beautiful as she was, Miss Millay did a great deal of harm with her double burning candles . . . made poetry seem so easy that we could all do it. But of course, we couldn't."

The year she won the Pulitzer Prize she met the Dutch-born entrepreneur Eugen Jan Boissevain at a house party in Croton-on-Hudson, New York. He was the widower of Inez Mulholland who shared similarities with Edna: Vassar graduate, fierce feminist, and proponent of free love. Yet Inez had done something Edna had not. The day before President Woodrow Wilson's inauguration, wearing a crown and a white cape, she rode a horse at the head of a suffrage procession in Washington, D.C. In her poem "Passer Mortuus Est," Edna expressed she also had a sentimental streak concerning affairs of the heart, "After all, my erstwhile dear / My no longer cherished / Need we say it was not love / Now that love is perished?" Their wedding elicited national headlines and three New York papers placed it on their front page. Suffering from intestinal pain, the bride went from the ceremony to the hospital for emergency surgery. Referring to her Pulitzer Prize, she told Eugen, "If I die now, at least I'll be immortal." An onslaught of health and other problems led to her observance, "It's not true that life is one damn thing after another—it's the same damn thing over and over."

To find a forever home after her nomadic existence, Edna and Eugen purchased an abandoned berry farm on a hilltop overlooking the Berkshire Hills. A proud homeowner, Edna christened it Steepletop after the pink-flowered steeplebush that grew wild in its meadow. The couple enjoyed wonderful years, but Steepletop's gate could not keep out evil spirits. In 1936 Edna fell through the door of a car, an accident that left her with chronic pain and segued to her morphine addiction. When Eugen died after surgery for lung cancer, Edna suffered a nervous breakdown and had to be institutionalized. Her elegy for Eugen can be expressed in the poem she had written years before, "Dirge without Music," in which she mourned, "Quietly they go, the intelligent, the witty, the brave. I know. But I do not approve. And I am not resigned." The following year, while at the top of her stairs, Edna suffered a heart attack, and tumbled to her death. Later in the day, caretaker James Pinnie discovered her body at the foot of the landing.

STEEPLETOP

Edna wrote, "Safe upon the solid rock the ugly houses stand: / Come and see my shining palace built upon the sand!" Visitors to Millay's shining palace, perched on a hill overlooking hundreds of acres of pastures and woods, sense the high priestesses of poetry's bohemian ghost.

The home is a fossil that remains the same as on the date of the poet's 1950 passing. In the foyer are walking sticks and hunting rifles. A jar of witch hazel sits on the shelf above her bathroom sink, next to her bottle of pills with a 1945 label. In her bedroom, the dresser drawer holds her purse; inside is a tube of lipstick etched—as were her hand towels and notepad—with the initials E. St. V. M. Wrapped in tissue is a lock of her red hair. The clothes from her reading tours, silk scarves, and monogrammed purse lie in readiness. Beside the four-poster bed is a nightstand on which rests Melachrino cigarettes, assorted lacquer and rhino-horn trinkets, souvenirs from her honeymoon across Asia.

Steepletop's sanctuary is Edna's second-floor library, which holds three thousand books, along with faded newspapers. One is tempted to curl up in her chair. Hung from the ceiling is a hand-lettered sign demanding "Silence," which is tongue-in-cheek, as she did not permit anyone to enter this domain. In the kitchen, stuffing spills from the salmon-colored Naugahyde cushions. The wine glasses in the cupboard once touched Edna's lips. In what Edna referred to as her "withdrawing room" rests her Remington typewriter, two pianos, and a life-size marble bust of Sappho.

Although Steepletop was a retreat from Hardy's "madding crowd," Edna and Eugen often invited guests to their home. At the outdoor bar, gin watered the flowers; in the spring-fed pool, one swam au naturel. The she-shack was where Edna wrote, accompanied by her German shepherd, Altair; after Cora's passing, Edna surrounded the cabin with thirty-one white pines in memory of her mother and Maine. A missing museum item: a candle with wicks on both ends.

A heart-rending sight is the railing's broken baluster: as Edna tumbled down the stairs, she grabbed hold of it to break her fall. The Steepletop Cemetery holds the graves of Cora, Edna, Eugen, her sister, Norma, and her brother-in-law, Charles Ellis. Edna's epitaph could have been the words from "First Fig": "My candle burns at both ends; / It will not last the night; / But ah, my foes, and oh, my friends— / It gives a lovely light!"

A View from Her Window
Looking from the window, Edna saw endless rows of pink-flowered steeplebush.

Nearby Attraction: The Circle Museum
The Circle Museum consists of eight acres filled with a hundred whimsical metal sculptures.

CHAPTER TEN

Deeds Not Words

Alice Paul

"The thing I think that was the most useful thing I ever did, was having a part in getting the vote for all the women."

—ALICE PAUL

Alice Paul Institute (Paulsdale) (opened 2002)
128 Hooton Road, Mount Laurel Township, New Jersey 08054
(856) 231-1885
info@alicepaul.org
https://www.alicepaul.org/

Parking: A parking lot is located at the rear of the property, marked by signs.

Hours of Operation: Thursday and Friday, 12–6 p.m.; occasional Saturdays, 10 a.m.–3 p.m.

Admission: Adults: $$; Children under 6: Free

Gift Shop: Yes

Accommodations near Paulsdale: Staybridge Suites / La Quinta Inn & Suites / Cinnaminson Motor Lodge

Nearby Eateries: Mezeh / Pho Xinh / Tommy's Taven & Tap

WHICH HISTORIC FIGURE ENDED UP BEHIND BARS SEVERAL TIMES FOR ACTS OF civil disobedience and protested through fasting? The answer is not only the dhoti-clad Hindu Mohandas Gandhi; it is also the Victorian-garbed Quaker Alice Paul. To experience the home of the firebrand, make your way to her former farm, Paulsdale.

Alice toasting—with grape juice—the passage of
the Nineteenth Amendment
WIKIMEDIA COMMONS, HARRIS & EWING, INC.

Alice Stokes Paul consecrated her life to the suffrage movement. While one can assume the derivative of suffrage is "suffering," the word originated from the Latin *suffregium*, which translates to the right to vote, as well as a prayer of intercession. A pillar of the movement was born in 1885 to a well-to-do family in Moorestown, New Jersey, in the residence Alice always referred to as the home farm. Her parents, Tacie and William, were Hicksite Quakers who taught their four children the principle of gender equality. Alice later remarked, "There is nothing complicated about ordinary equality." Tacie took Alice along to suffrage meetings, surely never imagining the role her daughter would one day play in the movement. Their church, however, still labored under the precepts of the era: married women could not attend university, the reason why Tacie had quit Swarthmore College.

Alice attended the Moorestown Friends School; after graduating at the top of her class, she studied biology at Swarthmore, founded in 1864, by her grandfather, Judge William Parry. The college years were golden: Alice participated in sports, was a member of the Phi Beta Kappa, and received the title Ivy Poetess. Her college yearbook, *Halcyon*, described her as "an open-hearted maiden, true and pure." A dedicated student, Alice spoke at her commencement ceremony. She earned a master's degree and a doctorate at the University of Pennsylvania. In the 1920s, Alice obtained three law degrees; she preferred the title Miss rather than doctor.

In 1907 Alice left for the Lower East Side of New York to apprentice in the fledgling field of social work. The city's slums opened her eyes to economic disparity, something she had been immune to in Mount Laurel Township, New Jersey. After receiving a scholarship from a Quaker group, Alice left for England with the aspiration of becoming a college professor.

Many Disney fans were introduced to the women's movement through Winifred Banks who sang the lyrics of "Sister Suffragette": "Political equality and equal rights with men! / Take heart! / For Missus Pankhurst has been clapped in irons again!" The Missus Pankhurst referred to was Emmeline Pankhurst, regarded by her countrymen as a homegrown terrorist. In protest of Emmeline's arrest—and disgusted by men ogling the nude goddess—Mary Richardson used a meat cleaver to slash Diego Velázquez's "Rokeby Venus." As

Paulsdale, birth home of Alice Paul
WIKIPEDIA COMMONS, ROBERT M. HUNT

she slashed the seventeenth century portrait, she stated, "I am a suffragette. I have tried to destroy the picture of the most beautiful woman in mythological history as protest against the government for destroying Miss Pankhurst, who is the most beautiful character in modern history." Her action left a half-dozen cuts in the canvass and earned her the epithet "Slasher Mary."

Alice transformed from unassuming Quaker to radical activist after meeting Emmeline and Christabel Pankhurst. The British mother and daughter subscribed to the ancient Greek oath of Hippocrates, "Desperate times call for desperate measures." While most women tried to effect change through letter-writing campaigns and speeches, the Pankhursts employed tactics that involved chaining themselves to lampposts and hurtling rocks through windows.

In 1909 Alice crashed the Lord Mayor's Banquet (Winston Churchill was in attendance), crying out, "How about votes for women?" Civil disobedience resulted in seven arrests and three incarcerations. In Holloway Prison, Alice embarked on a hunger strike that led to force-feeding through a nasal tube which she endured twice daily for four weeks. She recalled, "The largest wardress in Holloway sat astride my knees." What made horror endurable was "the militant policy is bringing success. The agitation has brought England out of her lethargy."

Physically weakened, but emotionally invigorated, Alice returned to the United States with the goal of advancing the clock for women's rights. The Paul platform was to "terrify the men in Congress" to allow female access to the ballot box. President Woodrow Wilson did not share her perspective, saying, "The principal objection to giving women the ballot is that they are too logical."

Alice founded and served as the head of the fifty-thousand-member National Woman's Party. To force the president's hand, Harriot Stanton Blatch (Elizabeth Cady Stanton's daughter), suggested picketing the White House as "silent sentinels," by which she advocated for nonviolent protest. Dressed in white, they carried purple, white, and gold banners that bore slogans such as, "How Much Longer Must Women Wait?" Another referenced America's involvement in World War I and attacked "Kaiser Wilson"; "An Autocrat at Home Is a Poor Champion of Democracy Abroad." Alice scaled a White House fence and set a fire on its lawn.

During President Wilson's 1923 inauguration, Alice, Helen Keller, along with thousands of suffragists, held their own Pennsylvania Avenue parade led by Inez Mulholland who rode in front mounted on a white horse. Infuriated men pushed into their ranks, and approximately one hundred female protestors needed hospitalization. The press covered the brutality, and the women's march overshadowed the inauguration. Police arrested NWP members who languished in brutal conditions in Occoquan workhouse in Virginia where guards subjected them to force-feedings. The suffragists received the name "the iron-jawed angels" from their refusal to eat. Dr. William A. White of St. Elizabeth's Hospital threatened that if Alice continued her shenanigans, he would have her committed. Amidst the inhumanity of Occoquan, from her cell, Alice heard the shouts of her fellow freedom fighters: "West Virginia greets you!" "Oklahoma is with you!" "New York salutes you!" In 1917 the Women's Party held an event to honor the eighty-nine women who had spent time behind bars. Each received a silver pin, designed by Alice, in the shape of a cell door with a chain and a heart-shaped lock. The pin now resides on the Belmont-Paul Women's Equality National Monument in Washington, D.C.

Realizing the thorn in his side would not go away, President Wilson ordered Congress to pass the 19th amendment. He encountered fierce opposition from the Southern states; Mississippi did not agree to its passing until 1984. The final vote for the amendment's passage arrived when Tennessee legislator Harry T. Burn changed his mind after receiving a telegram from his mother to "be a good boy." The winner of the election was Warren G. Harding—and the millions of women who voted. In her eighth decade, Alice reminisced that the adoption of the 19th amendment was the high point of her life.

With the actualization of her mission, Dr. Paul could have become a college professor, and accrued financial stability, thereby avoiding the destitution that dogged her twilight years. However, she still had hydra heads to slay. Indefatigable, she drafted the forerunner to the Equal Rights Amendment. If asked about her own "halcyon period," she likely would have recalled the struggle for suffrage: "I never saw a day when I stopped working for women's rights." Alice Paul passed away at the Quaker Greenleaf Extension Home in Moorestown at age ninety-two. Her bank account was empty; her idealism overflowing.

Alice Paul Institute

A quaint 224-year-old brick farmhouse is set so far back from Hooton Road that a passerby may not know of its existence. That is unfortunate as a giant in the fight for equality started her life in its upstairs room in a home that was her North Star of constancy.

Of the original 173 acres, only six and a half remain. The property has an expansive view, one the family would have enjoyed from their broad, wrap-around porch. The interior still has its random-width floorboards, some twenty inches wide. The large parlor, the hand-carved banister of the entrance hall staircase, and the ornate front door are original. The Alice Paul Centennial Foundation purchased the twelve-room structure as a memorial to Alice. Some of the people responsible for fundraising were Gloria Steinem and Marlo Thomas. The foundation, formed in 1984 to celebrate the centennial of the activist's birth, and to raise funds to buy Alice's personal effects. They donated her letters and records to the Arthur and Elizabeth Schlesinger Library at Radcliffe College; other memorabilia went to the Smithsonian. However, some artifacts remain. From her youth is a wooden pencil box with her initials and a pennant from Swarthmore College. Although the foundation used period colored paint and wallcoverings on the interior, they did not want the home to be a shrine to Alice—something of which she would have approved. Barbara Irvine, the president of the foundation stated, "It's got to be a living, breathing place, perpetuating the things she stood for." Paulsdale serves as a leadership training center for young people from across the country. The Alice Paul Institute website states, "The organization is a model of adaptive reuse of a historic site." One wonders how Alice, who always deflected praise, would have felt if she had been present at the 1995 ceremony, conducted at Paulsdale, when the postal service honored her with a seventy-eight-cent stamp.

Alice Paul's grave in the Westfield Friends Burial Ground in Burlington County, New Jersey, bears her name, date of birth, and death date. But her epitaph could have been that of the British suffragettes, "Deeds not Words."

A View from Her Window
From her window Alice would have looked upon her vast lawns at a copper beech and a white polar, a placid scene that would have provided a sense of calm in her storm-tossed life.

Nearby Attractions: Jacob's Chapel and the Colemantown Meeting House
The historic properties were stops for those seeking freedom on the Underground Railroad.

CHAPTER ELEVEN

Warmed the World

Eleanor Roosevelt

"No matter what happened to one in this world, one has to adjust to it."
—ELEANOR ROOSEVELT

Val-Kill Cottage (opened 1984)
106 Valkill Park Road, Haviland, New York 12538
(845) 229-9422
https://www.nps.gov/elro/index.htm

Parking: Parking is at the Eleanor Roosevelt National Historic Site parking lot.

Hours of Operation: Val-Kill is open seasonally. Tour times vary depending on season.

Admission: Free

Nearby Accommodations: Inn at Bellefield / Roosevelt Inn / Rocking Horse Ranch Resort

Nearby Eateries: Mizu Sushi / Essie's Restaurant / China Wok

WHEN THE WORLD'S FIRST LADY—THE HONORIFIC PRESIDENT HARRY S. TRU-man bestowed upon Eleanor Roosevelt—needed a refuge "far from the madding crowd" of Washington, D.C., she escaped to Val-Kill, her Hudson Valley hideaway. Of her beloved home, she stated, "Val-Kill is where I used to find myself. At Val-Kill, I emerged as an individual."

Anna Eleanor's parents, Elliott and Anna Roosevelt, were members of monied Manhattan. Her mother was a descendent of Philip Livingston whose signature graced the Declaration of Independence. Her father was the younger brother of Theodore Roosevelt, the twenty-sixth president. Elliott called Eleanor

Eleanor Roosevelt
WIKIMEDIA COMMONS, PHOTOGRAPHER UNKNOWN

Little Nell after the character in Charles Dickens's *The Little Curiosity Shop*. Her emotionally distant mother referred to her as "granny" because Eleanor rarely smiled—she was self-conscious over her protruding teeth.

A happy childhood chapter was a vacation when the family set sail for Europe on the *Britannic*. In Venice, father and daughter tossed coins into the volcano Vesuvius. A grim episode followed in France where Elliott checked into a hospital for his chronic drinking. With her husband in treatment, pregnant and caring for two children, Anna sent Eleanor to a boarding school run by nuns. Unable to speak French and missing her family, Eleanor was miserable.

When Eleanor was eight, her mother died from diphtheria. Anna had arranged for her children to live with her widowed mother, Mary Livingston Ludlow Hall at Tivoli, Duchess County, rather than with their feckless father. A year and a half later, Elliott passed away from the effects of alcohol withdrawal, and his eldest son succumbed to diphtheria. Her brother Hall was to follow in

Val-Kill, Eleanor Roosevelt's Hyde Park home
WIKIMEDIA COMMONS, ACROTERION

his father's inebriated footsteps. Fearful of molestation, the teenaged Eleanor installed triple locks on the inside of her bedroom door to deter her drunk uncles.

Escape arrived when Eleanor attended Allenswood Academy in Wimbledon, England, whose students were the daughters of European aristocrats. She was a favorite of the headmistress, Madame Marie Souvestre, who took her on trips to Florence. Through the experience, Eleanor gained self-confidence and no longer stooped to hide her almost six-foot frame.

Upon her return to New York City for her debut at the Waldorf-Astoria, she was on a train where Franklin Delano Roosevelt, her fifth cousin once removed, took the seat beside her. They had first met when he was four years old, and she was two, at his parents' Hyde Park estate. After her coming-out party, she described Franklin as "young and gay and good-looking, and I was shy and awkward and thrilled when he asked me to dance." He found her to be a welcome change from the other debutantes. After she took him to the tenements on the Lower East Side, he responded, "My God, I didn't know people lived like that."

After the nineteen-year-old Eleanor accepted the twenty-two-year-old Franklin's proposal, the couple married in Manhattan on March 17, 1905, as the president would be in the city to attend the St. Patrick's Day parade. Theodore Roosevelt walked his niece down the aisle as two hundred guests watched the exchange of vows.

As a wedding present, Franklin's mother, Sara Delano Roosevelt, gifted the couple a six-story house replete with elevator, butler's pantry, library; but it came with a catch: Sara lived in the adjoining house. Eleanor's domineering mother-in-law hired their staff, provided the furnishings, and described herself as her five grandchildren's real mother.

In 1918, while unpacking Franklin's suitcase, Eleanor found love letters from Lucy Mercer, her own social secretary. Further probing revealed that Alice Roosevelt Longworth, Theodore's daughter, had encouraged the affair. As a result, Alice and Eleanor were no longer kissing cousins. Devastated, Eleanor suggested a divorce, something Franklin desperately wanted to avoid as it would blight his political career. Franklin swore he would excise Lucy.

A second wrecking-ball arrived when Franklin came down with polio that necessitated leg braces and wheelchairs. Eleanor was a driving force in his successful campaign for governor of New York. Because his infirmity made travelling difficult, she appeared in his place.

The forty-eight-year-old Eleanor became the First Lady in 1933—the only woman in history who would hold the position for twelve years. Empathetic to the blight caused by the Great Depression, she travelled so much on the behalf of the downtrodden that she garnered the epithet "Everywhere Eleanor." Six years later, when the Daughters of the American Revolution refused to allow the African American Marian Anderson to perform at Constitution Hall in Washington, D.C., Eleanor resigned her membership. She helped organize the concert at the Lincoln Memorial where, on Easter Sunday, the audience of seventy-five thousand included senators, Supreme Court justices, and cabinet members—but no First Lady. Her explanation was she had been busy with a forthcoming book tour and the arrival of a grandchild. Eleanor was the only First Lady to have a Ku Klux Klan bounty on her head; her FBI file was four thousand pages long.

In 1945 Franklin passed away from a brain hemorrhage in their summer home in Warm Springs, Georgia; Lucy Mercer was at his bedside. A further blow was that Eleanor learned her daughter Anna had arranged for her father's mistress to share his final hours.

Post-Pennsylvania Avenue, when a journalist questioned Eleanor as to her plans, she responded, "The story is over." Her words did not prove prophetic. President Harry S. Truman appointed Eleanor as the representative to the newly minted United Nations. When the UN voted to adopt her Universal Declaration of Human Rights, her fellow delegates, for the first and last time, paid tribute in a standing ovation. At almost seventy years of age, Eleanor retired from her post, yet continued to work unofficially as a goodwill ambassador. She met with world leaders in the Soviet Union, Japan, and India.

VAL-KILL COTTAGE

When the world's fishbowl proved too stressful, Eleanor retreated to the Hudson Valley, a place that held her heart. In her youth, she had lived with her grandmother at Oak Terrace, a brick mansion that looked over the Hudson River and the Catskill Mountains. As Mrs. Roosevelt, she spent time at Springwood, Sara's thirty-five room estate, also on the banks of the Hudson. Val-Kill was her actualization of Eliza Doolittle's dream, of which she sang "All I want is a room somewhere."

The genesis of Val-Kill was a Springwood picnic that Franklin and Eleanor shared with Marion Dickerman and Nancy Cook. Franklin's nickname for the women was the Three Graces; Sara, no doubt, would have called the lesbian lovers, Marion and Nancy, something not as poetic. Franklin suggested he build his wife her own home on Roosevelt property that consisted of 179 acres of woods and lakes. The three women became the residents of Stone Cottage and its linens bore the monogram E.M.N. (Eleanor, Marion, Nancy).

In 1926 the trio established the Val-Kill furniture factory which provided employment for local workers. The enterprise produced impressive replicas of early American furniture. After its closure during the Depression, Eleanor converted the business to her own twenty-room residence which she called Val-Kill after a nearby stream by that name, Dutch for valley stream. She did not share Val-Kill with the other two graces. She wrote to her husband, "The peace of it is divine."

Although Val-Kill looked like any rustic retreat, it was unique as through its door passed John F. Kennedy, Nikita Khrushchev, King George VI and Queen Elizabeth of England, Charles de Gaulle, Prime Minister Jawaharlal Nehru, Prime Minister Winston Churchill, Marshal Tito, and Shirley Temple. Ernest Hemingway and Martha Gellhorn stayed there before their marriage. The driveway often held Franklin's 1936 Ford Phaeton.

Val-Kill has an oval dining-room table set with Eleanor's favorite china, a 1950s Philco television is in the living room. A desk holds a misspelt nameplate—Elanor Roosevelt—a gift from a child. The chairs have mismatched fabrics. In Eleanor's bedroom reside twin beds with chenille bedspreads. There are dozens of photographs of family members and her famous visitors. Several pieces from the Val-Kill factory are on display. The miniscule kitchen is where Eleanor prepared the only food she knew how to make: scrambled eggs and toast. (She had a live-in cook.) The grounds hold a swimming pool, tennis courts, horse barn, kennel, huge outdoor fireplace, and flower gardens. The National Park Service, which maintains Val-Kill, recognizes its importance as an LGBTQ site; Eleanor did not see gender as an impediment to love.

Eleanor and Franklin's final resting place is in the rose garden of Springwood; their graves are a simple white stone bearing their names, dates of birth, and deaths. The Roosevelt Library has a wing dedicated to Eleanor whose entrance bears a tribute by Adelaide Stevenson, "She would rather light a candle than curse the darkness and her glow has warmed the world."

A View from Her Window
From her second-floor bedroom, a room of her own, Eleanor could see a pond that reflected Val-Kill.

Nearby Attraction: Rockefeller Estate
The forty-room mansion that four generations of Rockefellers called home holds an impressive art collection and gardens.

CHAPTER TWELVE

A Band of Angels

Harriet Tubman

"There was one of two things I've got a right to, liberty or death. If I could not have one, I would have the other, for no man should take me alive."
—HARRIET TUBMAN

Harriet Tubman Home (opened 2017)
180 South St, Auburn, New York 13021
(315) 252-2081
https://www.harriettubmanhome.com

Parking: Yes

Hours of Operation: Tuesday–Saturday. Tours at 10 a.m. and 2 p.m.

Admission: $

Nearby Accommodations: Nightshade Inn & Gardens / Inn at the Finger Lakes / Lakefront Hotel

Nearby Eateries: Moro's Table / Elderberry Pond Restaurant / Patisserie

THE OLD NEGRO SPIRITUAL HOLDS THE PLAINTIVE WORDS, "SWING LOW, SWEET chariot / Coming for to carry me home." For the enslaved, home referred to heaven, the end of earthly misery. The Harriet Tubman Home is a testament that dreams do not have to wait for the hereafter.

In the comic strip, Wonder Woman wore a cape; the historic Harriet Tubman wore a shawl: both accomplished Amazonian feats. Araminta (Minty), later Harriet, was born around 1820 to Benjamin and Harriet (Rit) Ross, one of nine children. Her early years were spent on the Bucktown, Maryland, plantation of Edward Brodess. At age six, her owner hired out Harriet to a Mr. and Mrs. Cook who whipped her for not cleaning to their standards. They next tasked her

Harriet Tubman in Auburn, New York

Auburn home of Harriet Tubman
WIKIMEDIA COMMONS, LVKLOCK ACROTERION

with checking muskrat traps—valuable for food and fur—that entailed wading through cold water. One afternoon, suffering from measles, Harriet collapsed. After her mother nursed her back to health, her next job was with Miss Susan. Curious about the taste of a sugar cube, she snuck one from a bowl. Caught in the act, when Susan reached for the whip, Harriet took off and hid in a pigpen where she fought the animals for potato peelings. After five days of near starvation, she returned to face her punishment.

At age thirteen, Harriet was at a general store in Bucktown where an overseer threw a two-pound lead weight at a runaway slave that found its target on her forehead. The injury led to lifelong blackouts in which she claimed to converse with God. Love mitigated the horror and Harriet married John Tubman, a free black man. At the Bucktown village store, which still operates today, the owners display metal enslaved people's tags and shackles.

The event that altered the trajectory of Harriet's life was Brodess's plan to put her on the auction block. Conversing with the Lord, she asked Him to take the life of her master; Brodess died a week later. Knowing his widow would pursue the sale, Harriet plotted an escape. Because John refused to take the risk, Harriet left with three of her brothers. Fearful of capture, the men turned back, and Harriet undertook a solo journey from Maryland to Pennsylvania. She marked her transformation from slavery to emancipation by taking the name Harriet, after her mother, and her surname, Tubman, from her husband. Upon stepping onto the soil not polluted by human servitude, Harriet wept, "I looked at my hands to see if I was the same person now that I was free. There was such a glory over everything, the sun came like gold through the trees and over the fields and I felt like I was in Heaven."

Although no longer bound by shackles, Harriet suffered from loneliness revealed by a quotation from Exodus: "I was a stranger in a strange land." After a year working as a maid and saving as much as possible, the secretary of the Philadelphia vigilance committee, which helped runaway slaves, informed her of the imminent sale of her sister Mary and her children. Like the biblical Moses, Harriet set her sights on their deliverance.

The journey to Maryland was relatively safe insofar as no one would fathom a former slave returning South; however, the return was rife with danger. With a hefty reward for her capture, her Javerts—white and black bounty hunters— were relentless. Relying on her conversations with God, survival skills learned from her father, often disguised as a man or elderly woman, Harriet undertook nineteen trips to the South where she liberated seventy slaves. The activist declared, "I was the conductor of the Underground Railroad for eight years, and I can say what most conductors can't say—I never ran my train off the track and I never lost a passenger." What dampened the elation of her rescue mission was the discovery there was a new Mrs. Tubman.

As Harriet's fame grew, her admirers referred to her as Moses, for bringing slaves to the Promised Land and for her lyrics of "Go Down Moses"—code for "she had arrived." John Brown, who sought her advice for his raid on Harpers Ferry, dubbed her General Tubman. The five-foot-tall hellion let nothing stand in her way. While leading a group of slaves, she allegedly knocked out an infected tooth with her pistol; as Harriet never smiles in her few remaining photographs, the self-surgery cannot be verified.

Philadelphia, the hub of escaped slaves, stopped being a sanctuary after the passage of the Fugitive Slave Act: runaways living in free states could be returned to their former masters. Once again, Harriet was on the move; this time, the Promised Land was Canada, which had outlawed slavery in 1834. In her adopted country, she and her family had their base in St. Catharines, Ontario.

The nickname the General became even more apropos when Harriet offered her services to the Union Army. She explained, "The good Lord has come down to deliver my people, and I must go and help Him." She became the first woman to lead a military expedition during the Civil War. Union soldiers tore up railroad tracks, burned bridges, and set fire to Confederate plantations. During a raid on South Carolina, Harriet helped rescue seven hundred slaves. Of those who fled toward freedom, Harriet later recalled, "They reminded me of the children of Israel coming out of Egypt." During her Diamond Jubilee, Queen Victoria distributed presents to those who had demonstrated valor. She gifted the American woman-warrior with a white silk-and-lace shawl, now in the Smithsonian's National Museum of African American History and Culture. Harriet stated the queen had written that "anytime I was in England I could stop by the castle and share a spot of tea." In life post-freedom, Harriet wore white, as the color denoted strength in West Africa. One of her photographs shows her with a black shawl with fringes.

After a lifetime of extreme sacrifice, Harriet would have been justified in spending the remainder of her days in the tranquility of her Canadian home, her variation of the land of milk and honey, but because injustice still ruled the American roost, she returned to the United States to help right the wrongs. In Philadelphia, the Quaker Lucretia Coffin introduced Harriet to her sister Martha Coffin Wright, who lived in Auburn, New York. Martha's husband's law partner was Senator William Seward, later the secretary of state under President Lincoln. His wife, Frances, had inherited several properties from her father, one situated a mile away from the Seward mansion. In 1859, for twelve hundred dollars, with a down payment of twenty-five dollars, Frances sold a house with seven acres to Harriet despite the Fugitive Slave Act, which made the sale of a property to a runaway slave illegal and carried a penalty of a six-month jail term and a fine of fifteen hundred dollars (thirty thousand dollars in today's money). Due to the Sewards' political and social clout, they evaded repercussions.

HARRIET TUBMAN HOME

For the woman who had slept on a blanket in her slave quarters, in a pigpen, and on pine needles during her escapes, Harriet's home proved the culmination of an unimaginable dream. Her door was always open to the needy due to her earlier promise: "I would make a home for them in the North, and the Lord helping me, I would bring them all here." With several dependents, and as the army refused to pay her a pension, Harriet raised pigs for food and harvested crops. She rented out rooms and in 1869 she married her boarder, Nelson Davis, with whom she adopted daughter Gertie. Eleven years later, a tenant accidentally set Harriet's home on fire. The black community helped with the rebuilding; they substituted the wood with brick and added an extra story and an attic. In 1896 Harriet purchased an adjoining twenty-five-acre lot as a home for the elderly and ill. In 1911 Harriet, taking along her sewing machine, took up residence in the white wooden facility for the old, her once tremendous strength finally dissipated. Visitors to the building can see her sewing machine and original furniture. Treading in the footsteps of the Saint of the South leaves one with a sense of reverence.

At age ninety-three, Harriet passed away from pneumonia; her last words were, "I go to prepare a place for you." As she lay dying, she could have sung the words from "Swing Low, Sweet Chariot": "I looked over Jordan and what did I see / Coming for to carry me home / A band of angels coming after me / Coming for to carry me home."

A View from Her Window
Gazing from the windows of her red-brick house, Harriet saw her loved ones on the lawn, her crops, the wooden structure that housed the old and indigent. She might well have recalled the biblical words, "And God looked upon all that He had made, and, indeed, it was very good."

Nearby Attraction: Fort Hill Cemetery
Located in the colonial town of Auburn—sometimes referred to as "Prison City" as it is the birthplace of the electric chair—is an 1852 cemetery. In the mid-sixteenth century, the site was a fortified village of the Cayuga tribe. There is a fifty-six-foot obelisk dedicated to Logan, a Cayuga leader, who asked, "Who is there to mourn for Logan?" after Europeans murdered his family. A three-foot-tall granite marker erected in 1837 distinguishes Harriet Tubman's grave. On the front is carved: Harriet Tubman Davis 1820–1913. The back holds the words: "Servant of God, Well Done."

CHAPTER THIRTEEN

Semper Fidelis

Lois Wilson

"Hearts understand in ways our minds cannot."

—Lois Wilson

Stepping Stones (opened 1988)
62 Oak Road, Katonah, New York 10536
(914) 232-4822
https://www.steppingstones.org

Parking: Yes

Hours of Operation: Monday–Saturday. Tours start at 1 p.m.

Admission: Suggested donation: $10

Gift Shop: Yes

Nearby Accommodations: Hotel Zero Degrees / Ethan Allen Hotel / The J House Greenwich

Nearby Eateries: Blue Dolphin Diner / La Familia Katonah / Jewel of Himalaya Restaurant

VISITORS MIGRATE TO KATONAH, NEW YORK, FOR ITS INTRIGUING NAME OR TO scratch a historical itch as the region is dotted with sites ranging from pre-Revolutionary gristmills to Gilded Age mansions. Stepping Stones serves as a shrine to Lois Wilson, the First Lady of Sobriety.

Lois revealed that alcoholism is a cancer that also ravages the addict's loved ones. The remarkable individual was born in 1891 in Brooklyn Heights, the eldest of six children of Dr. Clark and Matilda Burnham. The family were members

Headstone of Lois Wilson at the East Dorset, Vermont, cemetery
WIKIMEDIA COMMONS, WHO IS JOHN GALT

Stepping Stones, home of Lois Wilson, founder of Al-Anon
WIKIMEDIA COMMONS, DANIEL CASE

of the Swedenborgian faith which counted amongst its followers Helen Keller and Robert Frost. The children attended the Pratt Institute in Brooklyn, one of the first American schools to offer kindergarten (German for "Children's garden"), followed by enrollment in the Quaker Friends School. The Burnhams spent summers in Manchester, Vermont, where the siblings played with Abraham Lincoln's grandchildren. Robert Todd Lincoln had constructed Hildene, a twenty-four-room mansion, converted to a home museum. In her memoir, *Lois Remembers*, she described her childhood as "idyllic."

While summering in Vermont, Lois met a friend of her younger brother, Rogers. Bill Wilson felt that the rich city girl viewed him with condescension. To impress Lois, who spent afternoons sailing on Lake Emerald, Bill outfitted his grandfather's rickety rowboat with a bed-sheet sail. A gust of wind flung him overboard; caught in the sheet, he looked like a water-borne mummy. Lois rescued Bill—the beginning of a life-long pattern.

Despite their rocky start, romance blossomed, and Lois was thrilled with her twenty-five-dollar amethyst engagement ring. With the outbreak of World War I, Second Lieutenant Wilson, at an army camp in New Bedford, Massachusetts, took his first drink—a Bronx cocktail—which he described as "the elixir of life." Before the army shipped Bill off to Europe, the couple married in the Swedenborg Church, followed by a reception in the Burnham's Clinton Street home. In his absence, Lois worried about her husband's safety and grieved a miscarriage. As an employee of the Young Women's Christian Association, Lois requested an overseas transfer so she could be near her spouse. The YWCA turned her down, explaining her religion was not Christian.

Bill returned home addicted to alcohol, which alleviated the horrors of war and masked his feelings of inadequacy. To ease his wife's mounting concern, Bill assured her that "men of genius conceive their best projects when drunk." Too intoxicated to pick up his diploma, Bill did not graduate from law school. Despite the setback, he obtained a lucrative position on Wall Street. Finding his career soul-sucking, his inebriation escalated. After Lois's second miscarriage and a hysterectomy, they turned to adoption. Agencies rejected their applications due to Bill's addiction. Unable to support themselves, they moved in with Lois's parents.

When Lois returned home from her job as a salesgirl at Macy's department store, Bill pilfered from her purse to buy booze; when she hid her money, he panhandled. One evening she opened the door to the sound of a lamp crashing as Bill grabbed it to help him stand. She pounded on his chest, screaming, "You don't even have the decency to die!" Contrite, he wrote in their Bible his pledge to never take another drink. Her unanswered prayers "turned to ashes in my mouth." Marriage proved the antithesis of idyllic.

Throughout seventeen years of Bill's alcoholism, Lois's pleading, prayers, and nagging fell on deaf ears. Salvation arrived with Bill's epiphany that only a drunk could help another drunk. Along with Ohio surgeon Dr. Bob Smith, Bill founded Alcoholics Anonymous. Sobriety should have meant that Lois finally enjoyed the better not the worse of her wedding vow, but as the wife of Bill Wilson, life was never smooth sailing.

Lois inherited the Clinton Street home Bill used to host Bowery drunks, who she plied with coffee while her husband ran AA meetings that he began with the words, "My name is Bill W. and I'm an alcoholic." He employed the initial "W" rather than his surname to provide anonymity.

For almost two decades, Lois's purpose had been to arm-wrestle the devil for her husband's soul; once he foreswore alcohol, she spiraled into a spiritual vacuum. In frustration, she used her shoe as a projectile with her hubby as its target. (In his drunk days, he had hurled a sewing machine in her direction.) Her salvation arrived with the realization that while her husband could help those locked in the purgatory of addiction, she could bring solace to their loved ones. In 1951, in keeping with AA's principle of privacy, she founded Al-Anon. Meetings began with her opening gambit, "I am Lois W."

Fired with purpose and rebuilding their fractured relationship, the Stock Market crash of 1929 resulted in the foreclosure of the only stable home Lois had ever known. They put their furniture into storage and for the next two years were urban nomads. The Wilsons stayed at fifty-one locations.

A home of their own arrived in 1941, when Helen Griffith, an AA supporter, sold her summer home to the Wilsons for six thousand four hundred dollars with no down payment. Initially, they christened their property "Bil-Los Break," but they renamed it Stepping Stones after the stones that led from their door and its spiritual connotation.

A reversal of fortune occurred with Bill's publication of *The Big Book*, one of the bestsellers of all time. The public feted Bill and Lois as the royal couple of recovery. Author Aldous Huxley stated that Bill was "the greatest social architect of our time." In keeping with his principle of anonymity, Bill turned down *Life* magazine's offer to put him on their cover; he also rejected their offer of appearing with his back to the camera. Whenever he displayed an inflated ego, Lois admonished, "Sweetheart, your halo's on crooked." On their 1954 wedding anniversary, Bill wrote on his wife's card, "Come any peril, we know that we are safe in each other's arms because we are in God's."

Although the victor in the battle of the bottle, Bill could not curb his addictive personality. A serial adulterer, after lecturing on the twelve steps, his thirteenth was making the moves on young women in recovery. Emotional as well as physical adultery intruded with Bill's fifteen-year relationship with actress Helen Wynn. Had bottles not been banned from Stepping Stones, Lois would have smashed one on his head. After putting his wife through twelve steps of hell, Bill refused to terminate his marriage. Other marital crosses were Bill's experimentation with LSD, which he wanted to distribute at AA meetings. His parting words about the organization he had birthed, "Let go and let God. Alcoholics Anonymous was safe—even from me." However, Bill was not safe from himself. His final addiction was to nicotine, and Lois hid his cigarettes as assiduously as she had once hidden his bottles. Despite his emphysema, Bill alternated between inhaling from his oxygen machine and inhaling nicotine.

At age ninety-seven, Lois joined her husband in a Vermont cemetery. Her obituary in the *Los Angeles Times* stated, "She had left no immediate survivors." But, in a sense, she had left thousands—those she had helped weather the scourge of addiction.

STEPPING STONES

Visitor Jean Z. compared touring Stepping Stones to a Christian visiting the Vatican. The 1920 two-story, brown-shingle Dutch-colonial house includes the couple's bed—the one on which Lois was born—and other furniture from Clinton Street. In the living room is Lois's piano; another room displays her dressmaker's dummy and a Wilcox & Gibbs sewing machine. The desk is the one on which she wrote the blueprint for Al-Anon. Nearby is a small, ornate stool, a gift from a British maiden aunt. A vanity table holds a bobby pin and a can of PermaSoft hair spray; on a table is a box of Wash 'n Dri, lighter fuel, and books. There are thousands of artifacts such as a letter from Carl Jung to Bill and a photograph of President Richard Nixon receiving the millionth copy of *Alcoholics Anonymous*. (The publisher released more than twenty-five million copies.)

In 1950 Bill built a cinder-block studio that he named "The Shack" and Lois called "Wit's End." One wall displays the Serenity Prayer in several languages. On his desk, pockmarked with cigarette burns, resides the home's sacred relic: the first edition of *Alcoholics Anonymous*. The book resulted in tears from Jean Z.'s sponsor, Louise. A tour guide reacted to the emotional response Stepping Stones elicits with the comment, "We always say it's not a successful tour unless at least one person cries."

Although the name Bill W. is on the cover of *Alcoholics Anonymous*, he could not have written it without his semper fidelis stepping stone.

A View from Her Window
From her window, Lois saw blue birdhouses, as well as a birdfeeder by her bedroom. In the eight acres roamed wildlife such as rabbits and deer.

Nearby Attraction: Sunnyside
The whimsical home museum of Washington Irving is nestled on the banks of the Hudson River. During the tour, his characters—the Headless Horseman, Rip Van Winkle, Diedrich Knickerbocker—accompany visitors.

CONNECTICUT

CHAPTER FOURTEEN

Connecticut's Canterbury Tale

Prudence Crandall

"My whole life has been one of opposition."
—PRUDENCE CRANDALL (AGE EIGHTY-FOUR)

Prudence Crandall Museum (opened 1984)
1 South Canterbury Road, Canterbury, Connecticut 06331
(860) 546-7800
crandall.museum@ct.gov

Parking: Free parking. Overflow across Route 169 behind church.

Hours of Operation: The museum is open for guided tours only, May through October. Visit the museum website for the most current information. May 6 through October 30: Friday–Monday. Tours at 10 a.m., 11:30 a.m., 1:30 p.m., 3 p.m.

Admission: Adults: $$; Seniors: $; Youth: $; Children 5 and under: Free

Nearby Accommodations: Inn at Fox Hill Farm / Spring Hill Inn / Heavitree B & B

Nearby Eateries: Pizzarama of Plainfield / The Victorian and Village Bakery / Horsebrook Cafe

A 1907 SONG BY WILL D. COBB AND GUS EDWARDS RECALLS, "SCHOOL DAYS, school days / Dear old Golden Rule Days." Not everyone waxes nostalgic about school days, which was the case with the girls who attended the Canterbury Female Boarding School. To enter the Prudence Crandall Museum is to step into a threshold where great courage walked together with great hate.

Not many connect Connecticut with intolerance, but a nineteenth-century Quaker turned the state into the epicenter of controversy. The aptly named

Portrait of Prudence Crandall Francis
WIKIMEDIA COMMONS, FRANCIS ALEXANDER

Prudence Crandall House Sign
WIKIPEDIA COMMONS, JJ BERS

Prudence, who created a tempest in a New England town, was born in Rhode Island, one of four children of farmer Pardon Crandall and his wife, Esther. When Prudence was ten, the Crandalls moved to Canterbury, Connecticut, due to inexpensive farmland and its acceptance of Quakers. Prudence attended the New England Friends' Boarding School in Providence, founded by abolitionist Moses Brown.

The town encouraged Prudence to open an academy for their daughters, and she obliged by purchasing a large house where she opened The Canterbury Female Boarding School. Her pupil Hannah was the daughter of Phillip Pearl, a state senator. On Sundays, church services were mandatory.

Outside the picturesque enclave, the country was aflame. In Boston, William Lloyd Garrison published an antislavery newspaper, *The Liberator*. In North Carolina, the editor of the *North Carolina Free Press* stated those who wanted to end slavery ought to be barbequed.

A historic chapter began when twenty-year-old African American Sarah Harris asked Prudence if she could enroll as a student as preparation for opening her own school. In January 1933, Sarah took her seat at one of the desks, thereby integrating the school, a fact that did not sit well with the town. (In tribute to her teacher, Sarah was to christen her baby Prudence Crandall Fayerweather.)

Petitions circulated that claimed bringing undesirables across Connecticut's border was "an evil of great magnitude." Citizens of Canterbury argued that educating blacks would lead to a bloody rebellion such as the one led by Nat Turner. The greatest opposition came from Andrew T. Judson who lived across the street from the school. He belonged to the American Colonization Society whose members, including President Andrew Jackson, held that it was God's will that the races remain separate. They threatened that if Prudence persisted, repercussions would follow. Prudence's response, "The school may sink, but I will not give up Sarah Harris."

In 1833 Prudence penned a letter to William Lloyd Garrison imploring his assistance. His response was an advertisement in *The Liberator* that requested "young ladies and little misses of color" to enroll in the Canterbury Female Boarding School. When word spread, a Mr. Frost visited Prudence to delineate the dangers of her enterprise, citing his concern blacks might start to believe they could marry whites. Her rejoinder, "Moses had a black wife."

Girls from New York, Rhode Island, Boston, and Providence arrived in Canterbury. While the Cobb and Edwards song recalled lessons in "Reading and 'riting and 'rithmetic / Taught to the tune of the hickory stick," the Crandall school taught history, chemistry, and moral philosophy—with never an inclusion of a hickory stick.

The first retaliation was from store owners who refused to sell Prudence groceries which led her father, Pardon, and brother, Hezekiah, to deliver supplies. Vandals smeared dung on the school's steps and door handles. After the Canterbury Congregational Church told the girls they were no longer welcome, they switched to the Packerville Baptist Church. On one occasion, heading home, fearing trouble, their carriage driver ordered them to dismount. His premonition was prescient; teenaged boys dragged the vehicle to the river and deposited it upside down. Pardon rescued the carriage; church services ended. Despite Canterbury's enmity, Prudence persevered, feeling her duty was to fight against prejudice that she called "the mother of all abominations."

When intimidation failed, the Connecticut state legislature passed the 1833 "black law" which prohibited instruction for "colored persons who are not inhabitants of this state." In celebration, the citizens of Canterbury fired a cannon thirteen times, the church bell chimed for hours. Prudence recalled those times were "weary, weary days."

An event Prudence knew was coming arrived when a deputy sheriff took her to court where she pled not guilty. The justice of the peace, Rufus Adams, offered her the choice of jail or posting bail. When she chose prison, the men were dumbstruck. Their concern was that incarcerating a white religious woman would reflect badly on them and make people sympathetic to the accused. When Sheriff Roger Coit escorted Prudence to her cell, she was pleased, as her fear had been the men would *not* put her behind bars. *The Liberator* denounced, "SAVAGE BARBARITY! Miss Crandall imprisoned!!!" Throughout the Northeast, the abolitionist presses publicized the trial. Poet John Greenleaf Whittier wrote in the *Essex Gazette*, "In prison for teaching colored sisters to read the Bible . . . Just God! Can this be possible?" The following afternoon, Prudence was free to await trial in her home. As in the lyric of "School Days," Prudence continued to stress to her students the Golden Rule. The first court hearing ended in a mistrial; in the second, the trial ended in a conviction. However, the court overturned the verdict on a technicality. *Crandall v. The State of Connecticut* (1834) influenced two United States Supreme Court Cases: *Dred Scott v. Sandford* (1875) and *Brown v. Board of Education of Topeka* (1954). Moreover, it laid the foundation for the 14th amendment to the U.S. Constitution.

On a winter afternoon, Frederick Olney, a black handyman, was at Prudence's parlor when he saw smoke rising from a corner of the room. He put out the fire that raged from a first-floor window. The police arrested Olney for arson.

To counteract the horror, romance entered when the thirty-one-year-old Prudence fell in love with the widowed Calvin Philleo, a Baptist minister she described as her "choicest blessing." In 1834, when a Canterbury minister refused to marry the couple, they took their vows in a Brooklyn church. After their honeymoon, Calvin, along with his son and daughter, moved into Prudence's home, and classes resumed. The honeymoon cocoon ended with a midnight attack where men used iron bars to shatter windows and furniture. A terrified student coughed up blood. Prudence closed the school and sold her home. Although the perpetrators of the violence felt vindicated with the demise of the Canterbury Female Boarding School, the repercussions of the closure had unexpected results. The short-lived school, which existed for seventeen months, helped the abolitionist movement gain momentum.

Shortly after their marriage, Calvin exhibited signs of mental instability, called his wife "old squash head," squandered their money, and left her to raise her stepchildren. His death ended their wretched union. Hezekiah and Prudence settled on a book-filled rundown farm in Elk Falls, Kansas, where Connecticut's state motto, *Qui Transtulit Sustinet*, which means, "He Who Transplanted Still

Sustains," came to pass. Her former town issued a mea culpa when the state legislature granted the eighty-four-year-old Prudence an annual four-hundred-dollar pension, as they were "mindful of the dark blot on our fair name and her straightened circumstances." Mark Twain offered to reinstate her in her old home; she refused but asked him to send her his books and photograph. A century after her death, Prudence became Connecticut's official state heroine. The Connecticut House of Representatives established her birthday as Prudence Crandall Day.

As Prudence lay dying, the presiding reverend, McKesson, asked what he should say at her eulogy, to which she responded, "Preach the truth."

Prudence Crandall Museum
The truth lies in her former home. The history of the museum echoes Romeo's words as he walked the streets of Verona that bore witness to the city's ancient feud, "Here's much to do with love but more with hate." Throughout the ground floor, the curators have instituted a banner-style exhibit entitled "The Canterbury Female Boarding School: Courage, Conscience, and Continuance." Through the message on the banners, visitors discover the story of the school, its teacher, and her students. The tour guides encourage guests to consider how they can make a difference by carrying out Prudence's precepts of justice and equality. Interactive questions, part of the exhibit, encourage visitors to examine current educational barriers and reflect on solutions. An emotional aspect of the tour is the newly discovered charred beam—the result of the arson attack on the school—that builders discovered during renovations. In the entry hall is a reproduction portrait of the schoolteacher-activist, her hair worn short, in defiance of the current Victorian fashion. The New England Anti-Slavery Society had invited Prudence to Boston where Francis Alexander painted her portrait. During her sitting, William Lloyd Garrison came to the studio to keep her company. The original 1834 painting resides in the Cornell University Library.

After completing a two-year restoration, the former schoolhouse focuses on sharing Prudence's principles of equal protection under the law whereby education is the great equalizer. The displays, which encompass all five rooms of the first floor, share the stories of teacher Prudence Crandall, her students, and a chapter from Canterbury's past. A banner showcases the subpoena that mandated the students testify against their teacher that leaves one with the horror of their conundrum. Another banner is of Prudence's arrest warrant, a smoking gun of the racial tempest of the era. Her incarceration presages the words of fellow New Englander Henry David Thoreau, who wrote in *Civil Disobedience*, "Under a government which imprisons any unjustly, the true place for a just man is also a prison."

The current zeitgeist in education is the belief that rather than teachers acting as the sage on the stage, they should be the guide by the side. The pedagogy is one that the museum follows as it makes the former students an integral part of the exhibits. Prudence would have been proud. Through documents and photographs, one can experience Sarah Harris's sampler, Eliza Hamilton's passport application. In a nod to nostalgia, the museum shares images of Prudence's signed schoolbooks from her years at the Moses Brown School. In a nod to the dearth of objects that are currently in storage, Joan DiMartino, the museum's curator and site superintendent, stated, "The building itself, site of the school, is our most important artifact."

In the fourteenth century, Geoffrey Chaucer's pilgrims journeyed from London to Canterbury; in the nineteenth century, Miss Crandall's students likewise made a pilgrimage, one that comprises Connecticut's Canterbury Tale.

A View from Her Window
In her times of sorrow, as Prudence glanced from her Palladian window, she would have seen the remains of egg yolks, cracks from stones, and those who desperately desired the demise of her school.

Nearby Attraction: Yale University Art Gallery
Yale University Art Gallery, the oldest college art museum in America, possesses 250,000 objects, many from antiquity.

CHAPTER FIFTEEN

A Heart Is Not Judged

Florence Griswold

"I'm going to have a wonderful season this summer."
—FLORENCE GRISWOLD

Florence Griswold Museum (opened 1947)
96 Lyme Street, Old Lyme, Connecticut 06371
(860) 434-5542
frontdesk@flogris.org
https://florencegriswoldmuseum.org

Parking: Yes

Hours of Operation: Tuesday–Saturday, 10 a.m.–5. p.m. Closed Mondays

Admission: General admission: $; Children 12 and under: Free

Gift Shop: Yes

Nearby Accommodations: Madison Beach Hotel / Rodeway Inn Waterford / HomeTowne Studios

Nearby Eateries: Café Flo / Old Lyme Inn / Papis Taqueria

IN FRANK L. BAUM'S *THE WONDERFUL WIZARD OF OZ*, DOROTHY SHARED HER insight: "If I ever go looking for my heart's desire again, I won't look any further than my own back yard." Unlike the girl from Kansas, the woman from Connecticut always understood "there's no place like home." To visit the Florence Griswold Museum is to connect with a special time, a special place, a special woman.

In the first decades of the twentieth century, Gertrude Stein, along with her partner, fellow Jewish American expat Alice B. Toklas, presided over their atelier on 27 Rue de Fleurus in Paris. Through their doors passed the legends Pablo

Florence Griswold House: Setting for Artist Colony
WIKIPEDIA COMMONS: PI 1415926535

Picasso, Henri Matisse, Georges Braque. At the same time, though worlds away, Miss Florence presided over her New England salon.

The artist's colony had its genesis with Florence, the daughter of Helen and Captain Robert Harper Griswold. Helen wrote to her husband, who was aboard his ship, the *Ocean Queen*, to announce Florence's birth on Christmas Day, 1850. Her parents dearly loved Florence and her siblings, Robert Jr., Helen Adele, and Louisa.

The Griswolds had an impressive heritage; Matthew Griswold had been a founding settler of Old Lyme, and the eastern shore of the Connecticut River bears the name Griswold Point. The family's ancestors included two governors of Connecticut, including Florence's grandfather, who was a U.S. congressman and a Connecticut Supreme Court judge.

Robert was a captain on his family's Black X Line; on one voyage, he bonded with his passenger Herman Melville and rewarded the author with a private stateroom. As a captain, Robert was away from his family for long periods of time; in compensation, his substantial income allowed him to purchase a grand home on tony Lyme Avenue. His daughters attended the private Perkins School in New London, run by their aunts. Florence became fluent in French and learned to play the harp and piano. Though the finishing school was supposed to enable the Griswold sisters to find eligible husbands, none of them married.

By 1855, as the age of sail had evolved into the age of steam, Robert retired, at age forty-nine. Unfortunately, he invested heavily in the South Lyme nail factory, which floundered; he sold off land and assumed three mortgages. Relatives paid the debt, but with Robert's 1882 death, his wife and four children were in dire financial straits. Their large house and several acres on the banks of the Lieutenant River was their only safety net. A further tragedy for the family was Robert Jr.'s death from diphtheria at age sixteen.

To earn a desperately needed income, in 1878 Helen and her daughters opened a girls' school in their home that offered classes in subjects including "the rich and elegant styles of French embroidery, ancient and modern, not elsewhere taught in this country." After fourteen years, due to competition from the Boxwood School, the Lyme Street School closed its doors. Further sorrow shadowed the Griswolds when Louise, an organist for the Congregational Church, died in an 1896 carriage accident. Three years later, Helen passed away from Bright's disease. In 1900 Helen Adele, the family artist, entered the Hartford Retreat for the Insane, where she died in 1913.

In 1900, destitute and with most jobs closed to women, in a bid to keep her beloved home, Florence opened it to boarders. Her idea proved prescient, as people were happy to take the train to flee from overcrowded New York and Boston for bucolic Old Lyme. Their hostess greeted them with a bottle of wine followed by a tour of her garden.

The first tenant was artist Henry Ward Ranger who was enchanted by the residence and felt its grounds would provide the perfect backdrop for his paintings. He viewed the Griswold home as the venue to start his own "American Barbizon Colony." The term alluded to the town of Barbizon located at the edge of the Forest of Fontainebleau, France, where painters specialized in rural themes. Ranger stated of his paradise found, "It looks like Barbizon, the land of Millet."

Word spread to his fellow artists, who in turn became boarders of—as they called her—Miss Florence. These core members instituted one of America's most famous Impressionist art colonies. The arrival of Childe Hassam in 1903 introduced Impressionism, a relatively new style in America. A resident artist, Edward Charles Voelkert, was famous for his paintings of cattle which he patterned after those on Old Lyme farms. While he painted the bovine, the house carried dozens of felines, the colony's mascots. Ellen Axson Wilson (the first wife of Woodrow Wilson), an avid painter, along with the future president, spent time in the colony where she befriended Florence. Heeding the advice of the Wilsons, Florence created a gallery in the front of her home to exhibit and sell her boarders' canvases. When the Old Lyme Art Association opened a galley next door on property she had donated, the chatelaine became its manager, and received commissions. Her boarders dubbed their home-away-from-home the Holy House, as it produced a font of inspiration. The moniker was also a play on the Bush Holley House in Greenwich, another artist boarding house.

In downtown Rome, the Villa Aurora's crown jewel is a ceiling on which the sixteenth-century painter Caravaggio painted a canvas, a work valued at $310 million. While the home in Old Lyme does not have the imprint of an Old Master, it does have souvenirs from its Impressionist boarders. To thank Miss Florence, her boarders showed their appreciation by using the dining room as their canvas, thus making the house itself a piece of art.

Despite the harmony between Florence and her "boys" as she called her tenants, economic worry hovered over the colony. Because she viewed her artists as family, Florence had only raised her modest seven-dollar weekly rent once. By trying to improve their accommodations, Florence had spiraled into debt. Along with artists, creditors began arriving at her doorstep. The threat of losing her house, where she had been born and which held the memories of her family, took a physical and psychological toll.

Discovering her plight, a boarder sent letters to everyone who would be willing to help, and they formed The Florence Griswold Association. A friend invited Florence to stay with them in New York for two weeks. In her absence, donations accumulated—some from the Wilsons—and her "boys" exchanged their paintbrushes for tools. The artisan Property Brothers repaired dilapidated furniture, mended torn carpet, and plastered cracking ceilings. For other tasks, they employed a mason, an electrician, and a plumber who installed hot and cold water. When Miss Florence returned and saw the renovation she was overcome with emotion. The self-described Keeper of the Artist Colony remained in her home until her 1937 passing.

FLORENCE GRISWOLD MUSEUM

For those looking to conjure a slice of New England's past and who want to tour a historic house that in itself is an art gallery, the white-pillared Florence Griswold Museum beckons. Samuel Belcher, the architect of the First Congregational Church of Old Lyme, planned the estate for William Noyes in 1817.

The Georgian-style mansion is representative of the affluence of Old Lyme's maritime era.

While the Sistine Chapel is famous for its ceiling, the Florence Griswold Museum is renowned for its murals. There are thirty-eight individual panels and eight double panels (on the doors that complete one scene) in the former boardinghouse. Highlights of the museum are the canvases of former members of the art colony. Willard L. Metcalf's *Kalmia*, 1905, depicts the mountain laurel that blooms along the banks of the Lieutenant River. Childe Hassam painted *Summer Evening* which captures a woman whose body leans to the shadows while a potted plant leans toward the sun. William Chadwick's Impressionist paintings convey the pastoral setting of the Griswold estate: grapevines cover its porch, along with a profusion of roses and perennials.

As a reminder the museum was once a home, there are toys and dolls, remnants from the Griswold children, and period furniture. The Griswold Garden is a delight and displays the flowers Florence cultivated. The thirteen-acre grounds overlook the lovely Lieutenant River, where one can envision the artists setting up their easels. The Georgian-style guesthouse retains its original furniture, art, and games. Visitors can also tour the Krieble Gallery, which hosts temporary exhibitions, a small cinema, bookshop, and quaint restaurant.

The Wizard of Oz might have been a charlatan, but he shared wisdom that applied to Miss Florence with his pronouncement, "A Heart is not judged by how much you love; but by how much you are loved by others."

A View from Her Window
From her window, Florence could see the Lieutenant River, salt marshes, white-spired churches, sheep and cows, cats and dogs. What also brought joy were the artists who shared her home and were her surrogate family.

Nearby Attraction: Mashantucket Pequot Museum
Dedicated to bringing the story of the Mashantucket Pequot Nation to life, visitors learn about the history and culture of Native Americans through dioramas, archival material, and exhibits.

Chapter Sixteen

Art Is Long

Theodate Pope

"I might perhaps write quite pretty fairy tales if I were only near the abodes of fairies and elves."

—Theodate Pope

Hill-Stead Museum (opened 1947)
35 Mountain Road, Farmington, Connecticut 06032
(860) 677-4787
https://www.hillstead.org

Parking: Yes

Hours of Operation: Wednesday–Sunday, 10 a.m.–4 p.m.

Admission: General admission: $$; Children under 6: Free

Gift Shop: Yes

Nearby Accommodations: Hampton Inn & Suites / Delamar / Farmington Inn

Nearby Eateries: Fork & Fire / Piccolo Arancio / Wood-n-Tap / J. Timothy's Taverne

Located in London's St. Paul's Cathedral is the tomb of the famed British architect Sir Christopher Wren, which bears his epitaph, "*Si monumentum requiris circumspice,*" which translates to: "If you would seek my monument, look around." In another time and place stands a different type of monument, the not-so-humble home: Hill-Stead.

Theodate Pope Riddle with classmates, when she was a student at Miss Porter's
School for Girls
ORIGINAL PHOTO PROPERTY OF MISS PORTER'S SCHOOL, FARMINGTON, CT. PHOTOGRAPHER:
WILLIAM ALLDERIGE. UPLOADED FROM WIKIMEDIA COMMONS, PHOTOGRAPHER: ELSA ROLLE

Historically, women have had a hard time breaking through the glass ceiling
of architecture. While Julia Morgan—architect of Hearst's Castle—succeeded
in "the gentleman's profession" on the West Coast, Theodate Pope did likewise
in the East.

The genesis of Hill-Stead began with Alfred Atmore Pope, the son of Maine
Quakers, and his childhood sweetheart, Ada Brooks. With his many-splendored

bank account earned from malleable iron, the midwestern millionaire built a mansion on Cleveland's Euclid Avenue, known as Millionaire's Row. Their only child, Effie Brooks (Theodate), was born in 1867. At age nineteen, Theodate confided to her diary her dream of "owning a fine country home in the east and a dairy farm." In the same year, feeling "Effie" lacked dignity, she assumed her paternal grandmother's name, Theodate, Greek for "gift of God." She attended Miss Mittleberger's School for Girls, whose fellow alumnae included the daughters of Presidents James Garfield and Rutherford Hayes.

During a family trip East to check out finishing schools, Ada was in favor of Miss Porter's School for Girls, which Sarah Porter, the daughter of the town's Congregational minister, had founded in 1843 in Farmington, Connecticut. Theodate was in accord as her favorite cousin was a student there. Enchanted by the New England village, Theodate declared it "one of the prettiest places I ever was in."

In midlife, Alfred developed a passion for French modernist paintings and through them developed friendships with artists Mary Cassatt and James Whis-

Hill-Stead Museum
WIKIMEDIA COMMONS, DADEROT

tler. Alfred also made the acquaintance of Claude Monet during an impromptu visit to the artist's home in Giverny, France. In 1888 the Popes embarked on a grand tour of Europe that lasted over ten months. On the return voyage to Cleveland, Alfred transported three Monets: *Grainstacks*, *White Frost Effect*, and *Grainstacks in Bright Sunlight*.

To alleviate their daughter's depression—she was miserable with life as a debutante—upon the family's return from Europe, her parents leased her a cottage in Farmington, two blocks from Miss Porter's School. Although an unmarried woman living on her own was scandalous, Theodate thrived in her newfound freedom in her adopted hometown. She restored the eighteenth-century saltbox house and furnished it with antiques. During this period, she became enamored with the Colonial Revival Movement that would set the stage for Hill-Stead.

Theodate had become interested in pursuing a career as an architect, following a conversation she had with her father during their European tour. Of the few women architects of the time, most had no formal training—as was the case with Theodate. Preparation for her chosen profession consisted of private lessons from Princeton University professor Allan Marquand. The art history notebooks from her lessons are in Hill-Stead's archives.

Upon completion of her studies, her parents supported Theodate's desire to design a family home in Farmington. Initially, Alfred hired the firm McKim, Mead & White, the leading architects of the Gilded Age. In an audacious move, Theodate made it clear that their help would only be an auxiliary. In a letter, she wrote, "It will be a Pope house instead of a McKim, Mead & White." Hill-Stead was a massive undertaking for a first project. After visiting George Washington's Mount Vernon estate, Theodate determined to include a portico similar to the one on the Potomac River side of his mansion. Consequently, Hill-Stead has six white-pillared columns. In 1916 Theodate attained her license in New York State; in 1933 she obtained another in Connecticut.

While plans were underway, in 1899, the family stayed at their apartment in the Windsor Hotel in Manhattan. On March 17th, Ada and Theodate had made plans to visit Mrs. Louisine Havemeyer, owner of an art-adorned mansion. Due to a headache, Theodate wanted to forego the excursion; however, at her mother's insistence, she went on the excursion. Had she not left the Windsor, she likely would have been a casualty of the fire that destroyed the building. When Alfred returned from his luncheon appointment at Delmonico's restaurant and saw the flames, he arranged for a man with a ladder to rescue three Monet paintings from his suite. The canvases were at the hotel as Alfred had planned to sell them at Durand-Ruel's New York gallery. The night before the fire, Ada had convinced him not to go through with the sale. Two of the salvaged Monets, one of the *Grainstacks* and *Fishing Boats at Sea,* are on view at Hill-Stead.

In 1915 Theodate had another rendezvous with death. Along with her maid, Emily Robinson, and fellow spiritualist, Edwin Friend, Theodate booked a passage on the RMS *Lusitania*, as she wanted to visit the British Society for Psychical Research. When a German submarine torpedoed the *Lusitania* off the Irish Coast, twelve hundred people lost their lives, including Emily and Edwin. Crew from the rescue ship, *The Julia*, discovered Theodate, unconscious, floating with her knee hooked over an oar that saved her from drowning. The sailors placed her in its makeshift morgue until Belle Naish, a fellow passenger, convinced them she was still breathing. Upon recovery, Theodate sent Ada a one-word telegram: SAVED. The nightmare shadowed her for the rest of her life.

Hill-Stead—the name derives from farmstead on a hill—represented the manifestation of Theodate's dream. In 1901, in her first summer at her once-upon-a-time home, she described it as "a large simple home." The adjective "large" is a given: it has thirty-six rooms for family use and servant's quarters; the house and connected carriage barn total thirty-three-thousand square feet. The adjective "simple" is subjective. How simple could the house be if it held paintings whose counterparts hang in the halls of museums and the homes of royalty and oligarchs?

Two years after surviving the *Lusitania* torpedoing, at age forty-nine, Theodate married John Wallace Riddle, a career diplomat who had been an ambassador to Russia. She had met him ten years earlier through her Hill-Stead neighbor, Anne Roosevelt Cowles, President Theodore Roosevelt's sister. The couple travelled extensively, including a 1919 trip to China, Japan, and Korea. Due to his height, she called him "Totem"; he referred to her as "dearest of geniuses." John was supportive of her architectural aspirations, such as her commission to work on the Theodore Roosevelt Birthplace National Historic Site in Manhattan.

In 1946 Theodate, whose parents and husband had predeceased her, passed away at Hill-Stead. Her fifty-page will directed her home to operate as a museum. A clause stipulated that nothing could be added to the collection in the house, and nothing could be removed or moved.

HILL-STEAD MUSEUM
Touring Hill-Stead with its stunning backdrop of the Litchfield Hills is to experience a house encased in amber where the first half of the twentieth century yet dwells. Henry James alluded to the estate in *The American Scene*, where he wrote,

"A great new house on the hill apparently conceived—and with great felicity—on the lines of a magnificent Mount Vernon."

In addition to the Claude Monet paintings, the two *Grainstacks, Fishing Boats at Sea,* and *View of Cap d'Antibes,* other treasures are Edgar Degas's *Dancers in Pink, Jockeys and the Tub,* Mary Cassatt's *Sara Handing a Toy to the Baby,* James McNeill Whistler's *The Blue Wave, Biarritz,* and *Symphony in Violet and Blue,* Édouard Monet's *The Guitar Player* and *Toreadors.* Paintings by the Impressionists' contemporaries Eugène Carrière, and Pierre Puvis de Chavannes also grace the walls. Visitors can also gaze upon bronzes by Antoine Louis Barye, Italian ceramics, Chinese porcelains, eighteen etchings by Whistler, and a sixth-century BCE Corinthian ceremonial head vessel called a pyxis.

In Hill-Stead's magnificent sunken garden is a sundial whose base bears the Latin inscription, *"Ars Longa Vita Brevis"* which means "Art Is Long Life Is Brief."

A View from Her Window
Through the window, Theodate could reminisce about those who had strolled in her gardens—her parents and three foster children, her beloved pets, and those whose names are legend: James McNeill Whistler, Mary Cassatt, Henry James, Edith Wharton, and President Theodore Roosevelt.

Nearby Attraction: Wadsworth Atheneum Museum of Art
Hartford, Connecticut's, 1844 art museum, housed in a building resembling a castle, is America's oldest institution in continuous operation. The initial funding and many artifacts came from millionaire philanthropist J. Pierpont Morgan. A nod to contemporary artists are works by Salvador Dali, Jackson Pollock, and Andy Warhol. Classic canvases are by Pieter Paul Reubens, Michelangelo Merisi da Caravaggio, and Pierre-Auguste Renoir.

CHAPTER SEVENTEEN

This Great War

Harriet Beecher Stowe

"There is more done with pens than swords."
—HARRIET BEECHER STOWE

Harriet Beecher Stowe Center (opened 1968)
77 Forest Street, Hartford, Connecticut 06105
(860) 522-9258
https://www.harrietbeecherstowecenter.org

Parking: Free parking in the Stowe parking lot on Forest Street.

Hours of Operation: Wednesday and Thursday, 11 a.m.–4 p.m.; Friday, 12–5 p.m.; Saturday, 10 a.m.–5 p.m.

Admission: Adults: $$$; Seniors: $$; Children: $$; Members, Hartford residents, Children under 6: Free

Gift Shop: Yes

Nearby Accommodations: The Connecticut River Valley Inn / Hilton Hartford / Atlantic Inn

Nearby Eateries: The Capital Grille / Indigo Indian Bistro / Treva

EXTRAORDINARY NOVELS HAVE HAD A GLOBAL IMPACT: JOHN STEINBECK'S *THE Grapes of Wrath*, Harper Lee's *To Kill a Mockingbird*, and George Orwell's *1984*. Harriet Beecher Stowe's *Uncle Tom's Cabin* altered history as it helped ignite the American Civil War. To learn about the female great emancipator, follow the road to the Harriet Beecher Stowe Center.

A historic irony is how a girl from New England became a persona gratis in the theater of the South. Harriet Elisabeth was born in the small town of

"The little lady that started this great war"—President Abraham Lincoln's greeting upon meeting Harriet

Harriet Beecher Stowe Center
WIKIMEDIA COMMONS, MIDNIGHTDREARY

Litchfield, Connecticut, in 1811, the seventh child of Reverend Lyman Beecher. When his wife, Roxanna, was pregnant, Lyman had hoped for a son he would call Henry. Upon the arrival of a girl, he christened her Harriet, nicknamed Hatty.

Roxanna, a mother of nine, passed away at age forty-one from tuberculosis when Harriet was five years old. Hoping a change of scenery would abate his daughter's grief, Lyman sent Harriet to relatives in Nut Plains, Connecticut. Her aunt, Harriet Foote, taught her that women were the intellectual equals of men. A year later, Harriet rejoined her family.

Along with second wife, Harriet Porter, with whom he had four children, and his nine from his first marriage, in 1832, Lyman moved the family to Cincinnati. He felt the city to be the moral equivalent of its first syllable, "sin," and believed it his duty to save its souls from the Catholics and the infidels.

The twenty-one-year-old Harriet joined the Semi-Colons, a literary gathering held in her Uncle Samuel's parlor. After the group praised her writing, her confidence soared. Another result of the Semi-Colons was it was there that she met fellow New Englander Calvin Ellis Stowe, an impoverished biblical scholar.

His late wife, Eliza—who had been Harriet's friend—had died in the cholera epidemic. A smitten Harriet gushed that Calvin was "rich in Greek & Hebrew, Latin & Arabic & alas, rich in nothing else." Calvin and Harriet married in 1836, and the new Mrs. Stowe described life in their Walnut Hills home as "tranquil, quiet, and happy." Twin daughters arrived, who Harriet wished to name Eliza, after Calvin's first wife, and Isabella. However, Calvin decided to honor both his former and current spouses and the final christening was Eliza Tyler and Harriet Beecher. Their other children: Henry Ellis, who Harriet called "the lamb of my flock"; Frederick William; Georgiana May; Samuel Charles; Charley (whose doting mother dubbed "my sunshine child"); and Charles Edward. To supplement their income, Harriet sold articles but lamented, "I am but a mere drudge with few ideas beyond babies and housekeeping." Charley's passing at eighteen months from cholera crushed his parents. Harriet later mined her heartache in *Uncle Tom's Cabin*, to describe the pain mothers experienced when their masters sold their children. When Calvin became a professor at Bowdoin College in Maine, Harriet was grateful to return to New England, in the hope a new environment would take the edge from her anguish.

Despite being overwhelmed with her children, Harriet paid attention to current events, and she was horrified over what the South referred to as their "peculiar little institution." She expressed her outrage: "No one can have the system of slavery brought before him without an irrepressible desire to *do* something, and what is there to be done?" In answer to her question, Isabella Porter Beecher, her sister-in-law, suggested, "If I could use a pen as you can, Hatty, I would write something that would make this whole nation feel what an accursed thing slavery is."

The impetus that led to the book that placed Harriet in the literary firmament was Congress's 1850 Fugitive Slave Act which made Northerners implicit in slavery. The law made the capture of former enslaved people, even in free states, legal. Harriet's response was to hide John Andrew Jackson, who had fled South Carolina. She sent abolitionist essays to the magazine *The National Era* and wrote her publisher, "The time is come when even a woman or a child who can speak a word for freedom and humanity is bound to speak."

The first segment appeared in the 1851 issue with the title, "Uncle Tom's Cabin" by Mrs. H. B. Stowe. Shying from praise, Harriet claimed the idea descended while she was taking communion, that she did not so much write it as she received it from God. Boston-based John P. Jewett published the articles as a novel in 1852; it sold ten thousand copies the first week and three hundred thousand copies in its first year. In three months, Harriet earned ten thousand dollars, a staggering figure for its time. Translations appeared in more than forty languages, and *Uncle Tom's Cabin* became the world's second-best seller, after the Bible. A marketing bonanza led to toys, games, wallpapers, plates, and candlesticks. Although vilified in the South—threatening letters arrived in the Stowe mailbox—the housewife transformed into a celebrity author who preached from her paper pulpit. In England, her novel sold three times as many copies as it did in America, and Queen Victoria reported she had enjoyed Mrs. Stowe's second book, *Dred*. At the invitation of antislavery European groups, Harriet visited Britain, France, Italy, and Switzerland.

Shortly after her return, a telegram informed her that her son, Henry, a student at Dartmouth College in New Hampshire, had drowned. A national tragedy followed the Stowes' personal one with the outbreak of the Civil War. Consumed with trepidation of losing a third child, Harriet nevertheless took her son Frederick, who had enlisted, to the New Jersey train depot. On New Year's Day, 1863, in attendance at a concert at the Boston Music Hall, she heard the announcement that President Lincoln had signed the Emancipation Proclamation. Aware the author was in the audience, shouts rang out, "Mrs. Stowe! Mrs. Stowe!"

As the war drew to its close, Calvin retired, and the Stowes built their forever home on Forest Street in Hartford, Connecticut. At last, she had the leisure to garden and paint. Another activity was sharing her history with her son Charles Edward, who published her autobiography. An ordained minister, he lived for a time with his wife and family in the Forest Street home. Hattie and Eliza never married and also lived with their parents. Georgina suffered from addiction to morphine, which a doctor had prescribed as a painkiller after she gave birth. She passed away at age forty-seven. The Stowes' youngest, Frederick William, had dropped out of Harvard Medical School to enlist in the Union Army and suffered a wound at the Battle of Gettysburg. Empathetic to Frederick's alcoholism, Harriet based the character Tom Boulton in *My Wife and I* after her suffering son. In a novel move for her era, Harriet portrayed addiction as an illness rather than a moral failure. Frederick took off for California, where he was never heard from again. Three of the Stowes' seven children outlived their parents.

In 1886 Calvin passed away, leaving his widow bereft. Another torment was that she was aware of her diminishing mental state. She confided her great fear to a friend, "My mind wanders like a running brook. My sun has set. The time of work for *me* is over. I have written all my words and thought all my thoughts." Descending into dementia, Harriet kept rewriting *Uncle Tom's Cabin*. She also took to wandering the halls of the house of her neighbor, famed writer

Samuel Clemens, mistaking it for her own. At age eighty-five, Harriet passed away in her home. Her final resting place was in Andover, Massachusetts, in a plot between Calvin and Henry.

HARRIET BEECHER STOWE CENTER

Harriet's forever home on 77 Forest Street is an expansive 1870s brick structure built on a hillside near the grounds of a mental institution—thus the neighborhood name Asylum Hill. The center holds the largest Harriet Beecher Stowe collection, with 228,000 items. Watching over her domain is Harriet's 1853 oil painting, painted by Alanson Fisher—in her black dress with white lace cuffs and collar, every inch the portrait of a Victorian lady. The dominant aspect of the house is the plethora of *Uncle Tom's Cabin* memorabilia. The center has a brown-and-gold embossed 1881 illustrated edition of the book, published by Houghton Mifflin. An 1855 Limoges vase depicts the titular character, hat in hand. An elaborate artifact is an 1850s girandole bearing the figures of Uncle Tom and Eva, Bible in hand. The center has an 1852 handwritten page from the manuscript of her groundbreaking novel. A room's wallpaper displays scenes based on 1850s prints from her book. The author's love of literature is apparent in the Henry Wadsworth Longfellow commemorative pitcher that bears his image and the names of his works "Hiawatha" and "Evangeline." During her European sojourn, admirers presented her with a twenty-six-volume petition supporting abolition, signed by 560,000 British women, currently on display. The Ladies of Surrey Chapel, London, presented Harriet with a magnificent silver inkstand in 1853. A primary-source document is a runaway-slave poster. A shocking artifact is a gold bracelet in the form of slave chains she received in 1853. A cache of letters bear the signatures of Henry Wadsworth Longfellow, Ralph Waldo Emerson, Elizabeth Cady Stanton, and Susan B. Anthony.

The center holds original and foreign editions of Stowe's novels. Bright-yellow women's suffrage ribbons, owned by Isabella Beecher Hooker, manifest the author's feminist affiliation. Her upstairs office, lined in blue-and-gold wallpaper, was where she retired to mourn the loss of her daughter Georgina. The adjoining room was Calvin's study. Early in their marriage, Harriet had persuaded her husband to provide her with a private space, "If I am to write, I must have a room to myself." He did not have to be convinced as Calvin had always encouraged his wife's writing, exhorting that she "must be a literary woman." An 1886 photograph shows the elderly Harriet sitting in a room of her Hartford home. On the wall is a copy of Raphael's *Madonna of the Goldfinch* encased in a gold frame with a leaf motif.

A popular anecdote concerning the diminutive author revolved around her 1862 visit to the White House. President Abraham greeted her, "So, you're the little woman who wrote the book that started this great war."

A View from Her Window
From her window, she must have marveled that she was the neighbor of Samuel Clemens, with whom she took tea.

Nearby Attraction: The Mark Twain House & Museum
The Mark Twain House & Museum, in the zip code of Nook Farm, is a nineteen-room, 11,500-square-foot mansion, with floor coverings designed by Louis Comfort Tiffany.

RHODE ISLAND

CHAPTER EIGHTEEN

Lucky Strike

Doris Duke

"Payback is a bitch, baby."

—DORIS DUKE

Rough Point (opened 2000)
680 Bellevue Avenue, Newport, Rhode Island 02852
(401) 849-7300
https://www.newportrestoration.org

Parking: On site

Hours of Operation: March/April through January. Museum times vary per season.

Admission: General admission: $$$; Students: $$; Children 12 and under: Free; Newport residents: Free. Discounts for active-service military and veterans.

Gift Shop: Yes

Nearby Accommodations: Hotel Providence / The Beatrice / The Renaissance Providence

Nearby Eateries: Perro Salado / Cru Café / Mamma Luisa Ristorante

As DOROTHY MADE HER WAY ALONG THE YELLOW BRICK ROAD, SHE CHANTED, "Lions and tigers and bears, oh my!" As Doris Duke strode along her estate's gilded walkway, her mantra could have been, "Alsatian hounds, Alaska malamute, camels, oh my!" Visitors to Rough Point will also gasp, "Oh, my!" when partaking of the mansion's treasure trove.

Doris Duke, 1951

Rough Point, view from Cliff Walk

Born in Manhattan in 1912 to tobacco czar James "Buck" Buchanan Duke and his social-climbing second wife, Nanaline, Doris rivaled Queen Elizabeth of England and Queen Juliana of the Netherlands for the title of the world's richest woman. Home was a five-story Fifth Avenue Greek-revival mansion, currently the site of NYU's Institute of Fine Arts. At the 2,740-acre Duke Farm, Doris dined on a hundred-thousand-dollar gold-plate dinner settings and bathed in marble tubs with gold spigots. The Dukes' summer cottage in Newport, Rough Point, on eleven oceanfront acres, was the playground for Doris and her friend, Alletta "Leta" Morris. The girls spent afternoons at Bailey's Beach building sandcastles; when older, the nearby Cliff Walk provided a place to flirt with sailors. The teenaged Doris told a reporter, "I am no different from anyone else. Really."

James adored his only child while Nanaline appeared closer to her son Walker Patterson Inman from her first marriage. On his deathbed, the titan cautioned his twelve-year-old daughter, "Trust no one." He bequeathed North Carolina's Trinity College forty million dollars on the condition they rename it Duke University; its football team served as his pallbearers. James's will endowed Doris with a one-billion-dollar fortune in contemporary currency.

The heiress's Rough Point debutante ball included six hundred guests and ended with the six-foot one-inch Doris leading a conga line to the ocean. Her British presentation took place at Buckingham Palace where she curtsied to King George V and Queen Mary.

Doris hoped marriage would free her from her mother's control, furnish the love she had lost with her father, and satiate her ravenous carnality. She stated, "Every member of the Duke family is oversexed. The government should test our chromosomes." At age twenty-two, Doris married James Cromwell—sixteen years her elder—whose first wife had been Delphine Dodge, heiress to her family's automobile fortune. The venue was the Manhattan mansion where Doris felt the spirit of her father. The Cromwells embarked on a nine-month round-the-globe cruise. Rather than exhibiting postnuptial passion, Jimmy inquired as what he could expect as his annual income. Her assessment of her husband, "Jimmy was no endowment. He wasn't even a small annuity." In India, Doris was overawed with the Taj Mahal—though she claimed she would have traded it for a good romp—and met with Mohandas Gandhi in his ashram. While Doris lost interest in her groom, she was enamored with Diamond Head, Hawaii, where she purchased five acres overlooking the Pacific. She erected the ethereally beautiful Shangri-La, which she named after the mythical kingdom in *Lost Horizon* where no one ever grew old. The white palace held floor-to-ceiling fish tanks and Islamic treasures dating from the twelfth century. Two stone camels stood sentry.

In her Hawaiian paradise, Doris had an alleged affair with surfing legend Duke Kahanamoku. She explained one Duke taught her about love and another taught her how to make love. When she discovered she was pregnant by a man not her husband, Doris had an abortion, knowing Jimmy would claim paternity. A year later, she gave birth to Arden, who lived for twenty-four hours. In her 1943 Reno divorce, on grounds of cruelty, Doris claimed Jimmy had demanded a seven-million-dollar payout.

During World War II, the debutante turned undercover agent where she went by the code name Daisy—after Daisy Mae Yokum from the "Li'l Abner" cartoon. She had a sexcapade with General George Patton in a chateau that had once belonged to Emperor Franz Joseph of Austria. As "Georgie" had a wife and several mistresses, Doris was once more on the prowl.

In Italy, Doris met the Dominican Don Juan, Porfirio Rubirosa, a relentless pursuer of women with deep pockets, known for his magnificent member. In the Riviera, he had the nickname "toujours pret"—Mr. Ever Ready; Parisien waiters call their pepper mills "Rubirosas." Her lawyers handed Doris's Latin lover a prenuptial agreement that reportedly caused him to faint. A biographer wrote of their relationship, "He kept her well-laid and she kept him well paid." The marriage ended after a year; his third wife was Woolworth heiress Barbara Hutton.

At age seventy-five, Doris adopted the thirty-five-year-old Chandi Heffner, a belly dancer and Hare Krishna devotee, who she met at a dance class in Hawaii. Doris believed that Chandi was the reincarnated Arden. Maternal associations came with an expiration date, and Doris called the adoption the biggest mistake of her life. After Doris disinherited her, Chandi sued and received a sixty-five-million-dollar settlement. Chandi participated in a mock wedding with Paul Reubens—stage name Pee Wee Herman—in a Hawaiian ceremony presided over by former Philippine First Lady Imelda Marcos. Oh, my.

In her later years, Doris, who desperately sought the eternal youth promised by the legendary Shangri-La, shattered at the loss of her beauty, became a recluse. She passed away in Falcon Lair (the former digs of Rudolph Valentino), under a cloud of suspicion involving murder and morphine. A court determined that her butler, Bernard Lafferty, coerced a heavily sedated Doris into signing a will that named him the recipient of a five-million-dollar bequest, as well as an annual five-hundred-thousand-dollar stipend. Lawsuits accused him of mishandling the estate's funds as he squandered more than a million dollars on Armani suits, a Cadillac, a thirty-five-thousand-dollar diamond-and-gold Cartier watch. However, he did spend a portion on his former employer: he purchased an eighteen-hundred-dollar Louis Vuitton valise to transport Doris's ashes, which he scattered over the Pacific Ocean.

Rough Point

When Shakespeare's Marc Anthony delivered Julius Caesar's funeral oration, he stated, "The evil that men do lives after them; the good is oft interred with their bones." The sentiment did not apply to Doris Duke, who used her tobacco empire for philanthropy. In 1962, in the days when Newport was a nondescript navy town, Doris instituted the nonprofit Newport Restoration Foundation to revitalize the city's colonial heritage. With the increased property values, people took to calling her "the lady." In her $1.2 billion dollar will, Doris left her 115-room mansion, Rough Point, one of the famous estates that line the ten-mile Bellevue Avenue, as a home museum.

Visitors might wonder why a magnificent estate bore the name Rough Point: Frederick William Vanderbilt, its original owner, christened it after the waves that crashed into the cliffs onto its beach. He sold the property to tin magnate William B. Leeds, whose son married Princess Xenia Georgievna of Russia. A Bolshevik firing squad had executed her father and uncle in St. Petersburg. The next owner was a duke, a self-made one.

Rough Point is awash with memories, some wonderful, one tragic. In 1966 Doris was responsible for the death of her interior decorator, Eduardo Tirella, when her car pinned him against the estate's massive gate. The inquest cleared her of homicide; a civil case resulted in a five-figure sum to his family.

The heiress's eccentric taste is evidenced in her bedroom, where the Charles X furniture bore a mother-of-pearl finish while the drapes were compliments of J. C. Penney. The solarium showcases the magnificent Newport coast; during Hurricane Bob, it became the stomping grounds of her pet camels, Princess and Baby, who left urine and dung souvenirs on precious Persian carpets. Another souvenir of her pets are the camel topiaries on the lawn that made visitors wonder if their shellfish had been a bit off. Ten large dogs also had the roam of the house.

Museum-quality pieces include canvases by van Dyck, Gainsborough, Reynolds, as well as family portraits of James, Nanaline, and Doris. Seventeenth-century tapestries cover walls with scenes such as amorous couples, another depicting the biblical Queen Esther. Everywhere is a treasure: a Tiffany swan centerpiece, a golden sunburst clock, and porcelain vases from the Ming dynasty. In the Yellow Room, there are side tables with ivory insets bearing the Russian Imperial Crest of Catherine the Great. A molded plaster ceiling captures likenesses of the heroes of the ancient world. Rough Point is also a fashion museum where mannequins model Doris's designer outfits. The clotheshorse was often on the world's best-dressed list—second only behind the Duchess of Windsor.

The heiress enjoyed everything from champagne to camels, yet she had a life plagued by loneliness and suspicion. After leaving Rough Point, one is left to ponder whether her destiny reflected the name of her tobacco empire's most popular cigarette, Lucky Strike.

A View from Her Window
Doris could have gazed on Bailey's Beach, upon which she built her first, and in a sense happiest, structure—the sandcastle from her childhood.

Nearby Attraction: Rose Lighthouse
If you are a fan of Virginia Woolf's *To the Lighthouse* (and even if you're not), embark on a one-of-a-kind overnight experience in Narragansett Bay. Rose Island offers visitors the opportunity to stay overnight in its museum, a re-creation of the 1870s lighthouse keeper's quarters.

MASSACHUSETTS

CHAPTER NINETEEN

Remember the Lady

Abigail Adams

"Give up the harsh title of Master for the more tender and endearing one of Friend."

—ABIGAIL ADAMS

Old House at Peacefield (opened 1946)
135 Adams Street, Quincy, Massachusetts
https://www.nps.gov/adam/learn/historyculture/places.htm

Parking: There is limited, untimed street parking available on Adams Street by Peacefield.

Hours of Operation: Museum times vary per season.

Admission: General admission: $$; Children under 16: Free

Nearby Accommodations: Marriott / Staybridge Suites / Hampton Inn

Nearby Eateries: Cloud Asian Fusion & Bar / Pho Pasteur

IF ONE LISTENS INTENTLY ENOUGH, THE WALLS OF PEACEFIELD DO TALK. THEY whisper of Founding Mother Abigail Adams, who admonished the periwigs to share power with the petticoats. To discover an intriguing slice of America, explore the Old House at Peacefield.

The leader of the pack of First Lady as political partner began with Abigail, born in 1744, in Weymouth, Massachusetts Bay Colony. (Her birthplace is now a home museum.) She was the second of four children of Elizabeth and the Reverend William Smith, a Congregationalist minister. The realization there was one paradigm for the lasses and another for the lads occurred when Abigail and her sisters, Mary and Elizabeth, remained home while their brother, William, attended school. To compensate, Abigail devoured her father's books

Portrait of Abigail Adams by Gilbert Charles Stuart
WIKIMEDIA COMMONS, GILBERT CHARLES STUART

on Shakespeare, history, and philosophy. Elizabeth worried about her headstrong daughter though her maternal grandmother approved of her rebellious streak, "Wild colts make the best horses."

Abigail understood the Thirteen Colonies' quest for independence as she feared losing her own. What she dearly desired was "a closet with a window that I can call my own."

When John Adams visited Reverend Smith, he met fifteen-year-old Abigail, ten years his junior. Two years later, he was calling Abigail "Miss Adorable";

she referred to him as "dearest friend." After John asked her father for her hand in marriage, Abigail felt her mother should likewise have been consulted. After overcoming their misgivings that the country lawyer would prove a poor provider, the couple wed in 1764 in a ceremony presided over by Reverend Smith.

Their home—inherited from John's father—was in Braintree, later known as Quincy. They had daughters Abigail (Nabby), Susanna (Suky), who passed away as a toddler, Elizabeth, who was stillborn, and sons John Quincy, Charles, and Thomas. The Adams relocated to Boston where their social circle included John's cousin Samuel Adams and John Hancock. John became the nonfictional Atticus Finch when, amidst public condemnation as the Redcoat lawyer, he defended eight British soldiers accused of killing five colonists during the Boston Massacre.

In 1774 John left for Philadelphia as a delegate for the First Continental Congress while his wife returned to Braintree. Duty dictated that the couple remained apart for more than half their marriage which led Abigail to write, "I shall assume the Signature of Penelope." John directed Abigail to "elevate the

Old House at Peacefield
WIKIMEDIA COMMONS, DADEROT

minds of our children and exalt their courage." Thomas contracted dysentery, and Elizabeth died from the disease while caring for her grandson.

At the Second Continental Congress, John received Abigail's plea regarding female inclusion in the new republic, "Remember the Ladies, and be more generous and favorable to them than your ancestors. Remember all Men would be tyrants if they could. If particular care and attention is not paid to the Ladies we are determined to ferment a Rebellion, and will not hold ourselves bound by any laws in which we have no voice." John called her saucy and said, "I cannot but laugh." He explained if he did her bidding to raise the political status of women, the heroic men would fight as bravely against the "Despotism of the Petticoat" as they had against the despotism of the British. In 2007 the U.S. Mint issued a medal featuring Abigail, quill in hand, inscribed with her famous words: REMEMBER THE LADIES. Nevertheless, a child of her epoch, Abigail believed women should remain in the shadow cast by their better halves, "However brilliant a woman's talents may be she ought never to shine at the expense of her Husband."

The minister's daughter's serrated teeth eviscerated contemporary Founding Fathers: Benjamin Franklin was an "old Sorcerer," Alexander Hamilton, "as ambitious as Julius Caesar," John Hancock, "a tinkling cymbal." She chided her grandson for preferring "Jack and Jill" over Isaac Watt's "Divine and Moral Songs for Children." She admonished John Quincy to never enter the Senate "with a Beard two days old" as she didn't want the "World to ask what kind of a Mother he had." John Quincy's wife, Louisa Catherine, viewed her mother-in-law as a tiny terror.

In 1789 John became the first vice president of the United States, a position that greatly impacted Abigail's life. The Adamses spent time in Philadelphia, the capital Abigail described as a place of "thorns without roses." Upon John's election as president, Abigail was recovering from an illness in a new home they had purchased in Braintree, christened Peacefield. In her forever home, Abigail had far more than "a closet with a window that I can call my own." The president wrote Abigail, "I pray heaven to bestow the best of blessings on this House and all that shall hereafter inhabit it. May none but honest and wise men ever rule under this roof." President Franklin D. Roosevelt had the words engraved over the fireplace in the state dining room.

As soon as she was well, Abigail took up the mantle of First Lady. Not impressed with Washington, D.C, she remarked, "It is the very dirtiest Hole I ever saw . . . a quagmire after every rain." John and Abigail were the first residents of the Executive Mansion (it was not called the White House until decades later), which was cold and damp; she used the East Room as a laundry room. A hovering cloud was anxiety over Nabby, Thomas, and Charles. The president confessed to his First Lady, "My children give me more pain than all my enemies."

In a nod to Charles Dickens's first line in *A Tale of Two Cities*, the year 1800 was "the best of times, the worst of times." The First Couple were extremely proud of John Quincy who was garnering accolades as the first U.S. minister to Russia, and later became secretary of state. In contrast, John had disowned Charles due to his marital infidelity and alcoholism—a disease that claimed his life at age thirty. A blow to John's ego was losing to Thomas Jefferson in the presidential election. Abigail wrote of her husband's heartaches, "When he is wounded I bleed."

The Adamses were delighted that Peacefield held their extended family, that they were once more in their native Massachusetts. However, the Grim Reaper came to call. Abby's sisters and John Quincy's one-year-old daughter died. Nabby's husband, William Smith, often abandoned his wife and four children for months, sometimes years, at a stretch. The Smiths lived in a cottage on the grounds of a debtor's prison. At age forty-eight, Nabby died from breast cancer at Peacefield. An indomitable spirit helped Abigail deflect the slings and arrows; she wrote to John Quincy, "I always thought a laughing philosophy much wiser than a sniveling one."

Abigail undertook her final act of rebellion by writing her will. The document was not legal—everything women owned was their husbands—but she knew her dearest friend would honor her dying wish. The disbursement went to her female relatives.

In 1818 Abigail Adams passed away from typhoid. Her husband of fifty-four years said, "I wish I could lay down beside her and die too." Six years later, John Quincy became the sixth president. Not until 176 years later would Barbara Bush have the same dual distinction of being a wife and mother of a president.

PEACEFIELD
Stepping across the vine-covered portico is to enter the cradle of a political dynasty. The mansion, the home of President John Adams, First Lady Abigail Adams, and of President John Quincy Adams, is known as The Old House because the Adams National Historical Park also includes the birthplaces of John and John Quincy Adams. John was more comfortable in his homestead than he was in the White House: "Let me have my Farm, Family, and Goose

Quill, and all the Honours and Offices this world can bestow, may go to those who deserve them better, and desire them more. I covet them not."

John and Abigail purchased their home in 1787, and it remained in their family until 1927. On view are the secondhand tables and chairs that the thrifty couple brought back from the sojourn in France. Louisa Catherine's handiwork is on display in the knitted bedspread. A wooden cradle likely held the infant John Quincy. The Memorial Room holds the locket John gifted his wife. In the Long Room are portraits of Abigail, John, and John Quincy. The furniture includes a Louis XV sofa that the family used in France, Philadelphia, Washington, and Quincy. On either side are chairs that could accommodate hoop skirts. A four-seat ottoman is in the center of the room. Behind the ottoman is a double Victorian chair with a built-in sewing box. The mantel over the fireplace displays a French clock, Chinese vases, and matching candelabras. On the second story is John's study, where he spent his retirement. His inlaid wood secretary desk stands against a wall; on its surface, he wrote the 1783 *Treaty of Paris*. At age ninety, John passed away in his study on July 4, 1826, the fiftieth anniversary of his signing the Declaration of Independence. Allegedly, his last words were, "Jefferson survives." He was wrong; Jefferson had died four hours earlier at Monticello. The building holds the desk where John drafted the Massachusetts Constitution. For all the fiery Founding Mother did on behalf of the new republic, America should remember the lady.

A View from Her Window
As Abigail looked out of the window, she may have imagined the cairn that holds the inscription: FROM THIS SPOT, WITH HER SON, JOHN QUINCY ADAMS, THEN A BOY OF SEVEN, BY HER SIDE, ABIGAIL ADAMS WATCHED THE SMOKE OF BURNING CHARLESTON WHILE LISTENING TO THE GUNS OF BUNKER HILL. 1775.

Nearby Attraction: The United First Parish Church
The white crypt of the United First Parish Church—the church of the presidents—holds four granite sarcophagi, the final resting place of John, Abigail, John Quincy, and Louisa Catherine Adams.

CHAPTER TWENTY

Anything But

Louisa May Alcott

"I would rather be a free spinster and paddle my own canoe."
—LOUISA MAY ALCOTT

Orchard House (opened in 1912)
399 Lexington Road, Concord, Massachusetts 01742
(978) 369-4118
https://louisamayalcott.org

Parking: In front of Orchard House. Additional parking is available in a lot one block away on Hawthorne Lane.

Hours of Operation: Museum times vary based on season.

Admission: Adults: $$; Seniors/College students: $$; Youth: $; Children under 6: Free; Annual pass: Free; Museum affiliates: Free

Gift Shop: Yes

Nearby Accommodations: Concord's Colonial Inn / Crescent Suites Hotel / Archer Hotel

Nearby Eateries: The Colonial Inn / Thoreau / Royal Indian Bistro

SOME OF AMERICA'S GREATEST AUTHORS, HAWTHORNE, EMERSON, AND Thoreau, slumber in Sleepy Hollow, a Concord cemetery. A notable grave belongs to the mother of young adult fiction, Louisa May Alcott. If, in *Spoon River Anthology* fashion, Louisa spoke from the afterlife, her story would involve her family, immortalized in her novel *Little Women*.

The cradle of America's literary homes is Concord, Massachusetts, New England's Bloomsbury. The town's clapboard houses have not changed much

Louisa May Alcott: anything but a little woman
WIKIMEDIA COMMONS, PHOTOGRAPHER UNKNOWN

since the 1776 arrival of the Redcoats, since the site birthed a beloved children's classic.

The author's father, Amos Bronson (he went by his middle name) Alcott, was a teacher and a transcendental philosopher whose radical theories destined his wife, Abigail, and their four daughters to grueling poverty. The penury was daunting to Abigail, of the affluent May family; her great aunt Dorothy Quincy married John Hancock, a signer of the Declaration of Independence. Bronson's Temple School collapsed after he admitted a black female. Enraged parents withdrew their children, and newspapers denounced him as "either insane or half-witted." Fleeing the tempest, Bronson left for a six-month visit to England financed by Ralph Waldo Emerson.

Upon his return, the Alcotts journeyed in a horse-drawn wagon to Fruit-lands, a Harvard, Massachusetts, utopian commune that consisted of thirteen members. Adherents could not wear cotton—a product of slavery; leather—it came from animals; or eat root vegetables—they grew in the direction of hell. Abigail took in boarders and worked as a seamstress. During the couple's first thirty years of marriage, they lived on family handouts and moved twenty times. One of the family's homes was Wayside, which they dubbed Hillside, a residence that doubled as a station on the Underground Railroad. Abolition brought the Alcotts into contact with Frederick Douglass, John Brown, and Harriet Tubman. After John Brown's execution, his wife and daughters took refuge with the Alcotts. When the Alcotts vacated, Nathaniel Hawthorne became the next tenant. Louisa is chiefly associated with the two-hundred-year-old Orchard House which Bronson purchased for less than a thousand dollars, a cost partially furnished by Emerson. The property received its name from its forty apple trees. Due to the house's poor condition, the Alcott women nicknamed it Apple Slump.

Bronson and Abigail proved to be devoted parents who encouraged creativity and allowed their youngest daughter, May, to paint on the walls. When Louisa showed an interest in writing, Abigail gifted her a fountain pen. An early

Orchard House, home of Louisa May Alcott
WIKIMEDIA COMMONS, VICTORGRIGAS

diary entry of Louisa's read, "I wish we were rich, I was good, and we were all a happy family."

Louisa (she preferred Lou) was born in Germantown, Pennsylvania, in 1832, on Bronson's thirty-third birthday. The family relocated to Concord, where Emerson offered her the use of his home library; Henry David Thoreau took her on nature walks in the woods near Walden Pond. In *Little Women*, Louisa's literary alter ego, Jo, states, "I can't get over my disappointment in not being a boy." When her older sister Meg admonished her to behave, as she was a young lady, Jo responded, "I ain't." Her litmus test for male companionship, "No boy could be my friend till I had beaten him in a race, and no girl if she refused to climb trees, leap fences."

At age fifteen, because of her financially hapless father and overworked mother, Louisa was determined to contribute to the family coffers. She vowed, "I will do something by and by. Don't care what, teach, sew, act, write, anything to help the family; and I'll be rich and famous and happy before I die, see if I won't!"

During the Civil War, Louisa worked as a Union nurse where she contracted typhoid, a condition that worsened when doctors treated her with mercury that led to poisoning. She never fully regained her health. Letters home describing her experiences made it into print as *Hospital Sketches*, which served as her first literary success. However, her preferred genre was suspense novels, for which she used the pen name A. M. Barnard. Her stories, which earned a pittance, showcased women on adventures in the high seas and glamorous locales.

Editor Thomas Niles urged Louisa to write a novel for girls, a task she dreaded as she deemed juvenile fiction "moral pap." Her resolve ended when Niles told her that he would publish her father's manuscript on his philosophical theories if she agreed. In 1868 Louisa wrote, "Mr. N. wants a girls' story, and I began *Little Women*. I plod away, though I don't enjoy this sort of thing. Never liked girls or knew many, except my sisters." Louisa's literary counterpart was Jo, Meg was Anna, Amy was May, Beth was Elizabeth, and her mother, Abigail, was Marmee. Niles's niece read some chapters and declared them "splendid." The novel sold two thousand copies within two weeks making the author a multimillionaire in contemporary currency. Louisa noted in her journal, "Goethe put his sorrows & joys into poems, I turn my adventures into bread & butter." With the windfall, Louisa fulfilled her father's dream of opening the Concord School of Philosophy in his study in Orchard House, the country's first school for adults.

Although grateful that the Alcott family was finally free of economic woe, Louisa was not comfortable with her role as a literary light. When fans knocked at her door, she pretended to be the maid and sent them away. When the first volume, covering the March sisters' childhood, proved rite-of-passage catnip, fans clamored for a sequel that would reveal the girls' fate. What irked Louisa was the outcry that clamored for Jo to marry a variation of Jane Austen's Mr. Darcy. She groused in her journal, "Girls write to ask who the little women marry, as if that was the only end aim of a woman's life. I *won't* marry Jo to Laurie to please anyone." Eventually bowing to pressure for Jo's wedding "out of perversity," Louisa "made a funny match" that failed to make readers' bosoms heave. She anticipated the fallout, "I expect vials of wrath to be poured upon my head but rather enjoy the prospect."

Louisa never married though she did spend time as a surrogate mother. In 1880 she became the guardian of her ten-month-old niece and namesake, Louisa May Nieriker, nicknamed Lulu. With her sister's largesse, May had moved to Paris to pursue her passion for art where she passed away from meningitis just after Lulu's birth. After her Aunt Louisa's death from a stroke, two days after Bronson's passing, Lulu joined her father in Switzerland.

ORCHARD HOUSE
After the Alcott family sold their house in 1911, the Concord Women's Club purchased the property to memorialize Louisa's life and legacy. Fans of *Little Women* pilgrimage to Orchard House to step into the Civil War era of the March sisters. The house, where 80 percent of the furnishings are authentic, is a time capsule of when the family walked its halls. The parlor has earth-toned wallpaper and a green patterned carpet. Portraits of Bronson and Abigail, along with May's watercolors, hang on the walls. The formal area displays "furniture very plain" and "a good picture or two hung on the walls," where visitors can conjure the images of the Alcott women darning their socks, playing their Chickering piano. The room holds the costumes the Alcott children wore in their home theatricals. Louisa adored her russet-colored boots to such an extent she only wrote parts for herself where she could wear them. Bronson arranged for arched niches to showcase busts of Plato and Socrates. The parlor retains the memory of guests Emerson, Thoreau, and Hawthorne waxing eloquent on literature and philosophy. Visitors are privy to Beth's piano, May's paintings, Anna's wedding gown, and Lulu's toys. An autobiographical element is Louisa's mood pillow: the author had a mercurial temper; when she put out her pillow it served as a sign for her family to give her space. When the pillow was sideways, it meant approach with caution.

In a journal entry from 1860, Louisa wrote, "All of the philosophy in our house is not in the study, a good deal is in the kitchen." The kitchen, where the family prepared their vegetarian meals, holds their scrubbed hutch table, the soapstone kitchen sink, replete with a drain, purchased with literary royalties. Bronson implemented a rack for drying laundry, and a hot-water boiler. During dinners in the dining room, conversations centered on suffrage, abolition, and child labor. The dining room is the repository of Abigail's family china, portraits of Elizabeth and Louisa, and May's paintings. Along with the original furnishings is Elizabeth's melodeon (a small red organ).

Before the Alcotts had taken residency of Orchard House, Elizabeth had recently passed away from scarlet fever. The shrine that her family set up in the dining room remains and includes May's portrait of her sister and two candles. A room of one's own was always a priority for Louisa. Her small bedchamber holds the bookcase her father built which she filled with works by Charles Dickens, George Eliot, and Johann Wolfgang von Goethe. Bronson also built a half-moon writing desk that he placed between the two windows. On the desk's small surface, which only had space for an inkwell and quill, within the span of ten weeks, Louisa wrote *Little Women*, the novel that impacted American literature and the Alcotts' lives.

Gazing upon a page from the manuscript of her famous work, penned in her distinctive backward-slanted handwriting, one can hear the scratching of a quill. Black-and-white photographs rest on antique furniture; the walls bear paintings of calla lilies and nasturtiums that May painted so her sister could see them from her bed as she convalesced from typhoid. Also present is May's painting of an owl that hangs by Louisa's bed. Given her immortality, Louisa was anything but a little woman.

A View from Her Window

From Louisa's semicircular desk, she looked upon Lexington Road which had an elm tree that dated from the period of the American Revolution.

Nearby Attraction: The Concord Museum

The 1930 brick building exhibits a lantern Paul Revere used to warn his fellow Bostonians, "The British are coming!" Visitors can view the bed, desk, and chair from Thoreau's cabin at Walden Pond, as well as the original study where Emerson wrote his famous essays.

CHAPTER TWENTY-ONE

Celestial Brethren

Clara Barton

"And if you chance to feel that the positions I occupied were rough and unseemly for a woman, I can only reply that they were rough and unseemly for men."

—CLARA BARTON (AT CEDAR MOUNTAIN)

Clara Barton Birthplace Museum (opened 1921)
66 Clara Barton Road, North Oxford, Massachusetts 01537
(508) 987-2056, ext. 2013
clarabartonbirthplace@bartoncenter.org
https://www.clarabartonbirthplace.org

Parking: Yes

Hours of Operation: From the last Friday in May to the last weekend in August the museum is open Friday–Sunday, 10 a.m.–4 p.m. In September the museum is open Saturdays only, 10 a.m.–4 p.m. From October through the last Thursday in May, tours are available on a limited basis by appointment only. Tours are not available on Tuesdays or Fridays. Not open in winter.

Admission: Adults and Children (6–12): $; Children 5 and under: Free; AAA members and Seniors: $

Gift Shop: Yes

Nearby Accommodations: Wellsworth Hotel / Homewood Suites / Hampton Inn

WHAT IS RED AND WHITE, CARRIES AN ICONOCLASTIC SYMBOL, AND IS AN inversion of the Swiss flag? The American Red Cross started with a shy New

Clara Barton
WIKIMEDIA COMMONS, MATTHEW BENJAMIN BRADY

England girl, born to be a nurse. To learn about Clarissa Harlow Barton, take a tour of the Clara Barton Museum.

Florence Nightingale, the founder of modern nursing, was named after Florence, Italy, the city of her birth. Sarah and Captain Stephen Barton christened their daughter Clarissa (Clara), after the protagonist of the British novel *Clarissa, Or, The History of a Young Lady* by Samuel Richardson. Raised in the Universalist Church, Clara started her life on a farm in Oxford, Massachusetts, on Christmas

Day, 1821, the youngest of five children. Fond memories were the times her father, a former army officer, shared stories of the Northwest Indian War.

When Clara was ten, her brother, David, fell while working on repairing a barn. She recalled of the medical practice of using leeches to suck out his "bad blood": "My little hands became schooled to the handling of the great, loathsome, crawling leeches which were at first so many snakes to me." The two years she spent nursing him endowed her with a sense of purpose.

Behind its quaint exterior, the Barton farm harbored horror. Her sister Dolly suffered from a mental disorder; her great-nieces shared anecdotes that Dolly became so deranged that Stephen instilled bars on her window and locked her in her room. Stephen and Sarah's shouting matches turned the house into a battleground. A cousin faced charges for a bank robbery. In her 1907 memoir, *The Story of My Childhood*, Clara reacted to those who commended her intrepid spirit: "[They] have been wont to dwell upon my courage, representing me as personally devoid of fear. However correct that may have become, it is evident I was not constructed that way, as in the earlier years of my life I remember nothing but fear."

Birthplace of the founder of the American Red Cross
EMILY THOMAS

To combat Clara's crippling shyness, the Bartons felt she should work as a teacher in North Oxford's one-room schoolhouse; the sixteen-year-old excelled in relating to her students—her "boys," as she referred to them. In 1852 she transferred to a school in Bordentown, New Jersey, where she taught from the recently published *Uncle Tom's Cabin*. To provide for the impoverished, Clara instituted New Jersey's first free public school where enrollment grew from six to six hundred. The town hired J. Kirby Burnham as the new principal had to possess testosterone. His salary was six hundred dollars; Clara's was $250. Her resignation elicited her statement, "I may sometimes be willing to teach for nothing, but if paid at all, I shall never do a man's work for less than a man's pay."

For a fresh start, Clara moved to Washington, D.C., where she became one of the first female employees of the federal government in her role as a copyist for the U.S. Patent Office. When Interior Secretary Robert McClelland pressured her supervisor into firing female federal workers, Clara did not lose her position, but her salary decreased to half of what her male coworkers earned. The office was rife with rumors that Clara was the mother of biracial children; she was subjected to jeers as she walked the gauntlet to her room. On March 4, 1861, the office closed so its employees could be part of the crowd of ten thousand to witness the inauguration of President Abraham Lincoln.

The motto of the Prince of Wales, "I serve," based on the German phrase "*Ich dien,*" was a precept Clara followed upon the eruption of the Civil War. The Baltimore Riot of 1861 resulted in the clash between the Massachusetts militia and Southern sympathizers, where the wounded ended up in the unfinished Capitol building. Clara hurried to the makeshift hospital and was aghast that some of injured men were her boys—her former students. She arranged for donations and delivered the supplies in her mule-drawn wagon.

Wherever the need was greatest, Clara was there. In Antietam, Maryland, she was in such proximity to the battlefield that a bullet passed through her sleeve and killed the soldier to whom she had been offering a sip of water. She shrugged off praise of her bravery by explaining its source, "It made no difference to anyone if I were shot or taken prisoner." Her tireless devotion led surgeon James Dunn to write, "General McClellan, with all his laurels, sinks into insignificance beside the true heroine of the age, the angel of the battlefield."

After the war, Clara organized a "missing man" bureau, authorized by President Lincoln, to discover the fate of soldiers to bring closure to their families. Her *New York Times* obituary stated that of the thirteen hundred graves in Andersonville Prison, she had identified all but four hundred. During a lecture tour after the war, Clara fought the hydra head of prejudice against the formerly enslaved and women. Through her activism, she befriended Susan B. Anthony and Elizabeth Cady Stanton.

Worn down physically and psychologically, in 1869 Clara boarded the *Caledonia*, bound for Switzerland, where she learned of an organization whose emblem was a reversed Swiss flag: a red cross on a white background. The following year, during the Franco-Prussian War, Grand Duchess Louise of Baden beseeched Clara to put the Red Cross principles into play. Several photographs of Clara show her wearing a large amethyst pin in the shape of a pansy, a gift from the Grand Duchess. Czar Nicholas II presented her with a silver cross of imperial Russia for her relief working during his empire's famine. When she returned home, Clara convinced President Chester Arthur to sign the American Red Cross into law.

At age seventy-five, she and her Red Cross workers travelled to the Ottoman Empire, the site of the Armenian genocide. As a Muslim country, Turkey objected to the cross insignia, and Clara arranged for its obliteration on flags and armbands. The five-foot dynamo was in Havana, Cuba, during the Spanish-American War where the seventy-seven-year-old worked sixteen-hour days.

After twenty-three years as president of the Red Cross, in 1904 Clara's opponents forced her to retire with the charge she was incapable of dealing with the behemoth she had willed into existence. Devastated, she remained indefatigable, and at age eighty-three, she started an association for emergency preparedness.

CLARA BARTON BIRTHPLACE MUSEUM

America's iconic nurse travelled the world, but the home of her birth retained a special niche in her soul. She recalled, "I love the old days all over again, every hour is as plain in my mental view as the best picture drawn before my eyes. The spot dearest to me there, the most like home, is the old house where my youth was passed.... It was a rather newly built house where I commenced my earthly pilgrimage."

The modest white structure with black shutters is located at 66 Clara Barton Road. On view is Sarah's wooden clock with fruit painted on its base, and a spinning wheel. A memento from Stephen is his brown leather wallet. David's photo, sword, and Civil War commission is the focus of the fireplace mantel. A highlight is the mobile field desk, either fashioned or purchased by David, that accompanied her on her travels. The desk holds a letter Clara wrote to her friend Mary Norton, whose framed photograph rests on its surface. Visitors tour the kitchen where a table holds period porcelain plates. Miscellaneous objects: a fountain-pen holder with several slots, a wooded bucket (a reproduction), metal pitcher, Clara's 1902 passport to Russia, a handheld brass school bell, her niece's porcelain doll.

In the parlor is Sarah's melodeon and her framed portrait hangs on the wall above the instrument. Clara's bedroom holds a quilt with the names of forty-eight Civil War veterans and the date, 1868, and the first Red Cross First-Aid kit. There are several World War II Red Cross outfits on display.

The woman born on Christmas Day passed away on Good Friday, at age ninety, at her home, Glen Echo, Maryland, now a historical site. Her last words were, "Let me go. Let me go." After seventy-five years of selfless devotion, it was time. Her burial was in North Cemetery, Oxford, in the family plot where her tombstone bears the names of the four battles in which she had participated. Nearby is a red granite cross. Upon her passing, the Angel of the Battlefield joined her celestial brethren.

A View from Her Window

When Clara looked from the window, she saw the adjacent barn—similar to the one in which her brother's accident had segued into her life's passion.

Nearby Attraction: Huguenot Fort

French Protestant refugees built the settlement, of which only a few stones remain. A stone cross bears the inscription, "In memory of the Huguenots / exiles for their faith / who made the first settlement of Oxford 1687."

CHAPTER TWENTY-TWO

Yes-No

Lizzie Borden

Joke at the time of the murders: Someone asked Miss Lizzie the time of the day.
"I don't know, but I'll ax father."

The Lizzie Borden House (opened 1996)
230 Second Street, Fall River, Massachusetts 02721
(508) 675-7333
https://lizzie-borden.com

Parking: Pearl Street; the lot behind the house; metered street parking

Hours of Operation: Tours are offered between 10 a.m.–3:30 p.m. daily.
The basement is reserved for ghost tours in the evening.

Admission: Tour of the entire house: $$$$; Overnight stays: $$$$$

Gift Shop: Yes

Nearby Accommodations: Bristol Harbor Inn / Fairfield Inn & Suites /
New Bedford Harbor Hotel

Nearby Eateries: Fall Rover Grill / Prime and Tapas / Sagres Restaurant

A POPULAR SEVENTEENTH-CENTURY NURSERY RHYME BEGINS: "THREE BLIND
mice. Three blind mice. See how they run. See how they run. She cut off their
tales with a carving knife." The dark story behind the light-hearted ditty: the
three blind mice were Protestant loyalists who Queen Mary burned at the stake.
A nineteenth-century American counterpart is similarly macabre: "Lizzie Borden took an axe / And gave her mother forty whacks / When she saw what she
had done / She gave her father forty-one." If the latter rhyme holds true, Lizzie
embodied King Lear's daughters, "Sharper than a serpent's tooth it is to have a
thankless child."

Lizzie Borden

Television viewers are smitten with *The Forensic Files* because of a thirst for tales involving murder and mayhem. And a headline that has whetted the public interest for 125 years involved Andrew Jackson Borden. He started his career as an undertaker and ended it as the president of the Union Savings Bank, and as a Fall River, Massachusetts, Scrooge. His wealth—$8.3 million in contemporary currency—could have bought a home on The Hill, the town's wealthy enclave, but he was too tight-fisted to leave the less expensive downtown sector. His backyard was far from a stately English garden: the Bordens used theirs to empty their slop pails, an easier approach than using their basement toilet. The backyard also doubled as a vomitorium when the need to upchuck arose.

After the passing of his wife, Sarah, needing a mother for Emma and Lizzie, Andrew married Abby Durfee Gray. The union proved joyless; Andrew never wore his wedding band. Never warming up to the woman she considered an interloper, Lizzie hostilely referred to her as Mrs. Borden. The sisters were cut from very different clothes. Emma, the elder sibling, was shy and unassuming. The only known photograph of her shows Emma covering her face with her left

Lizzie Borden House Bed and Breakfast: Would you want to book a room?
WIKIMEDIA COMMONS, LIZZIE BORDEN HOUSE

hand. The outgoing Lizzie worked as a Sunday school teacher and served as a member of the Women's Christian Temperance Union. Their commonality: ill will toward their stepmother, Abby.

Lizzie's link to infamy began on a stifling hot 1892 morning when the Bordens' maid, Bridget Sullivan (whom the family called Maggie), took ill and vomited in the backyard. Indeed, everyone in the household had been retching for days. Alarmed, Abby contacted Dr. Seabury W. Bowen with her fears regarding poisoning. The physician responded that the culprit was most likely warmed-over mutton—Andrew did not like to throw out food. Furious his wife was wasting money, Andrew refused to let the doctor examine his family.

On that fateful day, Lizzie ran into the street and called out to her neighbor, "Oh, Mrs. Churchill, do come over. Someone has killed father!" With those chilling words, Lizzie entered history as a victim, a villain, a jumping-rope chant, and a media sensation of the Gilded Age. When the hapless Adelaide Churchill entered the Borden house, she spied Andrew lying on the parlor's settee, hacked to death to a point where his face was unrecognizable. One eyeball was cut in half. He was dressed in black; on his pinkie finger, he wore a ring—a gift from Lizzie. His assailant had whacked him ten times with a hatchet-like weapon. Abby was on the floor of the guest bedroom, her body partially obscured by the bed. Her murderer had struck her nineteen times. The police discovered a hatchet with a broken handle in the cellar.

By the next morning, fifteen hundred gawkers had gathered outside the scene of the double homicide. Rumor was rife that Jack the Ripper had come to America to claim his next targets. However, the only serious suspect was Lizzie; Emma was out of town. Damning evidence was she had reportedly tried to buy highly poisonous prussic acid the day before the murders. The pharmacist refused her request despite her assurance she wanted the chemical to clean a seal-skin coat. There was also a widespread belief that she had burned her dress in the kitchen stove. Fall River residents took her alleged act as a nail in the coffin of culpability as the thrifty Borden women would have used a worn-out frock for a patchwork quilt or for rags.

The police arrested Lizzie who spent ten months in jail awaiting trial in New Bedford. Publicity surrounding the news surpassed coverage of the Chicago World's Fair. The all-male jury acquitted Lizzie due to the mindset that the white, Christian, New England daughter of a banker could not have perpetrated such a heinous act. In addition, they did not want to hang a woman. Perhaps the verdict was a foregone conclusion as the judge's charge to the jury was a thinly veiled instruction for acquittal.

Although the men of the jury gave Lizzie a pass, the finger of guilt can be pointed in her direction, as she was the possessor of motive. She hated her stepmother and was concerned that her father had deeded property to his in-laws. Moreover, with the removal of Andrew and Abby, she would no longer be under their financial thumb and could escape from an unhappy house to a beautiful residence.

The lawyer for the defense, Andrew J. Jennings, deposited everything related to the trial in storage, and never spoke of the case again. Seventy years later, his daughter donated the evidence to the town's historical society. The stash included Abby's dust cap, blood-stained pillow shams from the guest room, locks of the victims' hair, two paper tags labelling the Bordens' stomachs, and a hatchet missing a handle. Visitors to the center always make a beeline to gristly souvenirs, and there is a brisk trade selling tote bags and calendars emblazoned with Fall River's most infamous woman.

With their hefty inheritance, the sisters purchased Maplecroft, a four-bedroom house on The Hill. Free of Andrew's frugality, Lizzie applied gold leaf to her bedroom ceiling. To her consternation, although acquitted at her trial, she did not fare as well in the court of public opinion. At church, the townspeople would not sit beside her on the pew, children pelted her windows with rotten eggs, and randomly rang her doorbell. Lizzie again courted controversy when a jewelry store in nearby Providence accused her of shoplifting. Another scandal stemmed from her perceived crush on actress Nance O'Neil. The rumor mill resounded with the reason Lizzie threw a party for a theatrical troupe: to court Nance. Emma eventually moved out; the sisters remained estranged.

Lizzie, who had changed her name to Lizbeth after her move, died in 1927. Her internment was in Oak Grove Cemetery where her remains reside with the rest of the Borden family. The only people present for her burial were the undertakers. Her infamy has never disappeared, and over the years the curious have left mementos, ranging from graffiti on her tombstone to random gifts on her grave. Lizzie's will left thirty thousand dollars, as well as her stocks in the Steven Manufacturing Co., to the Animal Rescue League of Fall River.

THE LIZZIE BORDEN HOUSE

For those fascinated by unsolved crimes and comfortable with the macabre, the Lizzie Borden House beckons. Perched on a rocky hill that slopes toward the shore of Mount Hope Bay, the natural beauty provides a sharp contrast to a barbaric act. The three-story, bed and breakfast/museum, in some ways a beautifully furnished Victorian home, has jarring displays. On an entry table, there are photographs of the crime scene, a replica of the alleged weapon, and a magnifying glass for closer inspection. The atmosphere takes on a chill when entering the front room, the venue of Andrew's murder. A parlor portrait of Lizzie rests on the piano that also holds sheet music. Guests can sit on the settee from which Andrew never rose. (Due to the gore, the settee is, thankfully, a replica of the original.)

Climb the stairs to the guest bedroom where an assailant attacked Abby; her body fell between the bed and the dresser. One would assume the Borden house is the only one where a dining room holds an autopsy table that hangs from the wall and has replica skulls. (The real ones appeared during Lizzie's trial.) The gift shop offers creepy kitsch hatchets on keychains, earrings, and T-shirts. The most popular item is a blood-splattered Lizzie Borden bobble-head doll. The guests come for the museum's macabre element, or because they are amateur sleuths, trying to cast light on an unsolved murder. Visitors might try to sneak in a Ouija board to summon Lizzie, hoping for a posthumous breakthrough of the unsolved mystery.

The answer to America's longstanding Who Dunnit It? lies in the far left corners of a Ouija board: YES-NO.

A View from Her Window

Rather than Lizzie's view, in poet John Keats's words of "being a joy forever," she gazed upon her garden/vomitorium.

Nearby Attraction: Fall River Historical Society

Established in 1921, the French Second Empire mansion was once a stop on the Underground Railroad. The museum's mission is to preserve the history of Fall River. The interior of the estate showcases the beauty and authenticity of its era, while its lawn displays a beautiful Victorian garden. The museum's exhibits hold the world's largest collection of artifacts pertaining to the life and trial of Lizzie Borden, the town's notorious daughter.

CHAPTER TWENTY-THREE

Called Back

Emily Dickinson

"The Riddle we can guess / We speedily despise."

—EMILY DICKINSON

The Emily Dickinson Museum (opened 2003)
280 Main Street, Amherst, Massachusetts 01002
(413) 542-8161
https://www.emilydickinsonmuseum.org

Parking: All vehicles must park either at a meter (many available in front of The Homestead and Evergreens), in an Amherst town parking lot, or in the town parking garage on the north side of Main Street two blocks west of the museum.

Hours of Operation: Museum times vary based on seasons.

Admission: Adults: $$; Seniors: $$; Students 18 and over: $$; Youth 17 and under: Free; Teachers: $; Amherst College faculty and staff: Free

Gift Shop: Yes

Nearby Accommodations: Courtyard Hadley / Hampton Inn & Suites / Fairfield Inn

Nearby Eateries: The Black Sheep / Miss Saigon / Pasta E Basta

A WELL-KNOWN QUOTATION FROM EMILY DICKINSON IS, "BECAUSE I COULD not stop for Death– / He kindly stopped for me– / The Carriage held but just Ourselves–/And Immortality." Emily's immortality rests on her poetry; her legacy is enshrined in The Emily Dickinson Museum.

Emily Dickinson daguerreotype
WIKIMEDIA COMMONS, UNKNOWN ARTIST

The reclusive woman in white is as interwoven with The Homestead in Amherst as Emily Brontë was with the Parsonage in Haworth. The yellow-brick house was where Emily Dickinson was born in 1830, wrote her poetry, and died in 1886. The poet's grandfather, Samuel Fowler Dickinson (along with Noah Webster and others), founded Amherst College, named after Lord Jeffrey

Amherst, who plotted to decimate the Native Americans of New England by infecting them with smallpox. In 1813 Samuel built The Homestead on Main Street.

Emily's father, Edward, a Calvinist lawyer and politician, gave his family material comforts yet proved stingy with affection. His daughter Emily confessed, "I am not very well acquainted with father." Before marriage, he warned his fiancée, "I do not expect or wish for a life of pleasure." What counteracted frigid parents was Emily's bond with older brother Austin and younger sister Lavinia. In her youth, Emily entertained a vision of her future, "I am growing handsome very fast indeed! I expect I shall be the belle of Amherst when I reach my 17th year. I don't doubt that I will have crowds of admirers at that age." Although she never wed, evidence shows George H. Gould, a graduate of Amherst College, proposed.

Emily Dickinson House: The Homestead
WIKIMEDIA COMMONS, DADEROT

At age seventeen, Emily spent a year—the longest she was ever away from the place she always referred to as "her father's house"—at Holyoke Female Seminary, later Mount Holyoke College, where she caused administrative pursing of lips. When headmistress Mary Lyon pressured her students to be "saved," everyone acquiesced—except for Ms. Dickinson. Miss Lyons consigned her wayward pupil to the lowest of three categories—"the saved, the hopeful and the no hopers." The "no hoper" wrote, "Faith is a fine invention / When Gentlemen can see / But microscopes are prudent / In an Emergency." English teacher Margaret Mann's assessment, "She was somebody who walked on the diagonal while everybody else was keeping to the square." Letters to her brother reveal Emily's escalating alienation, "What makes a few of us so different from others? It's a question I often ask myself."

The portrait of the artist as a young woman took shape during the Civil War. (Austin paid for his replacement in the army.) Her disgust with the conflict is hinted at in her lines, "How martial is this place! / Had I a mighty gun / I think I'd shoot the human race / And then to glory run!" By age thirty-five, Emily had composed more than eleven hundred poems that plumbed the depths of grief, pain, love, nature, art, and death. She recorded eight hundred of her works in small, handmade booklets (fascicles) mostly earmarked for her eyes only. Ultimately, she toyed with publication, and contacted her literary mentor, Thomas Wentworth Higginson. Thomas was a member of the Secret Six, supporters of abolitionist John Brown. He rejected her poems with the pronouncement they were too odd. Thomas made two visits twice in the early 1870s and reported to his wife, "I never was with anyone who drained my nerve power so much."

Unlike their straitlaced parents, the Dickinson siblings were creatures of emotion rather than models of Puritan propriety. Lavinia was so hell-bent on marrying Yale student Joseph Lyman that she coiled her long hair around his neck. He resisted being reeled in and retreated to New Orleans. Her low-cut dresses distressed Edward who snapped, "Lavinia, put on a shawl!" Austin proposed to Susan Huntington (Emily's long-time friend), who was loathe to accept. He countered with the offer of a *mariage blanc*—a union devoid of sexual intimacy. After she became Mrs. Dickinson, the couple resided in The Evergreens, an Italianate mansion, a wedding present from Edward, separated by hedges from The Homestead. Emily doted on her nephews and niece, Ned, Martha, and Gilbert. Sue invited the leading intellectuals, such as Harriet Beecher Stowe and Ralph Waldo Emerson, to the Evergreens.

Susan had misgivings over marrying Austin as she was the love interest of both brother and sister. At age twenty, Emily expressed how she longed to hold

Susan "in my arms." In a letter to "Darling Sue," she wrote, "Susan knows / she is a Siren– / and that at a / word from her, / Emily would / forfeit Righteousness–." Letters with Susan outweighed any other. Susan served as Emily's "primary reader," influenced her literary output, and insisted her writing merited publication. Near the end of her life, Emily acknowledged Susan's influence, "With the Exception of Shakespeare, you have told me of more knowledge than any one living—To say that sincerely is strange praise—."

At age twenty-three, Emily began to retreat into her Homestead shell, as evidenced when she declined an invitation from her friend, "I'm so old-fashioned, Darling, that all your friends would stare." By age forty, communication was through partially closed doors, and her "attendance" at family events was observance from the top of the stairs. When she needed a new dress, the seamstress fitted it on Lavinia. During illness, her doctor made a diagnosis as he walked past her door. Once, Emily invited Martha into her bedroom, shut the door, and said, "This is freedom." Her reclusiveness may have been a shield against a society that wanted her to conform to the roles of wife and mother. Domesticity held little appeal: "House is being cleaned. I prefer pestilence." Expressing her desire to divest herself of the outside world, she wrote, "The Soul selects her own Society— Then—shuts the Door." The town referred to the mysterious recluse, who dressed only in white after her father's passing, as "The Myth."

The affair that greatly impacted her later life was not her own. Amour in Amherst ignited when the fifty-four-year-old Austin fell in love with the twenty-six-year-old Mabel, the wife of David Peck Todd, an assistant professor of astronomy at Amherst College. Austin's son, the twenty-year-old Ned, was the first to fall for Mabel. Austin noted the consummation of his extramarital affair in his diary with one word: Rubicon. David was compliant with his wife's adultery as he also sidestepped his wedding vows. Susan, the wife scorned, was furious. The couple's assignation was The Homestead where Austin and Mabel made love on its dining-room horsehair sofa. The woman in white was upset with the illicit relationship, which caused Susan pain and made Austin the object of gossip. Emily referred to Mabel as the "Lady Macbeth of Amherst." She refused to meet her brother's mistress; the only time Mabel laid eyes on Emily was when the poet lay in her coffin. Austin gifted his lover land across Main Street and helped pay for the erection of her thirteen-room house. The affair lasted until Austin's death thirteen years later. Mabel not only had to deal with her grief; she also had to commit Todd to a mental institution due to his increasingly erratic behavior.

At age fifty-six, the poet who "dwelt in possibility," passed away, ostensibly from Bright's disease. Susan dressed Emily in white satin and penned her obituary. After her sister's internment, Lavinia discovered roughly eleven hundred poems locked in a chest of drawers. She asked Susan to help transform Emily's words into a book. Frustrated with Susan's slow progress, Lavinia entrusted Mabel with obtaining a publisher.

THE EMILY DICKINSON MUSEUM

Emily's spirit hovers in The Homestead, where thousands of fans undergo a literary pilgrimage. Probably the first brick house in Amherst, the Dickinsons embellished the roof with a cupola, added a veranda, and built a conservatory for the poet's exotic plants. The downstairs library displays copies of *The Springfield Daily Republican* which published Dickinson poems anonymously in her lifetime; the newspapers sit on a table as if she had just put them down. Throughout the rooms are fragments of verse penned on envelopes, scraps of paper, and candy wrappers. The only incongruent element are the pinecones that the museum placed on chairs to discourage unwelcome seating.

The parlor's walls hold family portraits, and framed prints; the room has original furniture. The poet wrote of the room's instrument, "Cousin John has made us an Aeolian Harp, which plays beautifully, alone, whenever there is a breeze." The parlor's piano still plays. The museum has restored Emily's bedroom to its late 1870s appearance. It has a cream-colored trim, curtain of white lace and green damask which hang from brass rods, and rose-patterned wallpaper. A paisley shawl in shades of orange and red cover her original sleigh bed, in which Emily passed away. In the corner, by the window, is a writing table with an oil lamp. On her chest of drawers sits a china teacup, a framed photo of her nephew Gib, and a basket she used to lower gingerbread to the neighborhood children. Other items are a Franklin stove, and a cradle—an odd addition in a spinster's space. A plexiglass case displays a headless dressmaker's dummy draped in a facsimile of one of Emily's white dresses, seemingly a size eight. A reproduction of her writing desk (the original resides at Harvard) conjures Amherst's writer, quill in hand. Emily's room serves as a three-dimensional diary: her love of literature is manifested in the authors' likenesses that hang on her walls: George Eliot, Elizabeth Barrett Browning, Thomas Carlyle. Samplings of her poems remain.

To the degree Emily felt uncomfortable with strangers, she felt comfortable in The Homestead's garden, where she grew peas, marigolds, lilies, and pansies. She often sent cuttings to friends, bundled with her poems. The tour concludes with visitors descending the stairs that lead to the back door through which

Emily at last departed The Homestead. Her white coffin left for burial in the nearby West Cemetery. The inscription on her gravestone consists of her words from a letter: "Called back."

A View from Her Window
The windows of The Homestead provided Emily with a glimpse of a world from which she had retreated. From her cherry writing table in the corner of her bedroom, Emily gazed upon Mount Holyoke Range. Through the glass panes, she could also see the town's main thoroughfare which led to Boston.

Nearby Attraction: Smith College
Smith College is one of the largest women's colleges in the United States. The school's faculty lounge, Tyler Annex, is where Richard Burton and Elizabeth Taylor enacted their onscreen relationship in the film *Who's Afraid of Virginia Woolf?*

CHAPTER TWENTY-FOUR

Thinking Makes It So

Mary Baker Eddy

"Reject hatred without hating."

—MARY BAKER EDDY

Mary Baker Eddy Historic House (opened 1931)
8 Broad Street, Lynn, Massachusetts
(617) 278-9000
https://www.longyear.org

Parking: Parking lot behind the houses

Hours of Operation: Seasonal

Admission: Suggested donation: $10; Longyear Museum members and children under 12: Free

Gift Shop: Yes

Nearby Accommodations: Harborside Inn / The Bostonian Boston / The Row Hotel

Nearby Eateries: The Capital Grille / Seasons 52 / Legal Seafoods

THE MOST FAMOUS BATH IN HISTORY LED THE ANCIENT GREEK ARCHIMEDES to discern whether jewelers had added base metal to King Herod II's gold crown. After his discovery, Archimedes ran naked through the streets of Syracuse crying, "Eureka! I found it!" Another *aha!* moment that originated from a watery discovery occurred when Mary Baker Eddy slipped on a patch of ice. An intriguing destination is the Mary Baker Eddy Historic House.

The indomitable woman who achieved world renown started life on a modest farm in rural Bow, New Hampshire. Mary Morse was born in 1821,

Mary Eddy Baker in Lynn, Massachusetts
WIKIMEDIA COMMONS, PHOTOGRAPHER UNKNOWN

the youngest of six children of Mark and Abigail Baker, devout members of the Congregational Church. In her twilight years, Mary recounted the evening her father's home sermon lasted too long; as his eyes closed in prayer, she stuck a pin in his behind to terminate the session. Remembering Mark, she wrote, "Father kept the family in the tightest harness I have ever known." In contrast, she was extremely close to her mother, whom biographer Robert Peel referred to as "the summer to Mark's winter, the New Testament to his Old." In her autobiography, *Retrospection and Introspection*, Mary recalled at age eight hearing a voice thrice repeat her name. Sensing a holy presence, Abigail read her a passage from the prophet Samuel, "Speak, Lord; for Thy servant heareth."

When Mary was fourteen, the Bakers moved to a farm near Sanbornton Bridge, New Hampshire, where she attended Sanbornton Academy. As a woman in that era, she was unable to attend university; fortunately, her brother, Albert, a graduate of Dartmouth College, served as her tutor. Albert took over the law practice of Senator Franklin Pierce, later President Pierce. Albert's 1841 death from kidney failure devastated the twenty-year-old Mary. Two years after his passing, she wed thirty-three-year-old George Washington Glover. The couple moved to South Carolina, where George had business interests. Tragically, he contracted a fatal case of yellow fever six months later. Mary would recall, "I married young the one I loved."

Mary returned to her parents in Sanbornton, where her only child, George Washington Glover II, was born in 1844. Often bedridden and unable to care for him, Mary relied on housekeeper Mahala Sanborn to help with her son's care. After Abigail's passing, Mark remarried, and the active boy was no longer welcome in his home. A stay at Mary's sister's house was also short-lived, and well-meaning family members again placed George with Mahala, though it was against Mary's wishes.

Suffering from a toothache, Mary went to the nearby town of Franklin for an appointment with Dr. Daniel Patterson, her stepmother's relative. He wished

Mary Baker Eddy Home
WIKIMEDIA COMMONS, PHOTOGRAPHER UNKNOWN

to move their relationship to a personal plane, but the impediment was that Patterson was a Baptist, and Mary was reluctant to convert. However, as Daniel promised to make a home for her son, Mary took a second trip to the altar.

Mary convinced Daniel to move to North Groton to be near George. However, he reneged on his promise to help her regain custody. She was devastated when Mahala and her husband took George to Minnesota, then considered the Far West. His adoptive parents informed him Mary had died. Mother and son wouldn't be reunited for twenty-three years.

The loss sent Mary, already ill, into near invalidism. Left alone for stretches of time by her husband, she felt isolated in the remote mountain town. What made matters grimmer, Daniel, a poor provider, accumulated debts and they eventually lost their home.

During the Civil War, the governor of New Hampshire tasked Patterson with delivering funds to Northern sympathizers in the South. He stopped to see the battlefield of Bull Run, where Confederate soldiers incarcerated him in a Richmond jail. Six months later, Patterson escaped and rejoined Mary. Some years later, after an affair with a married patient, Patterson begged Mary for forgiveness. The wronged wife responded, "The same roof cannot shelter us. You may come in, certainly, if you desire, but in that case I must go elsewhere."

In 1865 Mark Baker passed away, leaving the bulk of his estate to his widow, and a dollar to each of his children. The following year, while walking to a temperance meeting in Lynn, Massachusetts, Mary slipped on a patch of ice and sustained a spinal injury. Christian Scientists view the episode as her burning-bush revelation. After reading the Bible, Mary regained her ability to walk. She wrote of the cure, "In the year 1866, I discovered the Christ Science or divine laws of Life, Truth, and Love, and named my discovery Christian Science."

She spent the next decade searching the Scriptures and began teaching others her Christian healing method. Mary published her findings in 1875 in her cornerstone work, *Science and Health with Key to the Scriptures*. Initial sales were dismal, though Queen Victoria, Thomas Carlyle, and the Archbishop of Canterbury received copies. Bronson Alcott, father of the author of *Little Women*, expressed initial interest.

In the spring of 1866, Mary met Asa Gilbert Eddy, a Singer Sewing Machine salesman, who came to her for treatment in Christian Science due to his heart condition. Upon his recovery, Gilbert, as he was known, became devoted to Mary and her doctrine. When they married a year later, the forty-six-year-old groom was a decade younger than his bride. Their union was chaste, but deeply spiritual. He took an office in downtown Lynn, advertising his services as a Christian Scientist practitioner—the first to do so publicly.

In 1879 Mary and a handful of students organized the Church of Christ (Scientist), and Mary became its pastor. Two years later, she obtained a charter for the Massachusetts Metaphysical College, authorized to teach Christian Science.

The Eddys relocated to Boston, where Gilbert passed away in 1882. Mary continued to heal, teach, write, and preach in ever-larger venues, until finally, in 1894, the original edifice of The First Church of Christ, Scientist, opened its doors. A little more than a decade later, an extension that seated five thousand accommodated the growing congregation.

Despite its struggling start, Mary's book *Science and Health* eventually sold more than nine million copies and has been translated into sixteen languages and English braille. In 1907 Clara Barton, founder of the American Red Cross, called her "our nation's greatest woman." Mary Baker Eddy founded *The Christian Science Monitor*, which has garnered numerous Pulitzer Prizes. The Christian Science Church has branches worldwide, in eighty countries. Her rise from obscurity to the acknowledged leader of a religious movement was phenomenal at a time when women did not have the vote. Mary passed away at age eighty-nine. Although her church's popularity has diminished, it has outlived the Gilded Age empires of Carnegie, Vanderbilt, and Rockefeller. Mary Baker Eddy remains controversial: some believe in her doctrine; others denounce the Church of Christ, Scientist, as neither Christian nor a science.

Mary's final resting place is on the shore of Halcyon Lake in Mount Auburn Cemetery, situated in Cambridge, Massachusetts. Her bronze casket holds a copper box containing her published works. Her Vermont white-granite memorial consists of eight fifteen-foot-high columns without a roof. The monument holds reliefs of roses (Mary's favorite flower) and morning glories, selected for their symbolism of opening to light and closing to darkness.

MARY BAKER EDDY HISTORIC HOUSE

With eight historic house museums tracing her life, Mary Baker Eddy may hold the record number. Her Broad Street residence in Lynn was the first home she purchased, and throughout her life she kept a photograph of it on her desk. She recalled, "Very sacred to me are the memories that cluster around my old home."

A modern glass foyer serves as the visitor's entrance. Visitors can stand in the attic under the skylight where Mary finished her manuscript of *Science and Health* and learn more about how she founded the Church of Christ, Scientist, and chartered the Massachusetts Metaphysical College. The house has two parlors—the first-floor parlor where she taught her classes and held the original modest church services; the second-floor parlor which was part of her private quarters, and likely where she wed Gilbert Eddy. The house, which now looks much as it would have when Mrs. Eddy lived there, displays wallpaper reproduced from original scraps found behind the door frames. Furnishings are of the period, though not original to the house.

In addition to touring the house, visitors are welcome to view an exhibit about her years in Lynn (1875–1882) and examine reproductions of the first three editions of *Science and Health* (the third carries an early iteration of what became the church's official seal: a cross and crown). To that edition, Mary also added a quote from Shakespeare's *Hamlet*, "There is nothing either good or bad, but thinking makes it so."

A View from Her Window
When Mary looked out the window, she saw the room she used to rent, a reminder of how fortunate she was to finally have a room of her own.

Nearby Attraction: Grand Army of the Republic Museum
Founded by the Union Army in 1885, it honors those who fought to save the Union in the Civil War. There are six rooms of memorabilia spanning the Revolutionary War to World War I.

CHAPTER TWENTY-FIVE

The Truth

Isabella Stewart Gardner

"C'est mon plaisir" (It's my pleasure)
—ISABELLA STEWART GARDNER

Isabella Stewart Gardner Museum (opened 1903)
25 Evans Way, Boston, Massachusetts 02115
(617) 566-1401
information@isgm.org
https://www.gardnermuseum.org

Parking: Limited free and metered parking near the Gardner Museum. Discounted parking at the nearby Simmons School of Management Garage.

Hours of Operation: Monday, 11 a.m.–5 p.m.; Tuesday closed; Wednesday, 11 a.m.–5 p.m.; Thursday, 11 a.m.–9 p.m.; Friday, 11 a.m.–5 p.m.; Saturday, 10 a.m.–5 p.m.; Sunday, 10 a.m.–5 p.m.

Admission: Adults: $$$; Seniors: $$; Students: $$; Children 17 and under: Free

Gift Shop: Yes

Cafe: Yes

Nearby Accommodations: Hotel Commonwealth / The Colonnade Hotel / Revere Hotel

Nearby Eateries: Siam Bistro Thai / The Gardner Café / Garden Cafeteria at the Museum of Fine Arts Boston / Sufra Mediterranean Food

G ODS BEHAVING BADLY IS EXEMPLIFIED IN T ITIAN'S SIXTEENTH-CENTURY painting *The Rape of Europa.* The canvas reveals Zeus, in the form of a bull, ravishing the maiden. The masterpiece served as the crown jewel in Isabella Stewart Gardner's gallery, the scene of a violation that involved the art world's greatest whodunit.

Isabella Stewart Gardner portrait by John Singer Sargent
WIKIMEDIA COMMONS, JOHN SINGER SARGENT

The consummate collector, one of Isabella's treasures was lace. Among her most precious was a tattered fragment of sixteenth-century Belgian material, once the possession of Mary Stuart, Queen of Scots. The artifact's appeal: Isabella professed she was a descendent of the royal despite the different spellings of their surnames. To bolster the blueblood connection, Isabella obtained William Ward's 1793 engraved print *Mary Queen of Scots Under Confinement*.

Although not a descendent of Mary, Isabella's family roots were in Scotland. The ultimate aesthete was born in New York City in 1840, the eldest of four children of Adelia and David. Despite her plain face, she had curves for which kings have scorned their scepters. A friend from her French finishing school, Julia Gardner, introduced Isabella to her brother, John "Jack" Lowell Gardner Jr. A Boston blueblood, he was the city's most eligible bachelor.

A few days before the bride's twentieth birthday, the couple married in Manhattan's Grace Church. A wedding present from her father was a home in pricey Back Bay from where she juggled Brahmin and Bohemian Boston. Known as Mrs. Jack, Isabella specialized in scandalous behavior. As Bostonians were either

Isabella Stewart Gardner Museum
WIKIMEDIA COMMONS, AMORAN002

Unitarian or Episcopalian, she presented herself as a Buddhist. *The Boston Globe* reported that the socialite, on a visit to the Boston Zoo, had taken Rex, a toothless lion, for a walk around his enclosure, while holding on to his mane. A sports fan, she attended the symphony with a hatband inscribed, "Oh You Red Sox." She packed a wallop of a fashion statement when she attached two of her knock-your-eyes-out diamonds to a gold headpiece with wires "so that she could wear them like an antenna of a butterfly." A culture vulture, Isabella dined with author Oscar Wilde, who sent her a copy of his salacious poems that he had penned for his lover, Lord Alfred Douglas. Other notable friends were Julia Ward Howe, Henry James, and T. S. Eliot. The music-mad Isabella held concerts at home where she recruited performers such as Dame Nellie Melba (the namesake of Melba toast), and actor/singer Paul Robeson.

Another thumbing of her nose at sedate society manifested itself in John Singer Sargent's 1888 portrait where the artist accentuated his model's hourglass figure with a skintight black dress and plunging neckline. At her husband's request, Isabella reserved the painting for their private viewing.

There are innumerable photographs of the heiress: with dogs Kitty Wink and Patty Boy, in Norway on a horse-drawn cart, in Italy on a gondola. However, the only picture where Isabella radiates joy is holding John "Jackie" Lowell Gardner III. After his passing from pneumonia just before his second birthday, Isabella fell into a deep depression. To restore his wife's spirit, John arranged a trip abroad. Ultimately, the couple visited thirty-eight countries.

Her father's will, coupled with John's fortune, left the Gardners with a fortune of, in today's money, approximately two hundred million dollars, which led to Isabella's passion. She bought art ranging from rare books and antique tchotchkes to Old Masters. One purchase occurred at a Paris auction where she arranged a signal with the dealer bidding on her behalf. She had instructed him to keep raising the stakes until she lowered her handkerchief. She outbid the Louvre and London's National Gallery.

After the death of her husband from a stroke, Isabella suffered a nervous breakdown. For an outlet, she founded a museum—the first American woman to do so—to showcase her treasure chest which included letters from Napoleon, Beethoven's death mask, and medieval rosaries. Boston buzzed over Mrs. Jack's "Eyetalian palace." Fenway Court, named after its locale, consisted of the façade of the Venetian palace Ca' d'Oro and held remnants of old Italian palazzi staircases, fountains, and balconies. The exterior displayed a coat of arms that featured a phoenix rising from the ashes, an emblem of immortality. Below the image is Isabella's motto, "*C'est mon plaisir*" which translates to "It's my pleasure."

From the balcony, one can envision the gondolas of the Grand Canal. Along with her pet terriers, Isabella moved into the Fenway's fourth-floor suite.

Eschewing traditional gallery austerity, she juxtaposed priceless paintings with everyday items so visitors would feel as if they were in a friend's home—if the friend had canvases bearing the names of the Old Masters. Family photographs, postcards, and novels held pride of place alongside cases that displayed correspondence with Johannes Brahms and Franz Liszt. The marble staircase featured an ornate wrought-iron railing taken from an Italian convent. A Roman mosaic of Medusa's head dominated the magnificent landscaping. A journalist described the gardens as "no less an artwork than the art itself."

Hundreds of bluebloods attended the grand opening of the Fenway to the strains of the Boston Symphony's overture to Mozart's *Magic Flute.* A thousand candle flames flickered in front of priceless displays. Lanterns illuminated the arched windows and the Fenway's eight balconies. Sheathed in a black gown and draped in pearls, Isabella greeted her guests. In 1924 Isabella passed away in her fourth-floor apartment. Her interment was in the Gardner Family Tomb in Mount Auburn Cemetery, Cambridge, Massachusetts, where she lies between her husband and son.

Not one to ever relinquish control, in her will, Isabella stipulated that her trustees hold an annual memorial service to commemorate her April 14th birthday in her chapel, which showcases thirteenth-century stained-glass windows. Another caveat directed the museum to change its name to her own. The third decree: should anything leave or be added to her collection, or if her placement of objects be altered, a Paris auction would sell her possessions with the proceeds earmarked for Harvard University.

Her edict that nothing be removed ended on the costliest St. Patrick's Day in art history. Two thieves, disguised as police officers, entered the gallery under the pretense of investigating a disturbance. Once inside, they shoved two guards against the wall and announced, "Gentlemen, this is a robbery." Leaving the men, bound with duct tape, in the basement, the pillage continued for eighty-one minutes. The thieves walked out with masterpieces and into the annals of one of the world's most infamous mysteries. The criminals left behind Whistlers, Raphaels, Sargents, and a Michelangelo *Pietà* sketch. What the interlopers failed to snatch: the jewel in the crown of the gallery, *The Rape of Europa.* Underneath the Titian, Isabella had placed a framed swatch of silk from her Worth of Paris gown. Unbelievably, Isabella had overseen every detail regarding her museum—except her failure to purchase insurance. Perhaps a violation of her temple was too terrifying to contemplate.

ISABELLA STEWART GARDNER MUSEUM

Since the heist, heavy gold frames reveal green brocade wallpaper where jewels of art once hung. A plaque reads: Stolen, March 18, 1990. Despite a ten-million-dollar reward, the ill-gotten gains (estimated at half a billion dollars) remain missing. Visitors must rely on imagination to visualize Vermeer's *The Concert* and to picture Rembrandt's only seascape, *Christ in the Storm on the Sea of Galilee.* One can imagine heartrending cries emanating from Mount Auburn Cemetery.

When Isabella installed her collection, she did not include labels as she wanted her museum to emulate a home. There are more priceless objects than you can shake a jeweled scepter at on the three floors; therefore, the descriptions only touch on the enormous treasure trove. The first floor's The Yellow Room has canvases by James McNeill Whistler, Edgar Degas, and J. M. W. Turner. The nod to the name of the room is the Italian wooden viola d'amore, and an Italian mandolin. The Spanish Chapel reflects Isabella's interest in the interplay between art and religion. From her European travels is an alabaster tomb figure of a knight, The Virgin of Mercy, that hangs above the altar, and a Venetian crucifix of bronze, wood, and ivory. The words "In Memoriam" are painted over the doorway. She left instructions that her body should lie in state just outside this room prior to her funeral. The third floor's Titian Room is the grandest of all the museum's galleries and showcases Isabella's love of Venice. Titian's *The Rape of Europa* dominates the room. Flanked on the left is an Italian bronze Cupid lying on his side. Other objects: a bronze Italian bust of Benvenuto Cellini, a banker and art collector. Michelangelo praised the sculpture and felt it to be the equivalent of the works of the ancient Greeks and Roman artisans.

Guests of the museum, surrounded by the founder's mementos, might feel they know Mrs. Jack. However, perhaps no one really knew Isabella, considering her words, "Don't spoil a good story by telling the truth."

A View from Her Window

When Isabella looked out her window, the vista was of the courtyard that housed gems of civilization such as a Renaissance Venetian canal-scape, an ancient Roman sculpture garden, and a medieval European cloister. Her nonpareil garden was her joy. In a letter to art dealer Bernard Berenson, American art's First Lady wrote, "My garden is riotous, unholy, deliriously glorious! I wish you were here."

Nearby Attraction: Fenway Park
Known as America's most beloved ball park, Fenway Park opened in 1912 as the home of the Boston Red Sox. Amidst the sea of green spectator seats is a solitary red one in the right-field bleachers. The distinctive color commemorates where the baseball landed after outfielder Ted Williams hit a 502-foot home run, the longest in the stadium's history. A distinctive characteristic of the park is The Green Monster, a thirty-seven-foot-high wall that stands in left field, home to hundreds of sacred signatures from past and present team members.

CHAPTER TWENTY-SIX

Rising of the Stars

Maria Mitchell

"We see most when we are most determined to see."

—MARIA MITCHELL

The Mitchell House (opened 1903)
4 Vestal Street, Nantucket, Massachusetts 02554
508.228.9198
https://www.mariamitchell.org/

Parking: Two-hour street parking on Main Street

Hours of Operation: Guided tours are available mid-June through early September, Monday– Friday, 10 a.m.–4 p.m.; Saturday, 10 a.m.–1 p.m.

Admission: Adults: $$; Youth & Children: $

Nearby Accommodations: The Nantucket Hotel & Resort / Harbor View Hotel

Nearby Eateries: Ships Inn Restaurant / The Nautilus / Seagrille

SINCE THE NINETEENTH CENTURY, CHILDREN HAVE RECITED THE NURSERY rhyme "Twinkle, twinkle, little star, how I wonder what you are . . ." In Nantucket, Maria Mitchell did more than wonder about the stars. To partake of the astronomer's "sweeping the sky," journey to the Maria Mitchell House.

Comets have long captured the popular imagination. In William Shakespeare's play *The Tragedy of Julius Caesar*, on the evening of her husband's assassination, Calpurnia observed, "When beggars die, there are no comets seen / The heavens themselves blaze forth the death of princes."

Maria (pronounced Ma-RYE-ah) was born in 1818, in Nantucket, the island Herman Melville, author of *Moby Dick*, described as an "elbow of sand."

Painting by Herminia Borchard Dassel. Gifted to the Maria Mitchell House by
Maria's grandniece, Virginia Barney
WIKIMEDIA COMMONS, HERMINIA BORCHARD DASSEL

The Mitchells lived on Prison Lane, so named after the jail located up the street. Currently, the location bears the address 1 Vestal Street. Vestal is an allusion to the Roman mythological Vesta, whose father swallowed her—along with his five other children—in fear they would partake of patricide. In contrast, Maria and her father, William, shared an unbreakable bond. Her mother, Lydia, a member of the Coleman family, was a distant relative of Abiah Folger, Benjamin Franklin's mother. Prior to marriage, Lydia was a librarian; however, with ten children and a husband who had his head in the clouds (or rather the sky), she no longer had leisure to read.

The Mitchells were members of the Nantucket Society of Friends though William occasionally sidestepped dogma. He enjoyed color and chose books with red covers, painted his telescope's stand a bright red, and hung a glass ball from the ceiling that created prisms on the walls. When the Mitchells moved, they purchased a piano, although his congregation considered the instrument a frivolity.

Aware Maria was a prodigy, William provided her with a room of her own at the bottom of the garret stairs. The space was the size of a closet but held shelves (one of which served as a desktop), a chair, and a whale-oil lamp. On the door, she hung a sign: MISS MITCHELL IS BUSY. DO NOT KNOCK. Father and daughter spent their nights "sweeping the sky." As they gazed into the heavens, William told his daughter, "Thee must wonder."

While the Mitchell sisters sought husbands, the only rings Maria was interested in were the ones around Saturn. Rather than socialize, Maria would put on her "regimentals"—her hood, coat, and mittens, and climbed the stairs to the rooftop observatory. Reluctance to marry may have stemmed from her mother, worn out from ten pregnancies (Eliza died at age three). Another theory: most men wanted wives in the kitchen, the nursery, the bedroom rather than on the roof.

At age seventeen, Maria founded a private school that caused a tempest in a Nantucket teapot as it was racially integrated. After a year, the school closed its doors when Maria left to become the first librarian at the Nantucket Atheneum, so named after Athena, the goddess of wisdom. Access to the library's thirty-two-hundred books was a substitute for college since the only university open to women was Ohio's Oberlin College. In the upstairs Lyceum room, the famous delivered lectures: philosopher Ralph Waldo Emerson, author Henry David Thoreau, artist John James Audubon, abolitionist Lucy Stone, and ex-slave Frederick Douglass. Her position, which Maria held for twenty years, allowed her to meet Herman Melville and Sojourner Truth. Partially due to the radical thinkers, Maria questioned her Quaker faith. Ultimately, she cut ties with her church when it excommunicated her brother Andrew for marrying a nonmember.

In 1836 William accepted a position at the Pacific Bank, situated in a large brick building, that allowed his family to reside on the top floor—far more spacious than their home on Vestal Street. William set up a small rooftop observatory.

Eleven years later, as the twenty-nine-year-old Maria peered through her telescope into the Nantucket night, she spied a comet just above Polaris. William exhorted, "Thee must tell the world," but Maria was too unassuming to announce she had discovered what had eluded distinguished European astronomers. William contacted members of the Harvard Observatory, but by the time his letter arrived, Father de Vico at the Vatican Observatory in Rome had received astronomy's coveted award. Eventually, official recognition fell on the woman from Nantucket. William and Maria called her great find, "the comet of the tenth month"; the scientific community dubbed it Comet 1847 VI; colloquially, it is Miss Mitchell's Comet. The event gained Maria a foothold amongst the stars, as well as earthly honors. King Frederick VI of Denmark (whose predecessor had, in 1831, promised a gold medal to anyone who discovered a new comet) bestowed the honor that made her the first woman and the first American to receive the award. She received recognition at the first women's rights conference in Seneca Falls and garnered international headlines. In 1844 Maria became the first female member of the American Association for the Advancement of Science.

As a child Maria had watched men sail away on their whaling ships, and she longed to travel, a dream realized in 1857. The first stage of her journey was in New Orleans where the slave markets brought home the horror of human bondage. In New York, she boarded the *Arabia*; in London, she paid tribute at Sir Isaac Newton's grave in Westminster Abby. In the company of author Nathaniel Hawthorne and his wife, Sophia, she departed for Rome. Her aspiration was to visit the Vatican's Observatory to end its edict that precluded women. Of her exclusion she wrote, "My woman's robe must not brush the seats of learning." Eventually, the Vatican allowed her entry, making Maria the first woman to set foot in the male domain. She wanted to remain in the observatory till dark to view the heavens through its telescope, but Father Angelo Secchi explained her visit could not extend beyond daylight.

The lives of a Poughkeepsie brewer and a Nantucket astronomer merged when Matthew Vassar founded Vassar College for women—though it excluded black women. Vassar hired Maria Mitchell as its Professor of Mathematics and

Director of the Observatory. Her students absorbed scientific knowledge along with exposure to the Suffrage Movement. Through her intercession, Julia Ward Howe, Louisa May Alcott, Lucy Stone, and Elizabeth Cady Stanton visited Vassar. Not surprisingly, Maria ruffled faculty feathers: she refused to give grades and argued against male professors' higher salaries.

The incomparable Maria Mitchell passed away in 1889. Her grave is at Prospect Hill Cemetery in Nantucket, near her parents, in the shadow of the Nantucket Maria Mitchell Association's Loines Observatory.

THE MITCHELL HOUSE

The museum is a 1790s Quaker-style structure that, as a guide explains, has "never been electrified, plumbed, or chopped up to accommodate modern conveniences. It remains exactly as it was when the family lived here in the early 1800s."

Visitors step into the past when they tour the two-story house covered with unpainted shingles, weathered gray by rain, fog, and age. An interesting exhibit is Maria's Thumbelina-size study. The parlor holds William's telescope, with which his daughter catapulted into history. Hanging on the wall is the 1848 invitation to the American Academy of Arts and Sciences. The organization's secretary, Asa Gray, opposed to a woman's inclusion, crossed out the salutation "Sir" since the occasion marked the first time a woman received the award. He also altered the word "Fellow" to "Honorary Member"—a change that reflected his disapproval of a female's appointment. For verisimilitude, the kitchen appears as if someone were preparing a meal. All the rooms, except the wood-grained kitchen and two that are wallpapered, retain their original white and gray-green color; furnishings are authentic to the era. Under the ledge of one of its desks, Maria's mother, Lydia, pasted a newspaper article about her husband's achievements; Quaker modesty frowned on boasting. Personal effects include: Lydia's childhood sampler; Maria's mother-of-pearl opera glasses, sewing box, a teacup souvenir from Europe, beer mugs (for medicinal purposes) and her Dollond telescope. The Maria Mitchell Association has 879 objects in its collection, in addition to 321 books from Maria's personal library. There is a "Peep at the Moon" frieze—a 1928 stencil created by Maria's cousin. The antique grandfather clock, a wedding present to William and Lydia, still ticks the passing of time. The roof walk recalls when father and daughter swept the skies.

The Maria Mitchell Association only brings out a crown jewel annually–on Maria's August 1st birthday—her astronomy award. One side of the solid gold 1848 medal depicts a portrait of the king of Denmark; the reverse portrays the

Greek mythological Urania, the muse of astronomy. Above her are the Latin words, "*Non Frustra Signorum Obitus Speculamur et Ortus*" which translates to "Not in vain do we watch the setting and rising of the stars."

A View from Her Window
When Maria looked from her window it was usually in the direction of the sky.

Nearby Attraction: The Whaling Museum
The museum was once the site of a nineteenth-century candle factory in which workers poured sperm oil (*spermaceti*) into candles. Nearby is an authentic whaleboat—a must-see for *Moby Dick* fans.

CHAPTER TWENTY-SEVEN

The Painted Bird

Rebecca Nurse

"I am as clear as the child unborn."

—Rebecca Nurse

The Rebecca Nurse Homestead (opened 1909)
149 Pine Street, Danvers, Massachusetts 01923
(978) 774-8799
info@rebeccanurse.org
https://www.rebeccanurse.org

Parking: Available

Hours of Operation: Museum times vary depending on season.

Admission: Adults: $$; Seniors 65+: $; Children 6–16: $; Children under 6: Free

Nearby Accommodations: Spring Hill Suites / Salem Waterfront Hotel & Suites / Harbor Light Inn

Nearby Eateries: Sawasdee / Century House / Pellana

WITCH HUNTS ARE THE THREAD THAT RUNS THROUGH THE TAPESTRY OF HIS-tory. The Romans fed the Christians to the lions; the Nazis consigned the Jews to the crematorium; the United States incarcerated the Japanese Americans. Three centuries ago, Salem targeted those the Puritans had decreed bore the mark of a witch. The importance of the Rebecca Nurse Homestead: it stands as sentry to the consequences of when hysteria and hatred triumph over humanity.

Witchy women have a prominent place in pockets of Massachusetts. Salem's police feature the image of a witch astride a broomstick; the local newspaper uses her as its logo; and the high school football team bears the name Witches. At

166

the end of the Essex Street pedestrian mall is an iconic landmark: a six-foot-tall statue of Elizabeth Montgomery, star of the television series *Bewitched*, in which she is riding a broom in front of a crescent moon. In a 1970 episode filmed in Danvers, Samantha tells her husband, Darrin, "There were no real witches involved in the witch trials." Endora, her mother, adds, "It was only mortal prejudice and hysteria." During Halloween, a hundred thousand tourists descend on

THE SHERIFF BROUGHT THE WITCH UP THE BROAD AISLE, HER CHAINS
CLANKING AS SHE STEPPED.

Rebecca Nurse on trial for witchcraft
WIKIMEDIA COMMONS, FREELAND A. CARTER

the town to snap cemetery selfies. Salons provide ghoulish makeup and garish hairdos; souvenir shops sell witch-kitsch. Lost in the spell of the season are the victims who made the town synonymous with sinister.

New England's link with infamy began in the winter of 1691. Tituba, a slave from Barbados, was babysitting the Reverend Samuel Parris's nine-year-old daughter, Betty, and her eleven-year-old cousin, Abigail Williams. Since the Puritans frowned on all activities except those church-sanctioned, and as the winter made life even more confining, Tituba became the Salem Scheherazade. She read the children's palms and spoke of voodoo, taboo topics in their Calvinist society. Had Tituba been a better fortune teller, she would have entertained the girls in a different fashion. The youngsters succumbed to "grievous fits," contorting and shouting gibberish. Members of the community gathered to sing psalms while Dr. William Griggs lay the blame at Satan's door. As the then zeitgeist held that the devil could assume the forms of his followers, Salem's elders cast about for the perpetrators. The blame landed on Tituba, a logical target, as she was a foreigner and a slave. Under pressure, Tituba "confessed" and impli-

Rebecca Nurse Homestead
WIKIMEDIA COMMONS, WILLJAY

cated others in casting spells on the youngsters. Her execution paved the way for nineteen more: fifteen women, four men, and two dogs met a gruesome death at the end of a rope. In the ensuing hysteria, children turned on their parents, spouses turned on one another.

The strange bedfellows of an ordinary woman and an extraordinary destiny began in 1621 with the birth of Rebecca in Yarmouth, England, the daughter of William Towne and Joanna Blessing. Desirous of escaping the religious intolerance of the Old World, the family set sail for the New World. Rebecca married Francis Nurse, also an immigrant from Yarmouth. He bought a three-hundred-acre farm where the devout churchgoers raised four sons and four daughters.

Rebecca would have remained a forgotten name on a headstone in a New England cemetery except for her unwitting role in an era when the insane ruled the asylum. A committee of four men visited the Nurses' home where the sickly, seventy-one-year-old Rebecca was on bed rest. Upon discovering her fellow citizens had accused her of causing them bodily harm through supernatural machinations, Rebecca questioned what she had done that God "should lay such an affliction on me in my old age." The Putnam family had lodged the complaint, a family with whom Francis and Rebecca had been involved in an acrimonious lawsuit. Sarah Cloyce and Mary Easty, Rebecca's sisters, rushed to her defense. For their pains, they ended up running afoul of the authorities.

During her trial, Judge John Hathorne stated, "It is awful to see your eye so dry when so many are wet." Rebecca responded, "You do not know my heart. I never afflicted no child, never in my life. I am as clear as the child unborn." The jury found her not guilty—the only such verdict in the Salem Witch Trial proceedings. Immediately, Rebecca's accusers began acting in a manner that indicated the need for an exorcist. In response, the alarmed judges barraged Rebecca with a series of questions that she was unable to answer due to advanced age, hearing loss, and exhaustion from a physical examination that searched for "the Devil's Mark." Construing silence as a sign of guilt, a judge signed her death warrant. The court informed her that they would spare her life if she confessed, to which she replied, "I cannot belie myself." Her daughter, Sarah, futilely testified she had seen Goody Bibber—one of her mother's accusers—prick her knees with pins while crying out blame. In 1692 the wife and mother of eight, who had lived an exemplary life, swung from a noose on Proctor's Lodge at Gallows Hill. Her children surreptitiously claimed her body from a shallow grave and gave her a Christian burial in the grounds of their home. Mary met the same fate as her sister. When the "hurly burly" of the annus horribilis ended nine months later, the jailers set Sarah free. After the execution of her sisters and her own narrow escape from meeting the same fate, Sarah and her family moved to Framingham, Massachusetts. Ironically, Salem derived its name from the Hebrew word for peace, *shalom*.

As an exposé of the Salem Witch Trials, Nathaniel Hawthorne wrote *The Scarlet Letter* that laid bare religious hypocrisy. The author, the great-great-grandson of Judge Hathorne, changed the spelling of his surname to distance himself from his ancestor. A poem by Emily Dickinson, "Witchcraft was hung, in History," concludes that witchcraft is "Around us, / every Day." Arthur Miller's parable of the witch hunt, *The Crucible*, shines a spotlight on the 1950s witch hunt against the Communists. The Simpson's *Treehouse of Horror* parodied the proceedings.

THE REBECCA NURSE HOMESTEAD

Perhaps the most damning denunciation of the mockery of justice is Rebecca's former residence, the only victim's home open to the public. The traditional saltbox-style museum is reached through a narrow path sandwiched between two nineteenth-century structures. The large clapboard landmark is topped with a brick chimney located at the end of a dirt lane bordered by thirty acres of fields and split-rail fences. The museum features three restored rooms, one that contains her spinning wheel. Located on the premise is an authentic-looking reproduction of the first Salem Village Meeting House, where the initial three victims—Tituba, Sarah Osborne, and Sarah Good—faced their accusers. Producers of the 1985 television movie *Three Sovereigns for Sarah* arranged for its construction. The show revolved around the three sisters who were plagued by the hounds of injustice; Vanessa Redgrave played the role of Rebecca's sister Sarah Cloyce. On the western edge of the property, nestled amongst trees, rests a monument in tribute to Rebecca. The inscription bears a poem, written for the occasion, by author John Greenleaf Whittier.

> O, Christian martyr! Who for truth could die,
> When all about thee owned the hideous lie!
> The world, redeemed from superstition's sway,
> Is breathing freer for thy sake today.

The other side of the stone reads:

Accused of witchcraft she declared "I am innocent and God will clear my innocency."

Once acquitted yet falsely condemned she suffered death July 19, 1692.

In loving memory of her Christian character even then fully attested by forty of her neighbors. This monument is erected July 1885.

A fourth author who wrote of the dangers of turning on one's own was the Polish-born Jerzy Kosiński. In his 1965 novel *The Painted Bird*, the boy-protagonist struggles to survive in Eastern Europe during World War II. The title comes from a horror the boy witnessed: a man painted a bird and then set it free. Others from his flock, fearful of its unfamiliar colors, tore it apart. The Rebecca Nurse Homestead bears the same message as *The Painted Bird*.

A View from Her Window

If Rebecca had really been a witch, she would have looked from her window and obliterated the hate-filled faces of those who sealed her fate, and rather looked upon her posthumous resurrection. The pious woman would have felt vindicated if Salem learned from her martyrdom of the injustice of turning on one's painted bird.

Nearby Attraction: Salem Witch Museum

The front entrance of the museum, located in an 1840s church, has a statue of Roger Conant, the founder of Salem. Inside is another statue—of a devil with glowing red eyes. The museum reenacts the accusations, the trial, and the punishments to provide a sobering reminder of the town's sordid past. The director admitted that the administrators are huge fans of the film *Hocus Pocus* set in modern-day Salem that features a fictionalized version of The Witches Museum.

CHAPTER TWENTY-EIGHT

Graves Are Always Tidy

Edith Wharton

"Life is always a tightrope or a feather bed. Give me the tightrope."
—EDITH WHARTON

The Mount (opened 2002)
2 Plunkett Street, Lenox, Massachusetts 01240-0974
413-551-5111
info@edithwharton.org

Parking: Yes

Hours of Operation: Generally open seven days a week from mid-May to October. On weekends in November and December.

Admission: Adults: $$$; Seniors 65+: $$; Students: $$; Children and teens 18 and under: Free

Cafe: Yes

Gift Shop: Yes

Nearby Accommodations: Hampton Terrace Inn / The Yankee / Garden Gables Inn

Nearby Eateries: 1894 Restaurant / Brava / Once Upon a Table

THE WRITER WHO PUNCTURED THE STEREOTYPE OF THE STARVING ARTIST, Edith Wharton comes across as a cosseted, stiff-necked dowager, with stays firmly fastened. However, if ardor had not beat under the primness, she could never have penned her passionate epics. To eavesdrop on her gilded world, grab your lorgnette and head to The Mount.

Portrait of Edith Wharton by Edward Harrison May
WIKIMEDIA COMMONS, EDWARD HARRISON MAY

Edith Jones (nicknamed "Pussy") was born in 1862 into New York society. (The phrase "keeping up with the Joneses" originated with her fabulously wealthy great-aunts, Mary and Rebecca Jones.) Her parents, George Frederick Jones and Lucretia, due to their irreproachable pedigree, were members of Manhattan's upper strata.

Edith was fond of her father, but relations with her mother—whose main diversion was acquiring fine clothing—were strained. As she did not attend school, the lonely child turned to books. She wrote of her reading salvation,

"Whenever I try to recall my childhood, it is in my father's library that it comes to life."

For the Joneses, civilization ended north of Central Park, except for jaunts to Newport, Rhode Island, and "the Continent." While in Paris, her parents found six-year-old Edith curled under the table engrossed in a book. They were shocked, as she had never been taught to read. The book, taken from the drawing room shelf, was a play about a prostitute. Lucretia (a Victorian "Mother Dearest") disapproved of novels and forbade Edith to read any—without her approval—until she was married.

Edith enjoyed making up stories, and at age eleven, she embarked on her first novel, which began: "'Oh, how do you do, Mrs. Brown?' said Mrs. Tomkins. 'If only I had known you were going to call I should have tidied up the drawing-room.'" The pain of her mother's response echoed through the years: "Never shall I forget, the sudden drop of my creative frenzy when she returned it with the icy comment, 'Drawing rooms are always tidy.'" At age fifteen, Edith sold her first poem at a church fair. Her circle viewed her writing with the distaste they reserved for manual labor. Blueblood ladies did not need brains. In her sixties, Edith recalled, "My childhood & youth were an intellectual desert."

The Mount, view from the flower garden
WIKIMEDIA COMMONS, DAVID DASHIELL

At age seventeen, Edith made the rounds of parties in New York and New-port. Although the brass ring for the debutantes was husband hunting, holy matrimony proved elusive. In 1882 Edith became engaged to Henry Leyden Stevens, whose father owned the Fifth Avenue Hotel. When their relation-ship ended, the *Town Topic* wrote, "The only reason for the breaking of the engagement . . . is an alleged preponderance of intellectuality on the part of the intended bride." Approaching "old maid status" at age twenty-three, Edith mar-ried Boston-born Edward "Teddy" Robbins Wharton, who had been Harvard's class of 1873 handsomest hunk. With the 1882 death of her father, she had been even more under her mother's thumb, and hoped marriage would provide escape—and the freedom to read novels. Despite the childhood book about the prostitute, Edith was naïve, and on the eve of her wedding, she asked Lucretia about marital dynamics. Her mother responded, "You've seen enough picture and statues in your life. Haven't you noticed that men are . . . made differently from women? You can't be as stupid as you pretend." In Trinity Chapel, Edith married the twelve-year-older Teddy who shared her passion for travel, deco-rating, and dogs. According to R. W. B. Lewis in *Edith Wharton: A Biography*, husband and wife did not consummate their marriage for three weeks, after which their sexual relations ceased.

The couple moved to Newport where Edith also felt like an outsider, saying, "I was a failure in Boston because they thought I was too fashionable to be intel-ligent, and a failure in New York because they were afraid I was too intelligent to be fashionable." What countered her alienation was her collaboration with Ogden Codman on *The Decoration of Houses*—a repudiation of the Gilded Age more-is-more décor. Railing against Victorian décor, she opted for lightness and classical simplicity.

In 1901 Edith purchased 113 acres in Lenox that overlooked the wooded shore of Laurel Lake in the Berkshire Mountains of Massachusetts. She chris-tened her residence "The Mount," after her great-grandfather's estate. The proud homeowner stated, "The Mount was my first real home." In a letter to her lover, Morton Fullerton, she wrote, "I was amazed at the success of my efforts. Decid-edly, I'm a better landscape gardener than novelist, and this place, every line of which is my own, far surpasses The House of Mirth."

While living at The Mount, Edith wrote *The House of Mirth* (1905), whose title was a biblical allusion, "The heart of fools is in the house of mirth," and *Ethan Frome* (1911), which a critic compared to the novels of Nathaniel Haw-thorne. However, while her career soared, The Mount was far from a house of mirth. Teddy, whom Henry James had pronounced "cerebrally compromised," withdrew fifty-thousand dollars from Edith's trust fund to support his Boston mistress. He spiraled into a morass of drink and depression.

Edith had also sidestepped her marriage vows when she fell for charming rotter Morton Fullerton, a journalist who had as many affairs as did characters in a Wharton work. His romantic past included homosexuality, a divorce, and a quasi-incestuous relationship with his adopted sister. Smitten with the man who had unleashed her from her emotional virginity in her mid-forties, Edith paid off his inconvenient mistress. She rendezvoused with Morton in France where he worked as a Paris correspondent for *The Times of London*. They plotted their Parisienne assignations via post messages, such as, "at the Louvre at one o'c in the shadow of Jean Gougon's Diana," an allusion to the marble sculpture of the Goddess of the Hunt. In letters, she poured out her passion, "You can't come into the room without my feeling all over me a ripple of flame."

By 1910 Morton's ardor had waned; Edith's love affair with France remained. After twenty-eight years of marriage, Edith filed for divorce from the increasingly unstable Teddy, though divorce was scandalous in her upper-class milieu. After spending only a decade in her fabulous forever home, Edith sold The Mount. In her memoir, *A Backward Glance*, Edith reminisced of the home into which she had entrusted her soul, "Its blessed influence still lives in me."

The lady of letters had met with the names of legend: Henry James, Theodore Roosevelt, and Aldous Huxley. Sinclair Lewis dedicated *Babbitt* to her. In 1925 the sixty-three-year-old Edith met the twenty-eight-year-old F. Scott Fitzgerald. She had sent him a letter praising *The Great Gatsby* and invited him and his wife, Zelda, to her chateau for tea. Zelda said she would be damned if she would travel fifty miles from Paris to let an old lady make her feel provincial. Fortified with alcohol, Fitzgerald met the Grand Dame.

"Mrs. Wharton, do you know what's the matter with you?"

"No, Mr. Fitzgerald, I've often wondered about that."

"You don't know anything about life. Why, when my wife and I first came to Paris we lived for two weeks in a bordello."

"But Mr. Fitzgerald, you haven't explained what they did in the bordello." Fitzgerald fled.

When World War I erupted, Edith provided for six hundred Belgian war refugees. At the front, she reported firsthand on the carnage. France awarded her the Cross of the Legion of Honor, and Belgium made her a Chevalier of the Order of Leopold. She paid a visit to the United States to receive an honorary doctorate of letters from Yale University, the first woman to be so honored. She did not visit The Mount; it would have proved too painful. In 1920 she published

The Age of Innocence, which skewered the upper echelon of New York, garnering her the Pulitzer Prize for Fiction. The Nobel Prize committee had nominated Edith three times for its award.

THE MOUNT

Henry James observed, "No one fully knows our Edith who hasn't seen her in the act of creating a habitation for herself." He described the stately pleasure dome as a "delicate French chateau mirrored in a Massachusetts pond." James dubbed her "The Lady of Lenox."

In The Mount, the rooms are windows into the soul of its chatelaine, a sentiment she expressed in *The Fulness of Life*, "I have sometimes thought that a woman's nature is like a great house full of rooms." The entrance hall resembles an Italian grotto and is the antechamber of the forty-room, sixteen thousand, eight-hundred-and-fifty-square-foot stucco green-shuttered estate. A broad terrace runs the length of the house; a Palladian double staircase leads to the magnificent gardens. The drawing room displays one of the dozens of marble fireplaces. Fans of Wharton novels can visit her third-floor bedroom where, dressed in an elegant bedjacket, lying on a pink bedspread strewn with papers and her dogs of the moment, she wrote *The House of Mirth* and *Ethan Frome*. The library on the second floor holds one thousand five hundred volumes. One bears an inscription to Edith from Morton Fullerton; others were gifts from Teddy Roosevelt and Henry James. In *A Backward Glance*, she wrote, "It was only at The Mount that I was really happy."

Edith's final resting place was in the Cimetière des Gonards at the Protestant cemetery in Versailles that holds a cross and the Latin inscription, "*O Crux Ave Spes Unica*" (The Cross Is Our Hope). Overrun with weeds, bird droppings, along with an ancient pot of flowers, one can hear Lucretia Jones's disapproving remark, "Graves are always tidy."

A View from Her Window
On a hill overlooking the formal French Flower Garden are the miniature markers that commemorated four of her devoted dogs: Toto, Jules, Miza, and Mimi.

Nearby Attraction: The Norman Rockwell Museum
Viewing the collection of Norman Rockwell paintings in Stockbridge is to walk down memory lane of rural America, an era encapsulated in idealized images.

MAINE

CHAPTER TWENTY-NINE

Wrong for Women

Sarah Orne Jewett

"Love isn't blind; it's only love that sees."

—SARAH ORNE JEWETT

Sarah Orne Jewett House (opened 1931)
5 Portland Street, South Berwick, Maine 03908
207-384-2454
historicnewengland.org

Parking: Street parking on Portland and Main Streets. Municipal lot on Portland Street

Hours of Operation: June–October 15, Friday, Saturday, and Sunday; Tours: 11 a.m.–3: p.m.

Admission: Adults: $$; Seniors: $$; Students: $; Free for Historic New England members

Nearby Accommodations: Juniper Hill Inn / The Garrison Hotel & Suites / Georges Grant Hotel

Nearby Eateries: Anatolia / Il Paradiso Del Chibo / Christopher's Third Street Grille

SARAH ORNE JEWETT OBSERVED, "WE UNCONSCIOUSLY CATCH THE TONE OF every house in which we live." The quotation rang true for the author, whose ancestral home formed the bedrock of her soul. To catch the author's tone, travel to the Sarah Orne Jewett House.

Rudyard Kipling said Jewett's 1896 *The Country of the Pointed Firs* was the female version of *Walden*. Theodora Sarah Orne Jewett hailed from South Berwick, Maine, situated on the Piscataqua River. In an essay she wrote, "I am proud to have been made of Berwick dust." The author was born in 1849 in her grandfather's, Captain Theodore Furber Jewett, grand eighteenth-century home.

After the captain's son, Theodore, and his daughter-in-law, Caroline, had children, Mary and Sarah, he built them a home of their own next door. In the

Sarah Orne Jewett
WIKIMEDIA COMMONS, PHOTOGRAPHER UNKNOWN

smaller residence, the Jewetts welcomed their third daughter, Caroline (Carrie). The townspeople referred to the sisters as "the doctor's girls."

At an early age, Sarah contracted rheumatoid arthritis, and her father thought it more beneficial for her to accompany him on his rounds than sit in a classroom. Through their horse-and-buggy rides to remote locales, Sarah made the acquaintance of every stratum of South Maine society: judges, shipowners, schoolmasters, and paupers. Cocooned in a magical childhood, Sarah was New England's Peter Pan, evidenced by a letter she wrote to Sara Norton, "This is my birthday, and I am always nine years old—not like George Sand who began a letter, 'It is now eight thousand years since I was born.'" Sarah wrote the letter in her forties.

What set Sarah apart from other South Berwick women can be gleaned from her teenage diary. An early infatuation was Cecily Burt who she met at church when visiting Cincinnati. After a prayer meeting, she wrote, "I do love her best of anyone here in the whole city." Before she headed home, Cecily

Sarah Orne Jewett House
WIKIMEDIA COMMONS, PHOTOGRAPHER UNKNOWN

gifted her a gold ring of which Sarah wrote, "I had rather have it than anything for I shall always have it with me." The news of Cecily's engagement delivered a crushing blow. Unable to follow her father into medicine because of her gender, and perhaps spurred by romantic rejection, Sarah turned to another aspiration.

At age nineteen, following several rejections, Sarah embraced her first success when the prestigious *Atlantic Monthly* published her short story "Mr. Bruce." Her most notable work was her bildungsroman (a word of German origin that refers to a coming-of-age novel), *A Country Doctor*. Other notable books that cemented her literary niche were *A White Heron and Other Stories* and *The Country of the Pointed Firs*. A common denominator of her work is they depict the color and character of rural Maine. Eventually, she earned enough income to achieve financial independence.

Not only did Sarah contribute to literature, she likely influenced the work of famed novelist Henry James. In 1886 James published his *The Bostonians*, inspired by the cohabitation of Sarah Orne Jewett and her partner, Annie Fields. Although he did not employ the term "Boston Marriage," his novel popularized the expression that referred to the turn-of-the-century relationships between two unmarried women who shared a home. These partnerships were accepted in New England, especially in Boston. The unions did not raise eyebrows (as was the situation with their male counterparts), due to the Victorian mindset that women were asexual and therefore nothing untoward took place behind closed doors.

Annie Fields, remembered as the beautiful society hostess of whom Charles Dickens was an admirer, was the wife of James T. Fields, the founder of *The Atlantic Monthly*. Extremely accomplished, she was an internationally acclaimed hostess of a literary salon she held at her home on 148 Charles Street, Boston. After James's death, she fell in love with Sarah, also a doctor's daughter, who shared her passion for writing and travel. Through Annie's publishing connections and Sarah's literary ones, their circle included some of the eminent people of the era: Harriet Beecher Stowe, Julia Ward Howe, Nathaniel Hawthorne, Ralph Waldo Emerson, William Makepeace Thackeray, among other literary luminaries. While South Berwick remained Sarah's base, she spent a great part of each year on Charles Street as well as at Annie's summer home in Manchester-by-the-Sea on the North Shore of Massachusetts. Annie and Sarah's wealth afforded the opportunity to travel, and the couple visited destinations such as Greece, Italy, England, and France. Their love was manifested in many ways, such as nicknames: Sarah was Pinny; Annie was Fuff. Their cache of love letters whispers their intimacy, "Are you sure you know how much I love you?" "And when I think it was my dear little Fuffy who wrote it . . ." "Half of me . . . stays with you . . ."

The blows that buffeted Sarah's life were the loss of loved ones. In 1878 Sarah learned of her father's passing through a telegram and wrote of his death, "I know that the later loneliness is harder to bear than the despair that comes at first." Thirteen years later, Caroline succumbed to the illness from which she had long suffered. The character of Almira in *The Country of the Pointed Firs* expressed the author's sorrow, "You never get over bein' a child long's you have a mother to go to." To convince herself that despite being an orphan, she was still nine years old, she borrowed her nephew's, Theodore (Stubby) Jewett Eastman, sled and careened down a slope. She was forty-one years old.

As a mentor to Willa Cather, Sarah impacted the Southern writer, as well as American literature. Sarah imbued Willa with the belief she could succeed in her literary aspiration and move in with her lover, Edith Lewis. In tribute, the dedication page to Willa's 1913 novel, *O Pioneers!*, states, "To the memory of Sarah Orne Jewett, in whose beautiful and delicate work there is the perfection that endures." In 1925, in the introduction to an edition of *The Country of the Pointed Firs,* Willa wrote that literary immortality was guaranteed to only three American novels: *The Scarlet Letter, The Adventures of Huckleberry Finn*, and *The Country of the Pointed Firs.*

In the fall of 1902, on Sarah's fifty-third birthday, she invited her sister Mary and friend Rebecca Young for a drive along the river marshes to enjoy the autumn foliage. As they descended a hill, their horse stumbled, causing Sarah and Rebecca's ejection from the carriage. Sarah suffered a concussion and a fractured vertebra and spent time convalescing on Charles Street. For years she suffered from the debilitating injury. Sarah passed away in the home that had remained a constant in her life.

SARAH ORNE JEWETT HOUSE

Willa Cather recounted that Sarah had once told her that "her heart was full of dear old houses and dear old women, and that when an old house and an old woman came together in her brain with a click, she knew that a story was under-way." The house on South Berwick was the fountain of her stories.

The house transports visitors to nineteenth-century New England. On display is Captain Jewett's imported furniture, silver, porcelain, tapestries, paintings, juxtaposed with the touches Mary and Sarah made when they inherited the house, such as a tulip-patterned wallpaper in the front hall. In the parlor Sarah entertained her Boston friends; books abound, as well as framed photographs of Annie Fields.

On the second-floor hallway is Sarah's desk—originally her grandfather's—where she wrote *The Country of the Pointed Firs*. Above the desk is a large window that overlooks the town square. The human comedy enacted outside her window became fodder for her novels. She would also have had a view of a stained-glass window and a glimpse into her garden. The desk holds innumerable objects, one of which is a quotation from Gustave Flaubert, "*Écrire la vie ordinaire comme on écrit l'histoire*," which translates to "Write ordinary life as we write history." The walls display portraits of literary figures George Sand and Alfred, Lord Tennyson. A copy of a poem, in Sarah's handwriting, shares her admiration of her acquaintance Rudyard Kipling.

The heartbeat of the house is Sarah's room that remains untouched since her 1909 death. Sarah had scratched her monogram into her window, the house's sacred graffiti. The mantel over the fireplace is filled with bric-a-brac: books, candles, and a wood owl. In the center of the shelf is a photograph of a forever-young Annie. Due to the strategic placing of two mirrors, Annie's image is reflected throughout the room.

A newspaper obituary referred to the passing of New England's most eminent "woman writer"; the inclusion of the word "woman" is one at which Sarah would have taken umbrage. As she had once observed, "God would not give us the same talents if what were right for men were wrong for women."

A View from Her Window
Sarah looked upon a garden filled with pear and apple trees, lilacs, and roses.

Nearby Attraction: Hamilton House
Hamilton House is a 1785 Georgian mansion that belonged to Colonel Jonathan Hamilton, situated on a bluff overlooking Salmon Falls River. Sarah used the estate as the setting of her Revolutionary War romance, *The Tory Lover*.

CHAPTER THIRTY

Lily of the North

Lillian Nordica

"People have voices equal to mine, plenty have talents equal to mine; but I have worked."

—LILLIAN NORDICA

The Nordica Homestead Museum (opened 1928)
116 Nordica Lane, Farmington, Maine 04938
lilliannordica@gmail.com
(207)778-2042
http://www.lilliannordica.com/homestead-museum

Parking: Onsite

Hours of Operation: Visits by appointment only

Admission: Donation: $

Gift Shop: Yes

Nearby Accommodations: Wilson Lake Inn / The Inn on Winter's Hill / Maine Evergreen Hotel

Nearby Eateries: Brickyard Café / White Fox Taverna

OPERA'S HEROINES STORM ACROSS THE STAGE, HOWLING ANGUISH BORN FROM betrayal, jealousy, vengeance. In a nod to life imitating art, Lillian Nordica's days were as tempestuous as those of the women she portrayed. To understand the saga of the Yankee diva, peek behind the curtain at the Nordica Homestead Museum.

Amanda Norton brought her daughter, Lillie, to Backus Corner to see Aunt Eunice, the neighborhood witch from Salem. The seamstress (her day job) read

Lillian Nordica as Brünnhilde in Wagnerian opera
WIKIMEDIA COMMONS, HOLLY CHENG

the two-year-old's palm and predicted, "You will sail the seven seas, and the Crowned Heads of Europe will bow before you." The local fortune-teller's words came to pass, but they did not give full justice to the fabulous fate that awaited the girl from Farmington.

Lillian's paternal grandfather was James Instance Norton. When Edwin, the youngest of his eleven sons, strummed his fiddle, his father banished "the devil's instrument." Edwin continued to play and sang in the Methodist church where he met his wife, Amanda. Her father, known as "Camp-Meeting John Allen," chided a cynic, "You ill-begotten, slab-sided, God-forsaken stack-pole of Hell." Far different than her father, Amanda's favorite aphorism was "Give me a spoon, and I won't hesitate to dig a tunnel through a mountain."

Edwin and Amanda had five daughters they christened with non–New Englander names: Imogene, Onie, Annie, Wilhelmina (Willie), and Lillian. When a sixth daughter arrived in 1857, her parents called her Lillian (Lillie) after her sister who had died at age two. Their farm resounded with music, but Edwin could not eke out a living on his grandfather Ephraim's land.

When Lillie was seven, the Nortons moved to Boston. After a series of boarding houses failed to generate income, Amanda worked as a saleslady at the department store Jordan Marsh and Edwin opened a photography studio until an experiment led to an explosion.

The Nortons believed Wilhelmina was Maine's Jenny Lind, an opera singer whose adoring public had dubbed her the Swedish Nightingale. Wilhelmina became one of the first students at the New England Conservatory of Music and studied under Irish-born professor John O'Neil. When her sister practiced at home, Lillie joined in until Amanda bribed her with pennies to hush. As she had not mentioned singing solo, Lillie announced, "I will sing the Old Section"—mispronouncing Sexton.

An October visit to Farmington coincided with a flood that caused much of the town to end up in the Sandy River. Water from a contaminated well led

Lillian Nordica birth home
WIKIMEDIA COMMONS, MAGICPIANO

to Wilhelmina's death from typhoid. Two years later, as Amanda was sewing, she believed she heard her deceased daughter's voice. Realizing Lillie shared her sister's gift, she took the fourteen-year-old to see Professor O'Neil. When Lillie hit a high C, she became his star pupil for the next four years.

After her graduation, the famous band leader Patrick Gilmore offered Lillie the opportunity to tour the great opera houses of Europe, heady fare for a girl whose only trip had been to her parents' native Martha's Vineyard. She sang at London's famous Crystal Palace, followed by a performance in Italy, the birthplace of opera. In Milan, her voice coach, Signor Sangiovanni, deemed she needed a stage name. As Lillie (Lily) translated to "Giglio" and Norton to North, she transformed to Giglio Nordica. Lillie starred as Violetta in Verdi's *La Traviata* in Brecia where audiences cried out *"Brava La Nordica!" "Bellissima Violetta!"* Nine curtain calls followed; the next morning a string band performed under her window. On a Venetian vacation, while on a moonlight gondola ride, mother and daughter heard an aria. At Amanda's urging, Lillian joined in. The other boats converged on the Nortons and Lillie held a solo performance.

After she sang at the Imperial Opera in St. Petersburg, Russia, Count Leo Tolstoy entertained mother and daughter at his palace where the countess played Chopin. In the Winter Palace, Lillie sang for Czar Alexander II; eight days later, he died from an assassin's bomb.

Another jewel appeared in the diva's tiara in Germany. Richard Wagner's widow, Cosima, had two consuming passions: hatred of the Jews and love of Richard. With his passing, she found purpose in their Festival Theater in Bayreuth. Cosima chose Lillie to sing the role of Elsa in *Lohengrin*, which proved such a resounding success Madame Nordica became the most celebrated of Wagnerian heroines and forever immortalized Brünnhilde, Isolde, Kundry, and Venus.

In the States, she toured with the Her Majesty's Opera Company and appeared in San Francisco, Boston, Chicago, and New York. Upon her return to London, the Prince of Wales was a fan. During the ground-breaking ceremony for the Panama-Pacific Exposition in San Francisco, with President Taft in the audience, Lillie performed the national anthem.

After years abroad, Lillie dreamed of a holiday in Farmington to visit her beloved father with whom "were passed so many happy days and years with him when I was young and cared for nothing more than his approbation and always agreeable society." Fate had other plans; on Christmas Eve, Edwin Norton passed away in Boston.

Madame Nordica spent time at her estate in Ardsley-on-Hudson which she named Villa Amanda in honor of her mother who had died in London. After receiving a thousand dollars for partaking in a musical, she donated the proceeds to the Suffrage Society. Lillie was infuriated over her obligation to pay taxes for a government in which she was disenfranchised. She also argued against male singers earning more than their female counterparts. Other social causes concerned animal welfare. After discovering that the snowy egret was an endangered species, she no longer used its feathers as part of her on-and-off-stage fashions. Although she spent years abroad, Lillie's allegiance remained with the country of her birth; by 1907 she stopped wearing Parisienne couture in favor of American-made gowns.

While Lillian actualized Aunt Eunice's prediction, her love life never matched the heights of her professional success. In Paris Lillie married Frederick Gower, her second cousin, from Maine, who had achieved wealth as Alexander Graham Bell's business manager. Frederick proved controlling, and when she insisted on performing, he burned her music and destroyed her gowns. Their union ended when Frederick attempted a solo crossing of the English Channel in a balloon and was never heard from again. Her second husband was Zoltán Döhme, a Hungarian tenor; his philandering and overspending led to divorce. In London, she became the wife of George Washington Young. His use of her money to bail himself out of floundering businesses led to their estrangement and separation. Lillie never had the children she desperately desired.

In 1914, during a world tour, after performing in Melbourne, Australia, after running late, she wired the captain of her ship, the *Tasman*, to wait for her arrival. In deference to the diva's fame, the captain complied. The *Tasman* ran aground off the coast of Indonesia. For days Lillie suffered from hypothermia, humidity, and mosquitoes until a Japanese coal ship rescued the passengers. In the grip of pneumonia, Lillie ended up in a Java hospital. To comfort a fellow patient, an American boy named George McDonald, she sang by his bedside in what was to be her final song. Her death provided a tragic end for Giglio Nordica, Lily of the North.

THE NORDICA HOMESTEAD MUSEUM

Although the opera star travelled the world, home was her Farmington roots where she performed several times at the peak of her career. Farmington reciprocates her affection. The post office has a large wood carving of Lillie as a child, lying on the grass; an auditorium bears her name. The town's greatest tribute to its famous daughter is the Nordica Homestead Museum, housed in the white, two-story farmhouse where she was born. Knowing how much Lillie had loved the home that her family had sold years before, her sisters, Annie and Onie, purchased the house for her on her birthday in 1911.

Guests enter the unassuming 183-year-old Cape-style farmhouse through the barn which displays a magnificent miniature model theater, a 1955 creation by Charles Tinkham, a New England craftsman. Tinkham incorporated three Boston theaters (Music Hall, the National Theater, and Symphony Hall) for his replica that includes sound, curtains, and lights. Lillie's bedroom holds her heavy wood-frame bed. Coca-Cola collectibles that bear the image of the opera star line the walls. A built-in china cabinet displays dinnerware. Throughout are the usual adornments of nineteenth-century families: Bibles, quilts, and tools; however, another room is vastly different from others in New England. A unique artifact is a helmet, a souvenir from when Lillie sang the role of Brünnhilde at the Metropolitan Opera.

Other treasures that distinguish the home are gifts from royalty. A teak-wood console was a present from a Chinese emperor. Lillian gave one of her sisters several silver spoons she received from Czar Alexander II that a family member recently donated. There is a bejeweled fan from Queen Victoria that bears the diva's name. Another fan, created from lace, was an 1894 gift that Cosima Wagner, gifted to Lillie in Bayreuth, Germany. Cosima included the name Elsa, a nod to Lillie's role in a Wagner opera. Vintage autographed photographs of composers and musicians abound. They are a testament to how far the girl from Farmington had travelled to perform a few feet from President Taft. A heavily carved chair was a present from financier Diamond Jim Brady. A front parlor holds stage jewelry, mostly made by Tiffany. A mannequin wears Brünnhilde's battle garb; another displays Madame's gown, sewn with golden thread that carried a 1890s price tag exceeding a thousand dollars. Another front parlor holds a white bust of Wagner.

In yellowing letters with European postage stamps, Amanda shared stories about a party where fellow guests were Baron and Baroness Rothschild, Prince Ronald Bonaparte. The proud mother described her daughter's dress of white silk and Lyons velvet, her fan made of beautiful flowers. The missive ends, "Many thought Lillie the handsomest woman there." A wall holds Lillie's first formal portrait, painted when she was twenty-three, wearing a gorgeous gown, a present from the czar. Crystal Williams, the Lillian Nordica Museum docent, remarked of the portrait, "Her eyes follow you around the room."

The great diva's death provided a tragic curtain call for Giglio Nordica, Lily of the North.

A View from Her Window

Looking out from her beloved farm's window, she could see a distant mountain peak, "Old Blue," which rose above the Sandy River Valley.

Nearby Attraction: Stephen King's House

In Bangor, Maine, one can stand outside horror writer Stephen King's house. The iron front gate has a spider and dragon motif; the yard has a fifteen-foot wooden sculpture of mystical creatures.

CATEGORIES: GENRES

The Activists
    Abigail Adams

    Susan B. Anthony

    Clara Barton

    Prudence Crandall

    Mary Baker Eddy

    Matilda Joslyn Gage

    Alice Paul

    Eleanor Roosevelt

    Harriet Tubman

    Lois Wilson

The Artists
    Alice Austen

    Lee Krasner

    Judith Leiber

    Lillian Nordica

    Theodate Pope

The Writers
    Louisa May Alcott

    Emily Dickinson

    Sarah Orne Jewett

    Edna St. Vincent Millay

    Harriet Beecher Stowe

    Edith Wharton

Miscellaneous
    Lizzie Borden

    Florence Griswold

    Eliza Hamilton

    Jacques Marchais

    Rebecca Nurse

The Wealthy
    Doris Duke

    Isabella Stewart Gardner

    Eliza Jumel

The Scientist
    Maria Mitchell

AFTERWORD
Wonderful Things

As much a recluse in Cornish, New Hampshire, as Emily Dickinson was in Amhurst, Massachusetts, J. D. Salinger's—the Garbo of the literary world—immortality rests on his novel *Catcher in the Rye.* His alienated protagonist, Holden Caufield, finds sanctuary in the Museum of Natural History, partially as it summoned memories of childhood field trips. The author reminisced, "It always smelled like it was raining outside, and you were in the only nice, dry, cozy place in the world. I loved that damn museum."

The first "damn museum" that I loved was in my hometown of Toronto. Canada's counterpart to Hearst Castle is Casa Loma, Spanish for "house on the hill." I was overawed when my yellow school bus pulled up to the once-upon-a-time Canadian Camelot, replete with turrets and towers. The estate was the domain of Sir Henry and Lady Mary Pellatt, the city's First Couple. The ninety-eight-room, thirty-bathroom estate had a plant-filled conservatory, marble floor, and a stained-glass ceiling. Steam pipes kept flowerbeds warm in winter. The architect E. J. Lennox, who had also designed Old City Hall, modelled the Long Hallway after the one in Windsor Castle. Each of the sixteen master bedrooms had a fireplace imported from European castles. The dining room could seat a hundred guests, who enjoyed bottles from the eighteen hundred stored in the wine cellar. Already a committed bibliophile, I envied the ten-thousand-book library. To stave off boredom during the winter months, the Pellatts could partake of their indoor swimming pool, billiard rooms (the 's' on rooms is not a typo), bowling alley, stables, greenhouse, and rifle range. I remember thinking, "Can such things be?" Fifty employees were tasked with changing five thousand light bulbs, maintaining the first electric elevator in the city's private residence, and polishing fifty-two telephones.

However, what made Casa Loma most memorable were the ghosts of Sir Henry and Lady Mary who yet haunt their twentieth-century feudal castle.

Rather than spend her days as a woman who lunched, Lady Mary was a passionate patron of the Girl Guides. How marvelous to have attended meetings in the venue of a castle. The first event took place in 1913 with 250 troops. When Lady Mary passed away in 1924, the Girl Guides formed a Guard of Honor at her St. James Cathedral funeral. In her casket, Lady Mary wore her Girl Guide uniform.

Sir Henry had accrued his many-splendored bank account from founding the Toronto Electric Light Company. Fame followed fortune and he received a knighthood from King Edward VII. The newly minted millionaire erected Casa Loma "because I wanted the finest house in Canada." His oversize ego was in proportion to his estate. As Sir Henry discovered, a spectacular rise is often accompanied by an equally spectacular fall. The modern Midas had invested $3.5 million ($75 million in contemporary currency) in his castle. By 1920 the Canadian government had nationalized the market in electricity, thereby eliminating his main source of income. In addition, the economy was in a slump following World War II. Unable to pay thirty-thousand dollars in back taxes, a bankrupt Sir Henry was no longer king of his castle. He died, two years later, in the Mimico home he shared with his former chauffeur.

The *dramatis personae* who once inhabited historic homes is what encases them in an aura of magic. Sir Henry Pellatt was a Shakespearean tragic hero, defeated by his fatal flaw of avarice. The man who loved pomp would have been gratified that at his 1939 passing thousands lined the streets to witness the largest military funeral in Toronto's history.

If one were to write the story of Sir Henry, the balancing act for a biographer would be how to objectively portray a life. If one is in awe of the subject, the writer might pen a hagiography—a term that refers to idealizing and idolizing an individual. In contrast, if one is not a fan of the profiled person, the result may be a hamartography, in which the author places every sin under a magnifying glass. When Sir Richard Attenborough was producing his epic film *Gandhi*, Prime Minister Jawaharlal Nehru told him, "Do not deify him. He was too great a man to be turned into a god." I have tried to portray the ladies of Women's Home Museums as accurately as I could. Their truth comes to light in their homes.

Museums serve as three-dimensional diaries where former chatelaines lay bare their secrets. Whether we visit these historic homes in person or as armchair travelers, they provide an emotional experience. Walking through Harriet Tubman's rooms in Auburn, New York, is an opportunity to interact with a woman who was truly a profile in courage. How many of us, after escaping from the bowels of hell, would be willing to return to save others? As a former high school English teacher in an inner-city San Diego school, I was not enamored of scrubbing graffiti and anatomical renditions of body parts from desks. However, after discovering Prudence Crandall's crucible in running her school, my challenges paled. In her role of teacher, Prudence endured arson, jail, and her town's condemnation. A chance to interact with history arrives with a trip to see, as Lincoln put it, the home of "the little lady who started this big war." The "little lady" was author Harriet Beecher Stowe; "the big war" was the Civil War. *Uncle Tom's Cabin* proves the veracity of the quotation "The pen is mightier than the sword." Though a trip to the site of a double homicide might not be everyone's cuppa, Lizzie Borden's Bed and Breakfast/Museum is a popular destination.

To resurrect the ladies who left their legacy, we can read their biographies and watch their biopics. But for the greatest resuscitation, we can look out their windows, sit at their vanity tables where ghostly shadows peer back, gaze upon what they once held dear. Their rooms are the repositories of yesteryear, the keeper of secrets, the storehouse of stories.

When Howard Carter first peered into the grate and beheld King Tutankhamun's mausoleum, untouched for three millennia, in answer to Lord Carnarvon's question, asking if he could see anything, the archaeologist replied, "Yes, wonderful things." My hope is that when you read about the women showcased in *Women's Home Museums of the Northeast: A Guidebook*, you will see, as I did on that long-ago field trip to Casa Loma, wonderful things.

A Note to Readers

Dear Readers, I truly appreciate you sharing my writer's journey—my once and future dream. An unexpected but wonderful result of publishing is interacting with those with whom I otherwise would never have crossed paths. An email from a stranger makes all the hours of solitary confinement—my only significant other being my laptop—worthwhile. In 2008, after I wrote my first book, *Once Again to Zelda: The Stories behind Literature's Most Intriguing Dedications*, I received an email from Georgia. Through the span of years, Jamie Lovett has been my Ethel Mertz.

Please let me know if you have visited any of the women's home museums profiled in this guidebook. If you know of an interesting one not included, I would love to hear about "the one that got away." Perhaps I can make it the subject of a blog. Are any of the women's museums on your bucket list?

During my research, I stumbled down interesting rabbit holes, which is how I discovered some of New England's quirkiest museums. Below are some of these niche emporiums.

NEW YORK: THE CONEY ISLAND MUSEUM

The museum brings the city's history to life through exhibits featuring old signs, postcards, and shooting galleries from the amusement park's heyday. The museum is situated on the first floor of a building on Surf Avenue, above Freak Bar, which offers vintage arcade games. In the *Seinfeld* episode "The Subway," Jerry takes a subway ride to Coney Island where he interacts with a naked commuter reading a newspaper.

CONNECTICUT: THE PEZ VISITOR CENTER

If you stop by Orange, you can meander through four thousand square feet of space dedicated to all things Pez. The museum's claim to fame is that it is home to the world's largest Pez display, in the form of a motorcycle. Originally manufactured in Austria in 1927 as a mint to help customers quit smoking, the first dispenser was—surprisingly—in the shape of a cigarette lighter. The product derived its name from the German word for peppermint, *pfefferminz*. Elaine disrupted George's girlfriend's piano recital by her raucous laugh at Jerry's Tweety Bird Pez dispenser. Yada, yada, she broke up with George.

RHODE ISLAND: GREEN ANIMALS TOPIARY GARDEN
Where can you go to see Don Quixote, unicorns, and camels? The Portsmouth grounds hold eighty sculptured trees and shrubs situated on an estate that overlooks Narragansett Bay. Perhaps Green Animals is what inspired Stephen King's topiary animals in his novel *The Shining*.

MASSACHUSETTS: WILLARD HOUSE & CLOCK MUSEUM
The Italian Geppetto would be in heaven in the Grafton Museum, which holds the world's most comprehensive collection of Willard timepieces. Visitors are enveloped in a chorus of ticking of historical clocks, some made two centuries ago. The museum is situated in an eighteenth-century red farmhouse, once the property of master clockmaker Simon Willard. One of his timepieces, known as the Boston Tea Party clock, sold for $440,000. His handiwork is in the U.S. Capitol building's Statuary Hall, the Old South Meeting House in Boston, and the University of Virginia.

VERMONT: BEN & JERRY'S
In 1972 Paul Simon released his song "Me and Julio Down by the School Yard." The nonlyrical Julio was Art Garfunkel, a student at Simon's Queens high school. The singer-songwriter duo became America's most beloved musicians. Ben Cohen and Jerry Greenfield met at their junior high school in Long Island, and their collaboration resulted in an iconic ice cream empire. Visitors to Waterbury can learn the ice cream–making process from cow to carton.

NEW HAMPSHIRE: LIBBY MUSEUM
For those who love the quirky, the Wolfeboro beckons. The century-old collection of dentist Henry Libby displays a taxidermist's delight: a seven-foot-long alligator, a tarantula, and a bobcat. Cultural artifacts are those from the Abenaki tribe, colonial-era weapons, a pair of Egyptian mummy hands. Who would not covet the necklace made from monkey teeth?

MAINE: THE TELEPHONE MUSEUM

A momentous moment in world history occurred in 1876 when, from his Boston laboratory, Alexander Graham Bell spoke the first words transmitted through a telephone, "Mr. Watson, come here." If you are in Ellsworth, you can visit the telephone is all its incarnations. Some of the items run the gamut from old crank phones to hand-operated switchboards. Guests can use the antique models to call one another. No doubt, selfies abound.

Thank you for accompanying me on the journey to New England's women's home museums. Please visit my Facebook page and share your photos of your museum experience. Your solidarity makes a writer's solitary journey less lonely.

Please contact me through:
    marlenewagmangeller.com
    wagmangeller@hotmail.com
    https://www.facebook.com/marlene.wagman.5/

Happy reading trails,
Marlene Wagman-Geller
San Diego, California

READER REQUEST:

If the spirit moves you, please consider leaving an online review on websites such as Amazon or Barnes & Noble. The good, the bad, and the ugly are all welcome. I subscribe to the Oscar Wilde quotation, "There is only one thing in life worse than being talked about, and that is not being talked about."

Dearest Docents

A touchstone of kindness is when a stranger reaches out from the proverbial blue and a helping hand is extended. The following were the helping hands of the women's home museums of the Northeast.

Alice Austen House
Kristine Allegretti, Director of Operations and Collections;
Victoria Munro, Executive Director

Matilda Joslyn Gage Foundation
Danielle Nagle, PhD, Executive Director

Morris-Jumel Mansion
Presley Rodriguez, Administrative Coordinator

Hill-Stead Museum
Melanie Bourbeau, Senior Curator

The Mount
Nicholas Hudson, Research Assistant

Florence Griswold Museum
Tammi Flynn, Director of Communications & Brand Strategy

Rough Point
Abigail Brewer, Visitor Services Newport Restoration Foundation

Sarah Orne Jewett House
Susanna M. Crampton, Public Relations Officer, Historic New England

The National Susan B. Anthony Museum & House
Allison Hinman, Deputy Director

The Mitchell House
Jascin N. Leonardo Finger, IMMA Deputy Director and Curator: Mitchell House, Archives, and Special Collections

The Leiber Collection
Ann Fristoe Stewart, Director and Curator

The Jacques Marchais Museum of Tibetan Art
Nico Simoni, Executive Director

Steepletop

Mark O'Berski, Vice President and Treasurer, The Millay Society; Krystyna Poray Goddu, Secretary/Literary Officer

Prudence Crandall Museum
Joan DiMaartino, Museum Curator & Site Superintendent

Alice Paul Institute/Paulsdale
Olivia Errico, Public Programs Manager

Clara Barton Birthplace Museum
Emily Thomas, Tour Guide and Researcher

The Nordica Homestead Museum
Crystal Williams, Collections Manager

DISCLAIMER:

I sent the relevant chapter to each museum profiled in *Women's Home Museums of the Northeast*. For the museums who responded, I incorporated all their revisions/suggestions. For those who did not reply, I used due diligence to describe their museum as accurately as possible.

Bibliography

Introduction

Berne, Suzanne. "Listening for the Scratch of a Pen." *The New York Times*, August 30, 1992. https://www.nytimes.com/1992/08/30/travel/listening-for-the-scratch-of-a-pen.html.

Graham, Ruth. "The Great Historic House Museum Debate." *The Boston Globe*, August 10, 2014. https://www.bostonglobe.com/ideas/2014/08/09/the-great-historic-house-museum-debate/jzFwE9tvJdHDCXehIWqK4O/story.html.

Mailman, Erika. "Six Female Writers' Homes You Can Tour, Including the One Where Alcott Penned 'Little Women'." *The Washington Post*, February 6, 2020. https://www.washingtonpost.com/lifestyle/travel/six-female-writers-homes-you-can-tour-including-the-one-where-alcott-penned-little-women/2020/02/05/aa2e8a4c-361f-11ea-bf30-ad313e4ec754_story.html.

Sheraton, Mimi. "Calling at the Houses Where History Lives." *The New York Times*, April 20, 2001. https://www.nytimes.com/2001/04/20/arts/calling-at-the-houses-where-history-lives.html.

Wagman-Geller, Marlene. *Fabulous Female Firsts: Because of Them, We Can.* Coral Gables, FL: Mango, 2020.

Chapter 1: Failure Is Impossible: Susan B. Anthony

Kanefield, Teri. *Susan B. Anthony: The Making of America.* New York: Harry N. Abrams, 2020.

Karnoutsos, Carmela. "Happy Birthday, Susan B. Anthony." *The New York Times*, April 8, 1979. https://www.nytimes.com/1979/04/08/archives/new-jersey-weekly-happy-birthday-susan-b-anthony.html.

National Susan B. Anthony Museum & House. Rochester, New York. https://susanb.org/. Accessed September 1, 2023.

Pollack, Pam, and Meg Belviso. *Who Was Susan B. Anthony?* New York: Penguin Workshop, 2014.

Salam, Maya. "When Susan B. Anthony's 'Little Band of 9 Ladies' Voted Illegally." *The New York Times*, November 5, 2017. https://www.nytimes.com/2017/11/05/us/womens-rights-suffrage-susan-b-anthony.html.

Schiff, Stacy. "Desperately Seeking Susan." *The New York Times*, October 13, 2006. https://www.nytimes.com/2006/10/13/opinion/13schiff.html.

CHAPTER 2: IT WAS, IT WAS: ALICE AUSTEN

"Alice Austen." *The Marginalian*. https://www.themarginalian.org/tag/alice-austen/. Accessed August 30, 2023.

Besonen, Julie. "She Did It Her Way." *The New York Times*, June 27, 2014. https://www.nytimes.com/2014/06/29/nyregion/she-did-it-her-way.html.

Kramer, Hilton. "E. Alice Austen Photographed Earlier Gracious Days of S.I." *The New York Times*, April 9, 1976. https://www.nytimes.com/1976/04/09/archives/e-alice-austen-photographed-earlier-gracious-days-of-si-e-alice.html.

"Welcome to the Alice Austen Museum." *Alice Austen House*. Staten Island, New York. https://aliceausten.org/. Accessed August 30, 2023.

CHAPTER 3: THAT WORD IS LIBERTY: MATILDA JOSLYN GAGE

Carpenter, Angelica Shirley. *Born Criminal: Matilda Joslyn Gage, Radical Suffragist*. Pierre, SD: South Dakota Historical Society Press, 2018.

Gage Museum. Fayetteville, New York. https://matildajoslyngage.org/. Accessed September 1, 2023.

"Matilda Joslyn Gage." *History of American Women*. https://www.womenhistoryblog.com/2012/03/matilda-joslyn-gage.html.

CHAPTER 4: THE OTHER HAMILTON: ELIZA HAMILTON

Begley, Sarah. "America's First Political Sex Scandal." *Time*, December 29, 2015. https://time.com/4149350/first-political-sex-scandal/.

Hamilton Grange. New York, New York. https://www.nps.gov/hagr/index.htm.

Roberts, Cokie. "The Hamilton I'd Put on the $10 Bill." *The New York Times*, April 20, 2016. https://www.nytimes.com/2016/04/20/opinion/the-hamilton-id-put-on-the-10-bill.html.

Rothstein, Edward. "A Founder's at Home." *The New York Times*, September 15, 2011. https://www.nytimes.com/2011/09/16/arts/design/alexander-hamiltons-renovated-grange-review.html.

Serratore, Angela. "Alexander Hamilton's Adultery and Apology." *Smithsonian Magazine*, July 25, 2013. https://www.smithsonianmag.com/history/alexander-hamiltons-adultery-and-apology-18021947/.

CHAPTER 5: QUEEN OF SUGAR HILL: ELIZA JUMEL

Bellafante, Ginia. "Why Has This 258-Year-Old Mansion Been Left to Fall Apart?" *The New York Times*, October 27, 2023. https://www.nytimes.com/2023/10/27/nyregion/morris-jumel-mansion-renovation-repair.html.

Gray, Christopher. "Streetscapes/The Morris-Jumel Mansion, 160th Street and Edgecombe Avenue; 1760's House Filled with History." *The New York Times*, March 24, 2002. https://www.nytimes.com/2002/03/24/realestate/streetscapes-morris-jumel-mansion-160th-street-edgecombe-avenue-1760-s-house.html.

Morris Jumel Mansion. New York, New York. https://morrisjumel.org/1187-2/.

Ward, Carol S. *Morris-Jumel Mansion*. Mount Pleasant, SC: Arcadia, 2015.

CHAPTER 6: NEVERMORE: LEE KRASNER

Blume, Leslie M. M. "The Canvas and the Triangle." *Vanity Fair*, August 22, 2012. https://www.vanityfair.com/culture/2012/09/jackson-pollock-ruth-kligman-love-triangle.

Brensen, Michael. "Lee Krasner Pollock Is Dead; Painter of New York School." *The New York Times*, June 21, 1984. https://www.nytimes.com/1984/06/21/obituaries/lee-krasner-pollock-is-dead-painter-of-new-york-school.html.

Cooke, Rachel. "Reframing Lee Krasner, the Artist Formerly Known as Mrs. Pollock." *The Guardian*, May 12, 2019. https://www.theguardian.com/artanddesign/2019/may/12/lee-krasner-artist-formerly-known-as-mrs-jackson-pollock-barbican-exhibition.

Delatiner, Barbara. "Lee Krasner: Beyond Pollock." *The New York Times*, August 9, 1981. https://www.nytimes.com/1981/08/09/nyregion/lee-krasner-beyond-pollock.html.

Farago, Jason. "Lee Krasner, Hiding in Plain Sight." *The New York Times*, August 19, 2019. https://www.nytimes.com/2019/08/19/arts/lee-krasner-barbican-schirn-kunsthalle.html.

Farrell, Michael P. "History Is Underfoot at Jackson Pollack's House." *Times Union*, August 5, 2010. https://www.timesunion.com/living/article/History-is-underfoot-at-Jackson-Pollock-s-house-605220.php.

Pollock-Krasner House and Study Center. East Hampton, New York. https://www.stonybrook.edu/pkhouse/.

CHAPTER 7: NEVER PASS INTO NOTHINGNESS: JUDITH LEIBER

Childs, Martin. "Judith Leiber: Fashion Designer Who Escaped the Holocaust and Went on to Produce Handbags for the Stars." *The Independent*, June 15, 2018. https://www.independent.co.uk/news/obituaries/judith-leiber-dead-death-fashion-designer-handbags-holocaust-new-york-andy-warhol-a8382551.html.

"Judith Leiber obituary." *The Sunday Times*, June 1, 2018. https://www.thetimes.co.uk/article/judith-leiber-obituary-wkkqjg2jh.

Leiber Collection. East Hampton, New York. http://www.leibermuseum.org/the-garden/.

Nemy, Enid. "Judith Leiber, 97, Dies; Turned Handbags into Objets d'Art." *The New York Times*, April 30, 2018. https://www.nytimes.com/2018/04/30/obituaries/judith-leiber-97-dies-turned-handbags-into-objets-dart.html.

Strugatch, Warren. "Judith and Gerson Leiber: 70 Years of Marriage, Fashion and Art." *The New York Times*, January 6, 2017. https://www.nytimes.com/2017/01/06/nyregion/judith-leiber-gerson-leiber-artists.html

Strugatch, Warren. "The Leibers Are Gone. But Their Bling Is Back." *The New York Times*, May 25, 2018. https://www.nytimes.com/2018/05/25/arts/design/judith-leiber-gerson-leiber-collection-reopens.html.

Sussman, Jeffrey. *No Mere Bagatelles*. New York: Judith Leiber LLC, 2009.

CHAPTER 8: STATEN ISLAND SHANGRI-LA: JACQUES MARCHAIS

Jacques Marchais Museum of Tibetan Art. Staten Island, New York. https://www.tibetanmuseum.org/.

Keane, Katharine. "Staten Island's Tibetan Gem." *National Trust for Historic Preservation*, February 17, 2016. https://savingplaces.org/stories/staten-island-tibetan -gem-jacques-marchais.

Lipton, Barbara, and Nima Dorjee Ragnubs. *Treasures of Tibetan Art: The Collections of the Jacques Marchais Museum of Tibetan Art*. Oxford: Oxford University Press, 1996.

Maitland, Leslie. "S.I. Museum Getting Glimpse of Tibet." *The New York Times*, June 2, 1978. https://www.nytimes.com/1978/06/02/archives/si-museum-getting -glimpse-of-tibet-never-before-exhibited-2500.html.

Shepard, Richard F. "Shangri-La on Staten Island." *The New York Times*, August 6, 1976. https://www.nytimes.com/1976/08/06/archives/shangrila-on-staten-island.html.

CHAPTER 9: A LOVELY LIGHT: EDNA ST. VINCENT MILLAY

Chow, Andrew R. "Edna St. Vincent Millay's Farmhouse Faces Closure." *The New York Times*, April 24, 2018. https://www.nytimes.com/2018/04/24/arts/edna-st-vincent -millays-farmhouse-steepletop-faces-closure.html.

Clark, Heather. "In Edna St. Vincent Millay's Diaries, the Private Life of a Celebrity Poet." *The New York Times*, April 15, 2022. https://www.nytimes.com/2022/04/15/ books/review/rapture-and-melancholy-edna-st-vincent-millay.html.

Conroy, Sarah Booth. "The Poet of Rhyme and Reason." *The Washington Post*, February 21, 1992. https://www.washingtonpost.com/archive/lifestyle/1992/02/22/the-poet-of -rhyme-and-reason/91f0151c-0e18-4d9a-abfd-d669082bac86/.

Doherty, Maggie. "How Fame Fed on Edna St. Vincent Millay." *The New Yorker*, May 9, 2022. https://www.newyorker.com/magazine/2022/05/16/how-fame-fed-on-edna -st-vincent-millay-diaries-rapture-melancholy.

Edna St. Vincent Millay Society at Steepletop. Austerlitz, New York. https://millay.org/.

Goddu, Krystyna Poray. *A Girl Called Vincent: The Life of Poet Edna St. Vincent Millay*. Chicago: Chicago Review Press, 2016.

McClatchy, J. D. "Like a Moth to the Flame." *The New York Times*, September 16, 2001. https://www.nytimes.com/2001/09/16/books/like-a-moth-to-the-flame.html.

Rojas, Rick. "Time Is Running Out for Edna St. Vincent Millay's Upstate Retreat." *The New York Times*, May 14, 2018. https://www.nytimes.com/2018/05/14/nyregion/ st-vincent-millay-steepletop.html.

Smith, Dinitia. "Romantic Rebel of the Jazz Age; In Two Biographies, a Portrait of Edna St. Vincent Millay as Poet and Free Spirit." *The New York Times*, August 30, 2001. https://www.nytimes.com/2001/08/30/books/romantic-rebel-jazz-age-two-bio graphies-portrait-edna-st-vincent-millay-poet.html.

CHAPTER 10: DEEDS NOT WORDS: ALICE PAUL

Alice Paul Institute. Mount Laurel, New Jersey. https://www.alicepaul.org/.

Cavna, Michael. "Alice Paul: Today's Google Doodle Salutes an American Suffrage Hero in Deed." *The Washington Post*, January 11, 2016. https://www.washingtonpost.com/ news/comic-riffs/wp/2016/01/11/alice-paul-todays-google-doodle-salutes-a-suf frage-hero-in-deed/.

Janson, Donald. "Honors Sought for a Women's Rights Leader." *The New York Times*, May 21, 1989. https://www.nytimes.com/1989/05/21/nyregion/honors-sought-for-a-women-s-rights-leader.html.

Kleiman, Dena. "Alice Paul, a Leader for Suffrage and Women's Rights, Dies at 92." *The New York Times*, July 10, 1977. https://www.nytimes.com/1977/07/10/archives/alice-paul-a-leader-for-suffrage-and-womens-rights-dies-at-92.html.

Kops, Deborah. *Alice Paul and the Fight for Women's Rights*. Westminster, MD: Calkins Creek, 2017.

"New Jersey Follow-up." *The New York Times*, December 3, 1989. https://www.nytimes.com/1989/12/03/nyregion/new-jersey-follow-up.html.

Shlaes, Amy. "Put Equal-Rights Champion Alice Paul on the $10 Bill." *Time*, June 19, 2015. https://time.com/3928988/amity-shlaes-10-bill-alice-paul/.

CHAPTER 11: WARMED THE WORLD: ELEANOR ROOSEVELT

Collins, Gail. "Eleanor Roosevelt, First Among First Ladies." *The New York Times*, October 6, 2020. https://www.nytimes.com/2020/10/06/books/review/eleanor-david-michaelis.html.

Collins, Glenn. "At Val-Kill, A Legacy That Lives in Empathy; Teaching Leadership as It Was Practiced by Eleanor Roosevelt." *The New York Times*, August 2, 2001. https://www.nytimes.com/2001/08/02/nyregion/val-kill-legacy-that-lives-empathy-teaching-leadership-it-was-practiced-eleanor.html.

"Discover Val-Kill." National Park Service. https://www.nps.gov/elro/index.htm.

Kennedy, David. M. "Up from Hyde Park." *The New York Times*, April 19, 1992. https://www.nytimes.com/1992/04/19/books/up-from-hyde-park.html.

La Gorce, Tammy. "Eleanor Roosevelt, Up Close." *The New York Times*, July 12, 2014. https://www.nytimes.com/2014/07/13/nyregion/eleanor-roosevelt-up-close.html.

"Mrs. Roosevelt, First Lady 12 Years, Often Called 'World's Most Admired Woman'." *The New York Times*, November 8, 1962. https://archive.nytimes.com/www.nytimes.com/learning/general/onthisday/bday/1011.html.

Tutelian, Louise. "Eleanor Roosevelt's Place Apart." *The New York Times*, December 17, 2004. https://www.nytimes.com/2004/12/17/travel/escapes/eleanor-roosevelts-place-apart.html.

Wilson, Emily Herring. *The Three Graces of Val-Kill: Eleanor Roosevelt, Marion Dickerman, and Nancy Cook in the Place They Made Their Own*. Chapel Hill: University of North Carolina Press, 2023.

CHAPTER 12: A BAND OF ANGELS: HARRIET TUBMAN

Brown, DeNeen L. "Renowned as a Black Liberator, Harriet Tubman Was Also a Brilliant Spy." *The Washington Post*, February 12, 2021. https://www.washingtonpost.com/history/2021/02/08/harriet-tubman-spy-civil-war-union/.

Clinton, Catherine. "Harriet Tubman." *The New York Times*, February 15, 2004. https://www.nytimes.com/2004/02/15/books/chapters/harriet-tubman.html.

Harriet Tubman's Auburn Home. Auburn, New York. https://www.nps.gov/hart/learn/historyculture/tubman-residence.htm. Accessed September 1, 2023.

Jackson, Kellie Carter. "What 'Harriet' Gets Right about Tubman." *The Washington Post*, November 1, 2019. https://www.washingtonpost.com/outlook/2019/11/01/what -harriet-gets-right-about-tubman/.

Waxman, Olivia B. "Why Harriet Tubman Wore White." *Time*, March 13, 2017. https:// time.com/4697549/harriet-tubman-day/.

CHAPTER 13: SEMPER FIDELIS: LOIS WILSON

Ames, Lynne. "The View From: Katonah; A Modest Shrine Where Sobriety Lived 'One Day at a Time'." *The New York Times*, November 20, 1994. https://www.nytimes .com/1994/11/20/nyregion/the-view-from-katonah-a-modest-shrine-where -sobriety-lived-one-day.html.

Foderaro, Lisa W. "Alcoholics Anonymous Founder's House Is a Self-Help Landmark." *The New York Times*, July 6, 2007. https://www.nytimes.com/2007/07/06/nyregion/ 06aa.html.

Pace, Eric. "Lois Burnham Wilson, a Founder of Al-Anon Groups, Is Dead at 97." *The New York Times*, October 6, 1988. https://www.nytimes.com/1988/10/06/obituar ies/lois-burnham-wilson-a-founder-of-al-anon-groups-is-dead-at-97.html.

Stepping Stones: Historic Home of Bill and Lois Wilson. Katonah, New York. https:// www.steppingstones.org/. Accessed September 1, 2023.

Wagman-Geller, Marlene. *Eureka!: The Surprising Stories Behind the Ideas That Shaped the World*. New York: TarcherPerigee, 2010.

Wagman-Geller, Marlene. *Still I Rise: The Persistence of Phenomenal Women*. Coral Gables, FL: Mango Media, 2017.

CHAPTER 14: CONNECTICUT'S CANTERBURY TALE: PRUDENCE CRANDALL

DiMartino, Joanie. "The Canterbury Female Boarding School Story in the 21st Century." *CT Explored*, Spring 2024. https://www.ctexplored.org/canterbury-female-board ing-school/.

Gold, Jack, dir. *She Stood Alone*. Mighty Fortress Publications, 1991. DVD.

Jurmain, Suzanne. *The Forbidden Schoolhouse: The True and Dramatic Story of Prudence Crandall and Her Students*. Boston: Clarion Books, 2018.

La Gorce, Tammy. "Honoring a Teacher Who Fought for Equality." *The New York Times*, September 13, 2014. https://www.nytimes.com/2014/09/14/nyregion/honoring-a -teacher-who-fought-for-equality.html.

Prudence Crandall Museum. Canterbury, Connecticut. https://portal.ct.gov/ECD-Pru denceCrandallMuseum.

CHAPTER 15: A HEART IS NOT JUDGED: FLORENCE GRISWOLD

Farrow, Liz. "The Spirit of Miss Florence Restored." *Connecticut Explored*, Winter 2005/2006. https://www.ctexplored.org/the-spirit-of-miss-florence-restored/.

Florence Griswold Museum. Old Lyme, Connecticut. https://florencegriswoldmuseum .org/.

Griswold, Wick. *Griswold Point: History from the Mouth of the Connecticut River.* Cheltenham, UK: The History Press, 2014.

CHAPTER 16: ART IS LONG: THEODATE POPE

Egan, James. "Fine Art in a Rare Setting." *The New York Times*, September 14, 1975. https://www.nytimes.com/1975/09/14/archives/fine-art-in-a-rare-setting-farmington-museum-if-you-go-.html.

Eiseman, Alberta. "The View from: The Hill-Stead Museum in Farmington. Art-Filled Mansion Fulfilled One Woman's Dream." *The New York Times*, April 22, 1990. https://www.nytimes.com/1990/04/22/nyregion/the-view-from-the-hillstead-museum-in-farmington-artfilled-mansion.html.

Glasberg, Eve. "A 'Village of Pretty Houses,' Where Women's Lives Were Reshaped." *The New York Times*, March 3, 2006. https://www.nytimes.com/2006/03/03/travel/a-village-of-pretty-houses-where-womens-lives-were-reshaped.html.

Katz, Sandra L. *Dearest of Geniuses: A Life of Theodate Pope Riddle.* West Hartford, CT: Tide-mark Press, 2003.

O'Gorman, James F. *Hill-Stead: The Country Place of Theodate Pope Riddle.* Princeton, NJ: Princeton Architectural Press, 2010.

Raynor, Vivien. "Art Sets Tone of Farmington Manor." *The New York Times*, August 16, 1981. https://www.nytimes.com/1981/08/16/nyregion/art-sets-tone-of-farmington-manor.html.

CHAPTER 17: THIS GREAT WAR: HARRIET BEECHER STOWE

Doctorow, E. L. "Out of the Parlor and into the Fray." *The New York Times*, February 13, 1994. https://www.nytimes.com/1994/02/13/books/out-of-the-parlor-and-into-the-fray.html.

Glass, Brent D. "3 Places Where American Women Made History." *Time*, March 11, 2016. https://time.com/4252992/american-women-history-places/.

Harriet Beecher Stowe Center. Hartford, Connecticut. https://www.harrietbeecherstowecenter.org/.

Kahn, Eve M. "Twain and Stowe Homes Being Renovated for Historical Accuracy." *The New York Times*, October 13, 2016. https://www.nytimes.com/2016/10/14/arts/design/twain-and-stowe-homes-being-renovated-for-historical-accuracy.html.

McDonough, Yona Zeldis. *Who Was Harriet Tubman?* New York: Penguin Workshop, 2019.

CHAPTER 18: LUCKY STRIKE: DORIS DUKE

Abbott, Elizabeth. "In Newport, the Many-Faceted Legacy of Doris Duke." *The New York Times*, September 7, 1997. https://www.nytimes.com/1997/09/07/realestate/in-newport-the-many-faceted-legacy-of-doris-duke.html.

Gordon, Meryl. "Reconsidering Doris Duke, the Debutante Who Broke All the Rules." *The New York Times*, April 7, 2020. https://www.nytimes.com/2020/04/07/books/review/sallie-bingham-doris-duke.html.

Mangin, Danny. "Doris Duke's Rough Point." *The New York Times*, accessed November 10, 2023. https://archive.nytimes.com/www.nytimes.com/fodors/top/features/travel/destinations/unitedstates/rhodeisland/newport/fdrs_feat_191_5.html.

Mansfield, Stephanie. "An Overdose of Greed." *The Washington Post*, April 27, 1995. https://www.washingtonpost.com/archive/lifestyle/1995/04/27/an-overdose-of-greed/f7b7899e-736d-4744-b9c0-704edd428d1f/.

Pace, Eric. "Doris Duke, 80, Heiress Whose Great Wealth Couldn't Buy Happiness, Is Dead." *The New York Times*, October 29, 1993. https://www.nytimes.com/1993/10/29/obituaries/doris-duke-80-heiress-whose-great-wealth-couldn-t-buy-happiness-is-dead.html.

Rough Point Museum. Newport, Rhode Island. https://www.newportrestoration.org/roughpoint/.

Wagman-Geller, Marlene. *Women of Means: The Fascinating Biographies of Royals, Heiresses, Eccentrics and Other Poor Little Rich Girls*. Coral Gables, FL: Mango, 2019.

CHAPTER 19: REMEMBER THE LADY: ABIGAIL ADAMS

"Cradle of a Political Dynasty." *The New York Times*, October 14, 2000. https://www.nytimes.com/2000/10/14/travel/cradle-of-a-political-dynasty.html.

Fritz, Jean. "Remember the Lady." *The New York Times*, June 7, 1987. https://www.nytimes.com/1987/06/07/books/remember-the-lady.html.

Old House at Peacefield. Quincy, Massachusetts. https://www.nps.gov/adam/index.htm.

U.S. National Archives. "A Virtual Tour of the Adams Mansion, Home of Two Presidents." Google Arts & Culture. https://artsandculture.google.com/story/a-virtual-tour-of-the-adams-mansion-home-to-two-presidents-u-s-national-archives/dAUBF2FZqC6kJw?hl=en.

West, Doug. *Abigail Adams: First Lady of the United States: A Short Biography*. Kansas City: self-published, 2021.

CHAPTER 20: ANYTHING BUT: LOUISA MAY ALCOTT

Berne, Suzanne. "Listening for the Scratch of a Pen." *The New York Times*, August 30, 1992. https://www.nytimes.com/1992/08/30/travel/listening-for-the-scratch-of-a-pen.html.

Brockell, Gillian. "Girls Adored 'Little Women.' Louisa May Alcott Did Not." *The Washington Post*, December 25, 2019. https://www.washingtonpost.com/history/2019/12/25/girls-adored-little-women-louisa-may-alcott-did-not/.

Louisa May Alcott's Orchard House. Concord, Massachusetts. https://louisamayalcott.org/. Accessed August 30, 2023.

Monk, Dave. "A Journey to the New England Home That Inspired Little Women." *The Telegraph*, December 26, 2019. https://www.telegraph.co.uk/travel/cruises/articles/louisa-may-alcott-orchard-house-by-cruise/.

Telegraph Reporters. "Who Was Louisa May Alcott and What Is Her Famous Book Little Women About?" *The Telegraph*, November 29, 2016. https://www.telegraph.co.uk/technology/2016/11/28/louisa-may-alcott-famous-book-little-women/.

Thomas, Peyton. "Did the Mother of Young Adult Literature Identify as a Man?" *The New York Times*, December 24, 2022. https://www.nytimes.com/2022/12/24/opinion/did-the-mother-of-young-adult-literature-identify-as-a-man.html.

Waxman, Olivia B. "The Real Family That Inspired *Little Women*." *Time*, May 11, 2018. https://time.com/5272624/little-women-history-real/.

CHAPTER 21: CELESTIAL BRETHREN: CLARA BARTON

Benge, Janet and Geoff. *Clara Barton: Courage under Fire*. Bend, OR: Emerald Books, 2003.

Clara Barton Birthplace Museum. North Oxford, Massachusetts. https://www.clarabartonbirthplace.org/.

Henneberger, Melinda. "Red Cross Founder Clara Barton Fought 'Thin Black Snakes' of Depression by Springing into Action." *The Washington Post*, April 6, 2012.https://www.washingtonpost.com/lifestyle/magazine/clara-bartons-enemy-depression/2012/04/04/gIQAdryXzS_story.html.

Tousignant, Marylou. "Clara Barton, Nurse and Activist, Spent a Lifetime Serving Others." *The Washington Post*, December 22, 2021. https://www.washingtonpost.com/kidspost/2021/12/22/clara-barton-200th-birthday/.

Webster, Adam. "Clara Barton Birthplace Tour in Oxford, MA." https://www.youtube.com/watch?v=YLa2CtLi8f4.

CHAPTER 22: YES-NO: LIZZIE BORDEN

Cantwell, Mary. "Lizzie Borden Took an Ax." *The New York Times*, July 26, 1992. https://www.nytimes.com/1992/07/26/magazine/lizzie-borden-took-an-ax.html.

de León, Concepción. "Lizzie Borden's Notoriety Is This Home's Selling Point." *The New York Times*, January 21, 2021. https://www.nytimes.com/2021/01/21/us/lizzie-borden-museum.html.

The Historic Lizzie Borden House. Fall River, Massachusetts. https://lizzie-borden.com/. Accessed September 1, 2023.

Gajanan, Mahita. "Did Lizzie Borden Really Take an Ax? The True Story Behind the Movie *Lizzie*." *Time*, September 14, 2018. https://time.com/5395515/lizzie-borden-history-chloe-sevigny-kristen-stewart/.

Latson, Jennifer. "How Lizzie Borden Was Punished Despite Her Acquittal." *Time*, August 4, 2015. https://time.com/3977000/lizzie-borden-history/.

Schmidt, Sarah. "Did This Woman Murder Her Parents with an Axe . . . and Get Away with It?" *The Telegraph*, May 5, 2017. https://www.telegraph.co.uk/news/2017/05/05/truth-americas-worst-daughter-lizzie-borden-axe-murderer-innocent/.

Sehgal, Parul. "An Enthralling New Look at the Mystery of Lizzie Borden." *The New York Times*, March 13, 2019. https://www.nytimes.com/2019/03/13/books/review-trial-lizzie-borden-cara-robertson.html.

CHAPTER 23: CALLED BACK: EMILY DICKINSON

Benfey, Christopher. "Explosive Inheritance." *The New York Times*, July 30, 2010. https://www.nytimes.com/2010/08/01/books/review/Benfey-t.html.

Burkey, Neil. *Writers' Retreats: Literary Cabins, Creative Hideaways, and Favorite Writing Spaces of Iconic Authors*. Watertown, MA: Charlesbridge, 2021.

Emily Dickinson Museum. Amherst, Massachusetts. https://www.emilydickinson museum.org/. Accessed September 1, 2023.

Gordon, Lyndall. "A Bomb in Her Bosom: Emily Dickinson's Secret Life." *The Guardian*, February 12, 2010. https://www.theguardian.com/books/2010/feb/13/emily-dick inson-lyndall-gordon.

Showalter, Elaine. "Lives Like Loaded Guns: Emily Dickinson and Her Family's Feuds by Lyndall Gordon." *The Guardian*, March 5, 2010. https://www.theguardian.com/books/2010/mar/06/loaded-guns-emily-dickinson-gordon.

Tursi, Renee. "Two Belles of Amherst." *The New York Times*, December 13, 1998. https://www.nytimes.com/1998/12/13/books/two-belles-of-amherst.html.

CHAPTER 24: THINKING MAKES IT SO: MARY BAKER EDDY

Fraser, Caroline. *God's Perfect Child*. London: Picador, 2019.

Fraser, Caroline. "Mrs. Eddy Builds Her Empire." *The New York Review*, July 11, 1996. https://www.nybooks.com/articles/1996/07/11/mrs-eddy-builds-her-empire/

Hourly History. *Mary Baker Eddy: A Life from Beginning to End*. Independently published, 2019.

Mary Baker Eddy Library. Boston, Massachusetts. https://www.marybakereddylibrary.org/research/memorial-in-mt-auburn-cemetery/.

Mary Baker Eddy Museum. Chestnut Hill, Massachusetts. https://www.longyear.org/.

Peel, Robert. *Mary Baker Eddy: The Years of Discovery*. Boston: The Christian Science Publishing Society, 2023.

CHAPTER 25: THE TRUTH: ISABELLA STEWART GARDNER

Butterfield, Fox. "Boston Thieves Loot a Museum of Masterpieces." *The New York Times*, March 19, 1990. https://www.nytimes.com/1990/03/19/arts/boston-thieves-loot -a-museum-of-masterpieces.html.

Diggins, Alex. "This Is a Robbery: Why the Biggest Art Heist of All Time Remains Unsolved to This Day." *The Telegraph*, April 14, 2021. https://www.telegraph.co.uk/tv/0/robbery-biggest-art-heist-time-remains-unsolved-day/.

Haverstick, Iola. "The Legend and the Lady." *The New York Times*, September 18, 1965. https://www.nytimes.com/1965/09/18/archives/the-legend-and-the-lady-mrs -jack-a-gographn-of-isabella-stewart.html.

Richard, Paul. "The Theft That Shook the Art World." *The Washington Post*, March 20, 1990. https://www.washingtonpost.com/archive/lifestyle/1990/03/20/the-theft -that-shook-the-art-world/e5d8d5b7-c3f2-4675-8bd7-56b0deb4972e/.

Silver, Daniel, and Diana Seave Greenwald. *Isabella Stewart Gardner: A Life*. Princeton, NJ: Princeton University Press, 2022.

Chapter 26: Rising of the Stars: Maria Mitchell

Barrett, Hayley. *What Miss Mitchell Saw*. San Diego, CA: Beach Lane Books, 2019.

Bergland, Renée. *Maria Mitchell and the Sexing of Science: An Astronomer among the American Romantics*. Boston: Beacon Press, 2008.

Brooks, Katherine, and Jascin Leonardo Finger. "What Is This? Maria Mitchell's Gold Medal." *Yesterday's Island*, November 16, 2023. https://yesterdaysisland.com/maria-mitchells-gold-medal/.

Folger, Tim. "Hot Science: Maria Mitchell House." *Discover*, February 5, 2004. https://www.discovermagazine.com/the-sciences/hot-science.

Gormley, Beatrice. *Maria Mitchell: The Soul of an Astronomer*. Grand Rapids, MI: Wm. B. Eerdmans, 2004.

Maria Mitchell Association. Nantucket, Massachusetts. https://www.mariamitchell.org/.

Salm, Dale. B. "Restored Home Helps a Star of Nantucket Shine Brightly." *South Coast Today*, July 27, 1997. https://www.southcoasttoday.com/story/lifestyle/1997/07/27/restored-home-helps-star-nantucket/50612090007/.

Stetson, Deb Boucher. "Nantucket's Brightest Star." *Cape Cod Life Publications*, June 2018. https://capecodlife.com/maria-mitchell/.

Chapter 27: The Painted Bird: Rebecca Nurse

Calta, Marialisa. "Salem Remembers, 300 Years Later." *The New York Times*, May 10, 1992. https://www.nytimes.com/1992/05/10/travel/salem-remembers-300-years-later.html.

Driscoll, Anne. "For Salem, a Reminder of a Dark Past." *The New York Times*, October 30, 1988. https://www.nytimes.com/1988/10/30/us/for-salem-a-reminder-of-a-dark-past.html.

"Rebecca Nurse Homestead." Salem Witch Museum, Salem, Massachusetts. https://salemwitchmuseum.com/locations/rebecca-nurse-homestead/. Accessed August 30, 2023.

The Rebecca Nurse Homestead. Danvers, Massachusetts. https://www.rebeccanurse.org/. https://www.rebeccanurse.org/. Accessed August 30, 2023.

Chapter 28: Graves Are Always Tidy: Edith Wharton

"Books: The Last Survivor." *Time*, September 1, 1975. https://content.time.com/time/subscriber/article/0,33009,938649-1,00.html.

Burkey, Neil. *Writers' Retreats: Literary Cabins, Creative Hideaways, and Favorite Writing Spaces of Iconic Authors*. Watertown, MA: Charlesbridge, 2021.

Clarke, Gerald. "Books: Popping the Stays." *Time*, September 1, 1975. https://content.time.com/time/subscriber/article/0,33009,947190-2,00.html.

"Edith Wharton, 75, Is Dead in France." *The New York Times*, August 13, 1937. https://archive.nytimes.com/www.nytimes.com/learning/general/onthisday/bday/0124.html.

Gray, Paul. "Public Triumph, Private Pain: The Letters of Edith Wharton." *Time*, July 25, 1988, https://content.time.com/time/subscriber/article/0,33009,967975-2,00 .html.

McGrath, Charles. "Edith Wharton's New York." *The New York Times*, August 13, 1937. https://www.nytimes.com/2004/10/01/books/arts/edith-whartons-new-york.html.

Saal, Rollene W. "Edith Wharton's Mountain Home." *The New York Times*, August 23, 1987. https://www.nytimes.com/1987/08/23/travel/edith-wharton-s-mountain -home.html.

Sciolino, Elaine. "Edith Wharton Always Had Paris." *The New York Times*, October 8, 2009. https://www.nytimes.com/2009/10/11/travel/11footsteps.html.

CHAPTER 29: WRONG FOR WOMEN: SARAH ORNE JEWETT

Bischof, Libby. "The Mantle of Love and Friendship." *Historic New England*, Fall 2018. https://issuu.com/historicnewengland/docs/hne.fall2018.

Grumbach, Doris. "A Life among the Pointed Firs." *The New York Times*, May 23, 1993. https://www.nytimes.com/1993/05/23/books/a-life-among-the-pointed-firs.html.

May, Stephen. "A Literary Tour of Small-Town Maine." *The New York Times*, May 4, 1997. https://www.nytimes.com/1997/05/04/travel/a-literary-tour-of-small-town -maine.html.

Sarah Orne Jewett House. South Berwick, Maine. https://jewett.house/.

Viera, Diane. "One Family Two Homes." *Historic New England*, Fall 2012. https://issuu .com/historicnewengland/docs/historic_new_england_fall_2012.

CHAPTER 30: LILY OF THE NORTH: LILLIAN NORDICA

Ericson, Raymond. "Brunnhilde From Maine." *The New York Times*, May 3, 1964. https:// www.nytimes.com/1964/05/03/archives/brunnhilde-from-maine-yankee-diva-lil lian-nordica-and-the-golden.html.

Glackens, Ira. *Yankee Diva: Lillian Nordica and the Golden Days of Opera; Hints to Singers.* London: Coleridge Press, 1963.

Nordica Homestead Museum. Farmington, Maine. http://www.lilliannordica.com/ homestead-museum.

Page, Tim. "Maine Recalls a Yankee Diva." *The New York Times*, June 9, 1985. https:// www.nytimes.com/1985/06/09/travel/maine-recalls-a-yankee-diva.html.

Parker, Jane, and Patricia Flint. *Lily of the North: The True Story of Lillian Nordica, a Maine Diva.* Thomaston, ME: Maine Authors Publishing, 2015.

Index

About the Author

Marlene Wagman-Geller received her bachelor of arts from York University and her teaching credentials from the University of Toronto and San Diego State University. She recently retired after teaching high school English and history for thirty-one years. Reviews from her books have appeared in *The New York Times* and dozens of other newspapers including *The Washington Post*, *The Chicago Tribune*, and the website/blog *The Huffington Post*. When not researching or writing, she devotes her time to her guilty pleasures—a Starbucks run (venti latte nonfat milk, extra hot extra foam) and reading.